From Practice to Competition

PROFESSIONAL DEVELOPMENT IN SPORT COACHING

Published in partnership with the United States Center for Coaching Excellence

Series Editor: Karen Collins

This book series provides coaches, sport organization leaders, directors of coaching, educators, and athletic directors with the skills, guidelines, and research-based best practices to support quality coach development. Offering practical, readily-implemented information, these books will help to improve coaching performance across multiple sport contexts.

To Be a Better Coach: A Guide for the Youth Sport Coach and Coach Developer by Pete Van Mullem and Lori Gano-Overway

Winning Well: Maximizing Coach and Athlete Wellness by Cara Cocchiarella and Camille Adana

From Practice to Competition: A Coach's Guide for Designing Training Sessions to Improve the Transfer of Learning by Gibson Darden and Sandra Wilson

From Practice to Competition

A Coach's Guide for Designing Training Sessions to Improve the Transfer of Learning

GIBSON DARDEN
SANDRA WILSON

ROWMAN & LITTLEFIELD
Lanham • Boulder • New York • London

Published by Rowman & Littlefield
An imprint of The Rowman & Littlefield Publishing Group, Inc.
4501 Forbes Boulevard, Suite 200, Lanham, Maryland 20706
www.rowman.com

86-90 Paul Street, London EC2A 4NE, United Kingdom

Copyright © 2023 by the Rowman & Littlefield Publishing Group, Inc.

All rights reserved. No part of this book may be reproduced in any form or by any electronic or mechanical means, including information storage and retrieval systems, without written permission from the publisher, except by a reviewer who may quote passages in a review.

British Library Cataloguing in Publication Information Available

Library of Congress Cataloging-in-Publication Data

Names: Darden, Gibson F. (Gibson Fisher), author. | Wilson, Sandra, 1965– author.
Title: From practice to competition : a coach's guide for designing training sessions to improve the transfer of learning / Gibson Darden, Sandra Wilson.
Description: Lanham, Maryland : Rowman & Littlefield, [2023] | Series: Professional development in sport coaching | Includes bibliographical references and index. | Summary: "Practice may be the most important predictive factor of athlete success in a sport. Designing and conducting effective practice sessions is therefore an essential element of all coach development efforts, and this book is a practical guide to help coaches make the most of training in order to yield greater transfer to the game for their athletes"— Provided by publisher.
Identifiers: LCCN 2022053873 (print) | LCCN 2022053874 (ebook) | ISBN 9781538166277 (paperback) | ISBN 9781538166284 (epub)
Subjects: LCSH: Coaching (Athletics) | Athletes—Training of. | Physical education and training.
Classification: LCC GV711 .D358 2023 (print) | LCC GV711 (ebook) | DDC 796.07/7—dc23/eng/20230109
LC record available at https://lccn.loc.gov/2022053873
LC ebook record available at https://lccn.loc.gov/2022053874

Contents

Introduction		vii
1	The True Purpose of Practice	1
2	The Science of Transfer	23
3	The Foundation for Transfer	45
4	Designing Practice for Transfer	69
5	Practice Analysis for Transfer	93
6	Skill Instruction That Transfers	111
7	Repetitions That Transfer	137
8	Feedback That Transfers	165
9	The Games That Transfer	189
Notes		213
Bibliography		229
Index		237
About the Authors		247

Introduction

WHY THE BOOK?

For most coaches, practice time is a valuable and limited resource. As such, effective coaches consistently evaluate the impact of their practice activities. They identify the merits of a practice activity by asking questions like: Why am I doing this drill? Is it time efficient? Does it effectively develop athletes' skills? This book makes the case that the most important question for coaches to ask when evaluating a practice condition is, Will it transfer? The primary reason for practice is to increase performance in the game or competitive environment. One of the seven core responsibilities of effective coaches is to conduct practices and prepare for competition. While we intuitively know that practice should prepare athletes for competition, sometimes our practice conditions don't align with this purpose. For example, the common use of drills where players dribble around cones or hit off tees may do little to prepare athletes for competition. Practice conditions (e.g., drills, instruction, repetitions, feedback) should be evaluated on the potential to transfer to competition. Doing so will help coaches get the most out of their practice time. Simply put, the premise behind this book is to explore key elements that increase the positive transfer of practice conditions.

Getting practice to transfer to the game is a common source of frustration for coaches. Consider the "perfect" practice that preceded a poorly played such claims, most would be unsupported by research and science. Much of transfer is about deep learning and the careful manipulation of learning conditions. True learning of any content (whether it be academic or sport skills) is not easy. Transferring knowledge and skills to later and different conditions is a developmental process that takes planning, effort, and most of all—patience (by both athlete and coach).

The content and sequence of the book reflects that developmental process. The book is organized into nine progressive and sequential chapters. We intend for the reader to "build toward transfer" by transferring content sequentially from one chapter to the next, beginning with the first chapter. For the most part, the reader will apply concepts from the previous chapter(s) as they progress through the book. However, some of the practice conditions and strategies can stand alone and be useful in isolation. For example, the coach interested in how to use repetitions more effectively might go straight to chapter 7. We try to help make connections in each chapter by pointing to supporting theories and concepts in the earlier chapters (which the coach can choose to explore).

Chapter 1 kicks it off by offering a reflection on the true purpose of practice. It asks coaches to reflect on misconceptions about the role of practice and the importance of different types of skill and practice. It makes a clear distinction between practice conditions that seek to get things right during practice vs. conditions that seek to transfer skills to competition. Chapter 2 captures the leading theories of transfer that support our recommended practice methods. We summarize their key elements and bring them to life with interesting reflections and examples. We encourage coaches to pick and choose parts of theories that are most relevant and connect with their own athletes and coaching situations. We want coaches to appreciate that the most effective practice conditions have research support from a variety of theoretical perspectives (not just one). Chapter 3 helps coaches build a foundation that is more conducive for transfer. Much like preparing the soil before planting seeds, conditions need to be right before "growing" transfer during practice. Transfer is more likely, for example, when practice conditions build on a culture of learning and communication. Chapter 4 identifies important planning and design concepts that apply specifically to the transfer of learning. These are the principles that help coaches design practice environments that optimally challenge athletes so that they continue to develop.

It encourages coaches to strategically manipulate aspects of the environment and/or balance practice activities among different practice goals. Chapter 5 provides a systematic approach for analyzing practice to increase the similarity between practice and the competition (game). Since some views of transfer emphasize the specificity and simulation of the competitive environment in practice, this chapter conducts a task analysis for similarity, and gives coaches the chance to conduct their own analysis.

The second half of the book builds on the role of the coach as a teacher and explores how coaches can better "teach for transfer." Chapter 6 discusses key concepts of coaches' instructions that are more likely to generate transfer of learning. Since coaches often express frustration when their instruction is not retained or transferred by athletes, the chapter seeks to narrow the gap between what is taught (instruction) and what is learned (and transferred). Chapter 7 gets into a popular coaching topic—repetitions. The emphasis is on the *quality* of repetitions rather than the quantity. Repetitions performed with increased variability, for example, offer more quality for transfer of learning than repetitions performed perfectly and repetitively. Chapter 8 explores how coaches can provide athletes with feedback that assists in the transfer of learning. While feedback is important and needed, we stress that coach feedback should seek the transfer of athlete independence to situations where athletes need to detect and correct their own mistakes and errors (e.g., individual practice or the game). Finally, in chapter 9 we make the argument that nothing offers more potential for the positive transfer of learning than a good game! This chapter connects most of the theories and concepts from earlier chapters by applying the games-based approach to practice. Contrasted with the traditional drills approach, it offers practice conditions that look and feel more like the real game, better developing the perceptual, tactical, and mental skills that transfer to the game.

1

The True Purpose of Practice

Coach Rodriguez is in her second year as a high school volleyball coach. She has a reputation for running the "perfect" practice session. Parents love to watch her practices, and administrators point to her sessions as a model for others to emulate. Her athletes rotate efficiently through skill stations in groups of three to four athletes, each station working on executing the fundamental volleyball skills (e.g., spiking, passing, serving stations). There is no wasted time, and players get plenty of consecutive repetitions of the skill at each station. When the whistle blows every 10 minutes, players hustle to the next station; they know where to go and what to expect. Each station has zones, cones, targets, and other equipment to facilitate the drill. Performance cues and video clips of expert performers are even posted at the stations (e.g., elbows in, stay low) to remind athletes to use good techniques. Coach Rodriguez rotates effectively, providing error corrections ensuring techniques look great. Despite her practice success and having good "talent," her teams have struggled to win and have had consecutive losing seasons, finishing near the bottom of the conference standings both years. Coach Rodriguez commented that they haven't quite been able to "get over the hump" yet. They still seem to be making lots of unforced and mental errors when they compete.

Practice. Why do we practice? What is the purpose of practice? It's a simple question, right? Suppose you posed the question to a group of athletes and coaches, what answers would you get? "Get better in your sport," "Improve your skills," "Develop muscle memory," "Master your sport," "Gain confidence," "Acquire the skills," or "Get ready for the game." Likely, the responses would be all over the place, and they can all be correct. But in the end, most coaches would agree that the primary role of practice is to improve our athletes' skills and prepare them for the upcoming competition or game. This is reinforced in the *National Standards for Sport Coaches*.[1] One of the seven essential areas of knowledge and skills for sport coaches is: conduct practices and prepare for competition.

Though the role of practice tends to be well accepted (prepare for competition), traditional practice methods often miss the target. Practice is often designed around skill acquisition with the assumption that if athletes acquire the skills in practice, they will be prepared for competition. However, this transfer of skill acquisition to the game should be an intentional effort, not an assumed byproduct of practice performance (skill acquisition). The true purpose of practice is ensuring the skill acquisition activities transfer to the competition. In this way, designing practice activities should start with and continually ask the question: "Will it transfer?" And that is the purpose of this book. Alignment with this purpose of practice often requires a certain mind-set by the coach. This mind-set enables coaches to try different practice methods to increase transfer. As well, it instills the confidence to replace some of the more traditional practice approaches in favor of the "Will it transfer?" approach.

LEARNING

You haven't taught until they've learned.

—John Wooden[2]

Wooden nailed it; we should teach (coach) so athletes learn. Learning should be the goal of practice. How we learn best should inform and support our practice activities. Effective learning should be directed toward a *target context*, and for coaches and athletes, the target context is most often the *game* (or the *competition*). However, sometimes the target context is not the game, but rather the *next* practice activity, such as a more complex drill. Regardless, practice should seek to transfer our efforts *forward*, in such a way that learning and transfer are interconnected and purposeful in all our practice activities.

Performance vs. Learning

Sometimes learning gets confused with performance. There are important differences between the terms "performance" and "learning." Performance is a temporary or transitory expression of skill. Learning is relatively permanent and generalizable to other contexts. Learning is harder to observe; it's often invisible and happens gradually over time. So, we often use practice performance to infer learning. Below are the key distinctions between *performance* and *learning*.[3]

Performance	*Learning*
Observable behavior	Inferred from performance (often invisible)
Temporary	Relatively permanent
Influenced by temporary factors	Resistant to temporary factors
Specific to performance situation	Generalizable to different performance situations

Since learning is the goal of practice, coaches must distinguish between performance in practice and real learning. As coaches, we intuitively evaluate our practice (effective or not) based on the short-term performance improvements in our athletes (e.g., during practice). For example, after instructing, demonstrating, drilling, and providing feedback to players for the forearm pass in volleyball, it is satisfying to see athletes successfully execute 8 out of 10 forearm passes to the setter at the end of practice. But is this performance indicative of learning, and will it transfer? Figure 1.1 is a hypothetical depiction of how two different practice conditions (amount of coach feedback) impact performance. What should the coach conclude from those results?

Should the coach provide more feedback? Yes! The results of figure 1.1 suggest more feedback from the coach is better to increase athlete performance. If the goal of that practice was to *perform* better in practice, we would agree. However, if the goal of the practice was for athletes to *learn* from practice (relatively permanent and generalizable), the better answer is, we don't know yet. Let's explore this further.

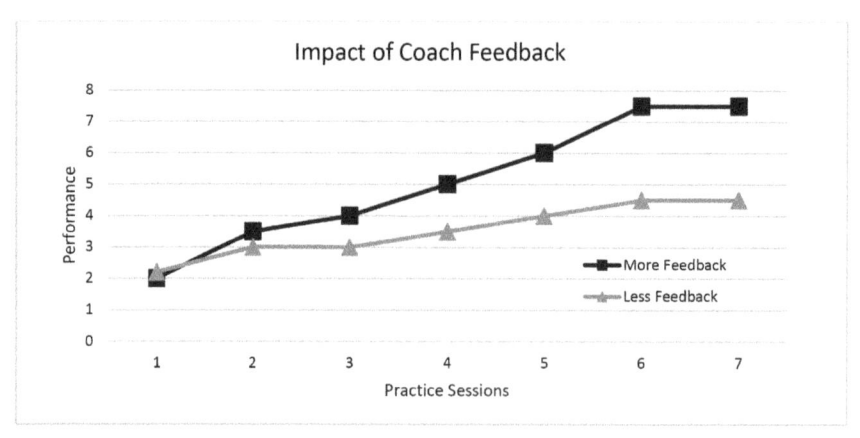

FIGURE 1.1
A hypothetical *performance* curve commonly mislabeled as a *learning* curve. The curve depicts performance of athletes practicing with different amounts of coach feedback across practice sessions.

The "Learning Curve"

Figure 1.1 is a *performance* curve commonly mislabeled as a "learning curve." Our reliance on learning curves to show improvements over time is deep and traditional. In all types of contexts in society, when we describe or depict improvements over time, we have historically termed them *learning* curves. When we try to perform a new task, we typically say we experience a *learning curve*. However, motor-learning research has clearly articulated that a performance improvement graphically depicted over time is more accurately termed a performance curve, rather than a learning curve. To be called a learning curve, it needs more—it needs to include some measure(s) of *learning*. While coaches want to see high-level performances in practice, they should be asking important questions such as: Can athletes sustain the level of performance over time? Can they consistently repeat the performance? Can they replicate the performance in a different environment? These types of questions help determine whether practice performance will transfer to the target context. Since learning and transfer are at the heart of evaluating practice effectiveness, we should modify the traditional conception of a performance curve.

Learning curves include tests of learning. In motor-learning research, this is most often done by including *retention* and *transfer* tests after a sustained amount of practice. A retention test would assess performance of athletes after some time away from practice, and performance is measured while receiving no feedback or instruction (like a game!). These tests are used to measure the more permanent effects of practice (e.g., memory) while letting the temporary aspects (e.g., fatigue) wear off or dissipate. A transfer test is used to represent how generalizable practice is to a slightly different target context. These tests might measure, for example, performance of the skill from a different distance/angle, at a different speed, or on a different surface. Again, no feedback or instruction is provided during the test. Transfer tests are designed to measure the depth of learning gained from practice, with the assumption that deeper learning is more transferable to different contexts (again, like a game!). The science of transfer (see chapter 2) supports the application of both tests to measure the effectiveness of practice.[4]

Figure 1.2 adds a learning measure to the performance curve so that it now depicts a learning curve. It adds a hypothetical transfer test as a measure of learning (it could also be a retention test). For our purposes, we combine transfer and retention as the measure of learning. The transfer test in figure 1.2 represents performance of the practiced skill in a different context (transfer), after some time off from practicing (retention). Remember, *different context* is any variation in the skill or environment that wasn't originally practiced, and the test was conducted without instruction or feedback. The

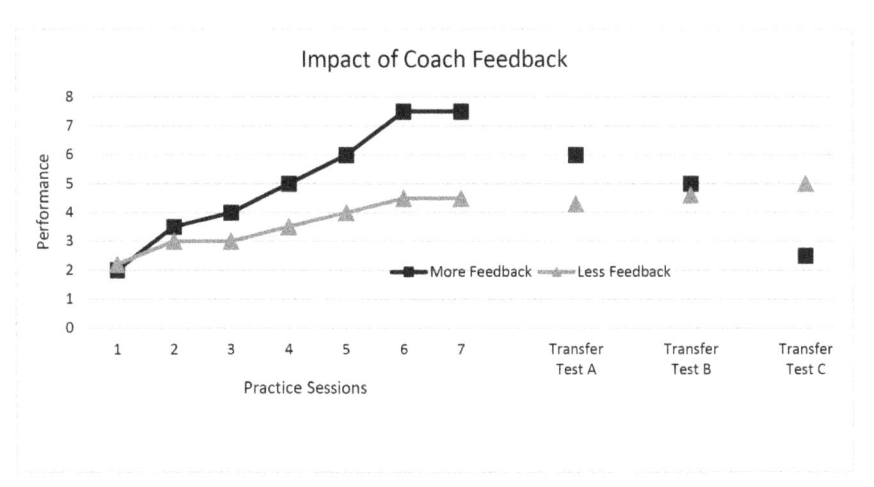

FIGURE 1.2
A true *learning curve* (hypothetical) depicting performance of athletes practicing with different amounts of coach feedback. Three possible outcomes are shown when a learning measure is applied after practice (Transfer Test A, Transfer Test B, or Transfer Test C).

learning curve in figure 1.2 shows three possible learning outcomes of applying the transfer test (Transfer Tests A, B, and C).

Let's interpret each possible outcome:

Test A: Some of the impact of more coach feedback had worn off. The learning impact of more feedback was not as great as it appeared in practice (performance curve), but it is still something coaches should provide.

Test B: There was little learning impact of more coach feedback. That is, more feedback was beneficial during practice, but it did not cause a permanent, transferable change in performance. This *performance vs. learning distinction* is commonly seen in motor-learning and practice research. And of course, this is like the "they did great in practice but didn't transfer it to the game" phenomenon.

Test C: More coach feedback artificially inflated practice performance relative to the learning measure (transfer test). This is a *performance-learning trade-off*. The "less feedback" condition had lower practice performance, but athletes learned more, when measured on the transfer test. The "more feedback" condition showed higher practice performance, but less learning. Motor-learning studies often show that practice masks the amount of true learning that is occurring.[5] Sometimes athletes' practice performance can mislead coaches, causing them to overestimate or underestimate their athletes' game performance based on their practice performance.

Performance Variables vs. Learning Variables

The application of transfer and retention tests in practice research allows us to tease out practice conditions that generate more permanent skill improvements in our athletes compared to more temporary improvements. More specifically, we can identify between practice conditions that (a) increase practice performance only, (b) increase both practice and learning, and (c) increase learning only. Research has identified a variety of practice conditions (or variables) that impact performance and learning differently. In figure 1.1, the specific (and hypothetical) variable is the *amount of coach feedback* (more or less). Transfer Test A in figure 1.2 is an example that the amount of coach feedback is both a *performance* and a *learning variable*, as more feedback increases practice performance and shows a higher transfer test score (learning). Transfer Test B is an example that more feedback is a *performance variable*, as it impacts performance in a more temporary way, during practice, but it has no impact on learning. Transfer Test C is again an example that more feedback is both a *performance* and *learning variable*. However, the impact on learning is in the wrong direction, as it depresses transfer test performance.

Since the purpose of practice is to learn and transfer what we practice, determining practice conditions that are more learning oriented (relatively permanent and generalizable) vs. performance oriented (temporary) is an important target for both researchers and coaches. While we know of obvious and controllable performance variables (e.g., fatigue, anxiety, injury, boredom, weather), transfer of learning is dependent on identifying and then implementing important learning variables into practice.

TYPES OF PRACTICE
One of the responses to our initial question of "why do we practice?" could very well have been, "It depends." It would be a good answer. Practice *depends* on a variety of factors related to our athletes' development, and several types of practice can produce transfer of learning. How we practice should match our athletes' level of readiness with respect to factors such as athlete goals, age, maturation, and competitive level. Why we practice for 8-year-olds in a recreation league (e.g., socialization, fun) will of course differ from why we practice for 18-year-olds in high school (e.g., competition, mastery, winning, fun). The important point is that skill acquisition and expertise is developmental, and the role of practice changes as athletes progress through a variety of developmental phases. To recognize the developmental nature of skill acquisition, different types of practice have been conceptualized for athletes as they develop their skills.

"Deliberate" Practice vs. "Purposeful" Practice
In 2016 Anders Ericsson and Robert Pool's book called *Peak: Secrets from the New Science of Expertise* clarified the role of different types of practice to achieve expertise in areas such as music, art, dance, and sport.[6]

Deliberate practice is the type of practice necessary to achieve expert levels. This type of training is highly structured and demands high levels of commitment, effort, and instruction. Key aspects of the original definition of deliberate practice are excerpted below.

Deliberate practice is a highly structured activity . . . specific tasks are invented to overcome weaknesses, and performance is carefully monitored . . . deliberate practice requires effort and is not inherently enjoyable. Individuals are motivated to practice because practice improves performance . . . engaging in deliberate practice generates no immediate monetary rewards and generates costs associated with access to teachers and training environments . . . an understanding of the long-term consequences of deliberate practice is important . . . to assure effective learning, subjects ideally should be given explicit instructions about the best method and be supervised by a qualified teacher.[7]

While elements of deliberate practice sound attractive (expert level!), it may not fit into the reason most of our athletes practice. It's characterized by unusually high levels of long-term effort and commitment and a reliance on high amounts of specialized instruction, training methods, and resources. As well, it is practice that's *not inherently enjoyable*. It's often viewed as an "unbalanced" devotion to the "job" of becoming an expert. For the readers of this book, deliberate practice is unrealistic and often ill advised. For example, our athletes are at a variety of developmental and readiness levels, and intrinsically enjoyable sport experiences are important for their motivation and long-term development (discussed in chapter 3). So, let's take it down a notch with the next type of practice that better fits our purpose.

Purposeful practice fits better with why most of our athletes practice. The characteristics of purposeful practice include:

1. *Well-defined and specific goals.* Achieving a series of small improvements while working toward longer-term and specific goals, adding challenge as practice continues.
2. *Focused effort.* Full and focused attention is on the practice activity and the skills to be improved.
3. *Feedback and guidance.* Feedback is needed to improve skills, reinforce behaviors, and enhance motivation, and is provided from someone who can guide practice.
4. *Work outside the comfort zone.* Skill improvement is under conditions of continual challenge. Instead of repetitive practice that is comfortable or easy, challenges are added to continue improvement.

Here is how Ericsson and Pool summarize purposeful practice:

> Get outside your comfort zone, but do it in a focused way, with clear goals, a plan for reaching those goals, and a way to monitor your progress. Oh, and figure out a way to maintain your motivation.[8]

So, the purpose of practice should include lots of purposeful practice! However, we also recognize that transfer of learning can also occur under conditions that don't fit the characteristics of purposeful practice. While purposeful practice implies a coach-led approach with athletes that have extrinsic goals (e.g., performance outcomes), there is growing support for practice conditions that are more indirect, where implicit learning occurs or when athletes may have more intrinsic goals. As such, we recommend coaches consider other types of practice that fit the developmental levels of their athletes and promote transfer of learning.

Play and Spontaneous Practice

These two forms of practice depend on who leads or shapes the practice activity (coach, athlete, or peer) and the athlete's goal of practice (extrinsic on the outcome or intrinsic on the process). Figure 1.3 shows a matrix where the different practice types can be situated.[9]

Play practice. There is growing support for *play practice* activities that can be incorporated into structured practice to help develop skills. These types of practice maintain the intrinsic enjoyment of the sport while still under coach supervision. We discuss more of this type of practice in chapter 9, the games-based chapter. *Deliberate play* is more intrinsically focused athlete-led activities. These sport activities are intrinsically motivating, provide immediate gratification, and are specifically designed to maximize enjoyment. *Spontaneous practice* constitutes a form of informal learning that is athlete-determined and is not supervised by adults. In sport, it is structured by athletes in their free time with the goal of improving aspects of their sport skills (e.g., extrinsic value). In this practice, athletes work on what they choose, and they don't necessarily identify the most important skills to work on or follow a coach-specified progression or plan.

There are other types or forms of practice that can be differentiated from purposeful practice.[10] *Maintenance practice* is the practice of skills that can al-

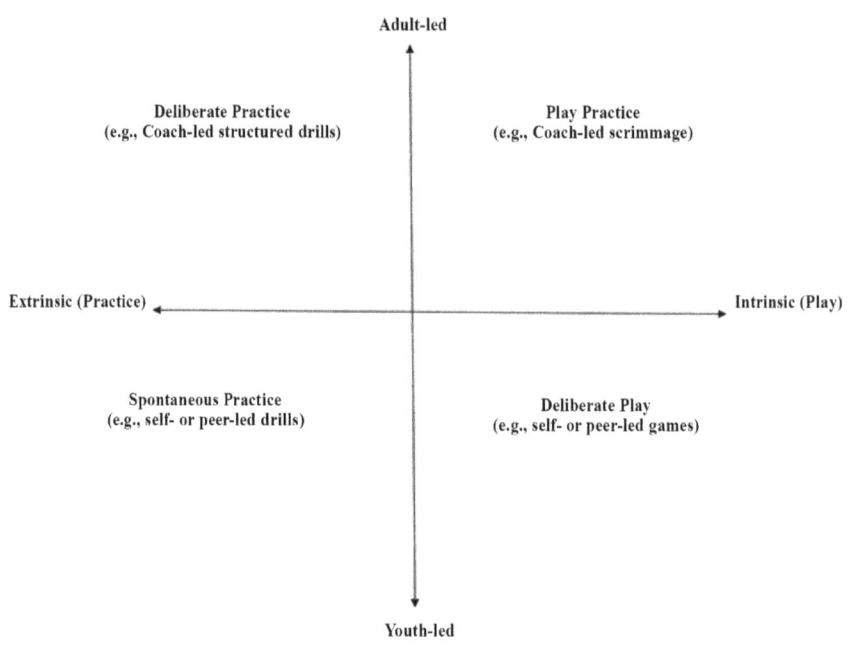

```
                        Adult-led
                           ▲
                           │
   Deliberate Practice     │    Play Practice
(e.g., Coach-led structured│  (e.g., Coach-led scrimmage)
         drills)           │
                           │
Extrinsic (Practice) ◄─────┼─────► Intrinsic (Play)
                           │
   Spontaneous Practice    │    Deliberate Play
 (e.g., self- or peer-led  │  (e.g., self- or peer-led games)
         drills)           │
                           │
                           ▼
                        Youth-led
```

FIGURE 1.3
Matrix of different types of sport and practice activities. All are potentially valuable to transfer of learning. (Adapted from Côté and Erickson, "Diversification and Deliberate Play")

ready be successfully performed, rather than for new learning. *Naïve practice* is the repetitive practice of skill(s) without having a goal or set purpose, hoping it will lead to improvement but not being challenged out of your comfort zone. *Competition practice* is practice that seeks to win against other athletes, not explicitly seeking to improve performance or increase learning. We discuss more of these practice types in chapter 4, the design chapter.

The important point about types of practice is that the "best" type of practice often depends on the coach's practice objectives or the developmental readiness of athletes. For example, late in the season, the coach may conduct more maintenance and competition practice, rather than purposeful practice. And to enhance fun and motivation for less-skilled athletes, the coach may integrate deliberate play games before or after competition practice. While the purpose of practice remains the same (learn and transfer what we practice), it is important for coaches to balance purposeful practice with other forms of practice. The good news is that there is value in all the types of practice discussed above, and each can provide positive transfer of learning.

TYPES OF SKILL

Becoming skilled in a sport is complicated. Skill is made up of different types of abilities, and they are all important to performance in the game. Coaches should first consider what types of skill are most important for their athletes to practice. An understanding of skill types can help coaches better design practice to increase transfer.

Technical, Tactical, and Mental Skills

Skill developed with practice can be placed into three categories.[11] These include *technical*, *tactical*, and *mental* skills. Below are these skill types, with examples:

> *Technical skills*: Effective execution of movement pattern or technique. Examples: serving a tennis ball, dribbling a soccer ball, dismount off a high bar (sometimes called *physical* skills).
>
> *Tactical skills*: Decision-making that enables athletes to gain an advantage over their opponents. Examples: deciding to dribble or pass, anticipating type and location of serve, game or team strategy.
>
> *Mental skills*: Mobilization of thoughts and feelings to enhance performance of the skill(s) in competition. Examples: maintaining composure, focus of attention, managing anxiety.

Coaches should balance practice activities that develop athletes in all three types of skills. An overemphasis on one or two types over the other type(s) may compromise overall athlete skill development and reduce the potential for transfer. For example, an athlete's inability to manage anxiety (mental skill) will reduce the transfer of their practice to the competition, even if they are highly skilled in the technical (movement) and tactical (decision-making) elements. The *National Standards for Sport Coaches*[12] reinforces the importance of developing all types of skill in athletes. Skills that should be taught by coaches include competition strategies and tactics (standard 26), mental and psychological skills (standard 27), team and life skills (standard 28), and sport-specific skills and techniques (standards 30–32).

Hard and Soft Skills

A second way to conceptualize important skill types is borrowed from Daniel Coyle's *The Little Book of Talent*, which is a spin-off of his earlier book, *The Talent Code*. He asserts the two primary forms of skill are "hard skills" and "soft skills"[13] and that before practice starts, we should figure out if our skill is a hard or soft one.

Hard skills are "robotic" skills that consist of reliably executing a mechanically similar movement pattern repeatedly, such as shooting a free throw in basketball, a golf swing, or a gymnastic bar routine. These skills are executed in predictable and stable environments where there is one best movement solution (sometimes called "closed" skills in the motor-learning literature). This contrasts with soft skills that consist of manipulating the environment to skillfully perform. These skills are executed in dynamic, unpredictable, and variable environments where there are multiple solutions to the problem (sometimes called "open" skills in the motor-learning literature), and successful performance relies heavily on *perception*. Soft skills would be soccer, basketball, or hockey players manipulating the defense and the ball to create openings or passing lanes. Table 1.1 highlights the elements of skill on the hard–soft continuum.

What's important is that hard and soft skills require different elements of skill that need be developed. Soft skills require awareness of and decision-making within chaotic environments, while hard skills require lots of pre-planning in controlled environments. This impacts how coaches should design practice. If a sport is soft-skill dominant, then practice should be about developing players who can solve problems and discover solutions with teammates and against opponents in game-like settings, rather than developing players who can repeat the same movement patterns identically from trial to trial. It's likely that many sport skills are more soft-skill dominant than we think. Even in an assumed hard-skill sport such as golf, there is unpredictability from hole to hole, lie to lie, and course to course. And as discussed later, there is even more variation in those repeatable swings than we think. As such, skill may be more about the ability to discover movement solutions

Table 1.1. Overview of "hard" and "soft" skills, with distinguishing elements for each skill type.

	Hard Skills	Hard/Soft Blend	Soft Skills
Elements	Individual competition Aesthetic sports Track and field events, golf, gymnastics events	Partner competition Court sports Baseball, tennis, volleyball	Team competition Invasion sports Soccer, lacrosse, basketball
Element: Movement Planning	Preplanned Choreographed	Some preplanned Some reactive	Reactive Some preplanned
Element: Decision-Making	Long time to make decisions Few options/choices	Long and short time to make decisions Some options/choices	Very little time to make decisions
Element: Environmental Variability	Stable Predictable Controlled Long wait times Many restrictions (e.g., rules, distances)	Stable and dynamic Predictable and unpredictable Controlled and chaotic Long stoppages of play Some restrictions (e.g., positions, zones)	Dynamic Unpredictable Chaotic Short stoppages of play Few restrictions (e.g., full-field play)

in dynamic game-like environments than about repeating perfect movements in predictable controlled environments.

FOCUS PRACTICE ON THE MOST IMPORTANT THINGS

To quote Stephen Covey, "The main thing is to keep the main thing the main thing."[14] This message reminds us that keeping our focus and efforts on the most important goals helps us accomplish them. The "main thing" in this book is to achieve the purpose of practice, or the transfer of learning. In this section, we present some common beliefs that can take our focus away from this main thing. We then provide a list of skill elements that will keep our focus on the main thing. This reflection should help shape how coaches view the purpose of practice.

Practice Beliefs That Take Our Focus off the Main Thing

The following assumptions or beliefs stem from years of tradition as well as human tendencies that we all struggle with. We provide them in a "Top 10" list, with brief explanations, not ranked in order of importance.

1. *Repetitions, Repetitions, Repetitions.* Wait, how can repetitions be a distraction? Those who study practice generally agree that repetitions are one of the most important aspects of skill acquisition. Even legendary John Wooden believed in the power of repetitions when he said, "Repetition is the key to learning."[15] But there is a need to modify the well-accepted notion that *more* repetitions are better for skill acquisition. Motor-learning research is replete with studies stressing the quality of repetitions or showing how repetitions are often more important for learning. Like the number of hours spent studying (or cramming) for a test, the number of repetitions performed may not correlate with test or game performance.

2. *Looking Good in Practice.* The common sentiment is "we play like we practice." Most of us appreciate "good" practice sessions where our players demonstrate high levels of success. We are drawn to drills that can be mastered by our athletes. Coaches and athletes feel satisfied in controlled drills and activities where feedback is plentiful and large amounts of improvements can be seen. This yields a tendency to conduct "pretty" drills in practice that may not transfer well to less-predictable game conditions. Looking good in practice often doesn't transfer well to the chaos of the game.

3. *Perfect Practice.* There is also a deep-rooted belief that "practice makes perfect" or the notion that "perfect practice makes perfect." These quotes often refer to using an ideal or perfect movement or technique (e.g., a perfect golf swing). It implies one perfect solution to a movement, with the practice goal to mimic or replicate the perfect technique. Such an emphasis may discourage individuals from taking risks and discovering solutions that best fit their individual characteristics. Mistakes (and failures) are an important part of the learning process. While there may be no such thing as a perfect practice, there is value in striving for perfection. Most likely we get closer to "perfect" through making errors and discovering new solutions. In many ways, "imperfect" practice transfers better than "perfect" practice.

4. *Immediate Results.* Our societal norms often reinforce the concept of immediate gratification. Getting answers quickly (e.g., Google and Wikipedia research) is enticing and sometimes addictive. However, these immediate results may sometimes sacrifice the depth and quality of learning. Helping athletes hit 9 out of 10 shots at the end of a practice drill is immediately gratifying. It suggests our drill and instruction was effective. Delayed gratification might better align with the notion that expertise and learning take time and patience. And as Wooden also said, "It takes time to create excellence. If it could be done quickly, more people would do it."[16]
5. *The Physical.* Sports are physical competitions. As such, it becomes easy to focus our practice time on the physical and technical skills needed for success. As well, it's often easy to see and evaluate physical techniques, with newer technologies making it even easier. The emphasis on the technical skills sometimes comes at the expense of the other skill types. Tactical and mental skills such as perception, decision-making, attentional focus, and game awareness are equally important for performance. Whether or not practice transfers to the competition depends on much more than mastering the physical techniques.
6. *Coach Control.* As coaches, we are responsible for the skill development of our athletes. This sometimes gets converted to the message that athlete development depends on the coach. While elements of this may hold true, there is agreement that when athletes assume responsibility for some of their own skill development, learning increases. Practice conditions that are coach-driven, where coaches make all decisions and provide all the instruction, can create a sense of dependence that doesn't transfer well. Maximizing athlete development and avoiding this dependence often requires the uncomfortable—giving up some control of practice conditions to our athletes.
7. *The Explicit.* Related to coach control is the notion that instruction provided to athletes by the coach must be *explicit*. That is, for athletes to improve, instruction needs to be direct, clear, loud, and obvious, and the more direct the instruction, the better. However, *implicit* methods of coaching have also proven effective to increase athlete learning. For example, a coach might manipulate practice conditions to improve targeted athlete skills or behaviors *without* directly instructing. Implicit learning

(without awareness) can facilitate athletes' attention and problem-solving skills that transfer well to competition.

8. *The Outcome.* Since coaches are often judged by outcomes (e.g., wins and losses, beating others), it stands to reason that this outcome emphasis is important during practice sessions. A problem with an overuse of "outcome-oriented" practice activities is that athletes learn to judge their development compared to others, rather than to their own levels of improvement. Coaches that are more "process oriented" might help athletes to understand the importance of improving those things under their own control (e.g., effort and improvement). Maintaining effort regardless of competitive outcomes (i.e., winning or losing) is important for athletes to reach their skill potential. When the goal of practice activities is for athletes to master their own skills, then continued athlete improvement (and a desirable outcome) is often more likely.

9. *Automaticity.* Practice is necessary to make a skill "automatic," and athletes need to develop "muscle memory." This implies that athletes should practice until skills can be executed with little or no conscious thought or attention. This is often translated to an emphasis on high numbers of "mindless" repetitions until automaticity is established. Sometimes this can come at the expense of developing "thinking" athletes who can problem-solve and adapt their skill to the unpredictable nature of competition. Since "no two shots are exactly the same" in many competitions, players need to practice repetitions where they learn adaptability to the changing environment. This skill of adaptability can be practiced, and it transfers well to competition.

10. *Copycats.* Coaches tend to emulate success. We often design our practice conditions around (a) how successful (winning) coaches do it, and/or (b) how we practiced and were coached when we played. This "copycat" approach to practice can be useful, with valid reasons, but it can also be a flawed approach. Coaching situations are unique to specific environments (e.g., community, parents, available athletes, and resources). While we advocate copying many of John Wooden's practice methods, we also recognize that his methods were unique to his era, his athletes, and likely a different coaching environment. As such, replicating all his practice methods may not be advisable. A copycat approach may also come at the

expense of discovering better methods based on new research. A lot has changed in the science of practice, and new findings consistently update "best practice" for coaches. Best practice is likely a blend of experience, sharing ideas, and applying new, research-supported practice methods (e.g., this book!).

Sharpen Our Focus on the Main Thing

Above, we identified some practice beliefs that take our focus off the purpose of practice. Now let's identify some elements we should focus on to improve the transfer of learning. Based on the motor-skill learning literature, if we keep our focus on practice conditions that create these skill elements in our athletes, we are more likely to achieve transfer of learning. These skill elements are provided again in a "Top 10" list below, with brief explanations, not ranked in order of importance.

1. *Independence.* Skilled independent athletes rely less on others and more on themselves to build their abilities and guide their performance. They are able to self-improve, making their own skill adjustments both in practice and competitions.
2. *Growth Mind-Set.* Skilled athletes with this mind-set have a deep belief that effort, feedback, and mistakes are essential for growth and skill development. Their mind-set embraces the learning *process* and increases their perseverance in practicing skills and their resilience in the face of failures.
3. *Attention Skills.* Skilled athletes with focused attention can control, allocate, and direct their attention effectively. They can maximize their capacity by strategically shifting their focus of attention or by selectively attending to key elements.
4. *Anticipation Skills.* Skilled athletes with this tactical ability have a "game sense" or seem to know what and when something is coming and "react" faster and more accurately than others. They know where and when to look for the most important information. They can "quiet" their vision or speed up their visual scan to match the situation.
5. *Decision-Making.* Skilled athletes with this tactical ability can sort through information to make accurate decisions. In fast-paced competitions, they can quickly work through options, or for slower-paced situations, they are

able to sift through and select the most important information. They have game IQ; they understand the tactics and strategies needed in competition.
6. *Memory Skills.* Skilled athletes can store and retrieve information accurately and quickly. They can retain skills after periods of time off, and they tend to forget less during times of interference and stress. Instead of memorizing a skill or a solution for one situation, they can adapt what they remember to different situations.
7. *Movement Stability and Consistency.* Skilled athletes with this technical ability can consistently show highly similar movements and techniques over time and in different environments. They are able to maintain their form or technique in a variety of situations (e.g., from different body positions or locations). These movements require little attention or thought from the athlete, allowing them to attend to other game-related elements.
8. *Adaptability.* Skilled athletes can adapt their movements and abilities to meet the demands of the competition. This adaptability can apply to all the skill types. For example, they can adapt their stable movement by changing speeds, or they can change their strategy based on different teammate and opponent locations and movements. Adaptable players can quickly apply "movement solutions" to the wide range of problems that appear in the real game environment.
9. *Error Detection and Correction.* Skilled athletes can detect their own errors and make appropriate movement adjustments to increase their performance. They rely on a high level of movement sense or "kinesthetic" awareness, combined with a high level of knowledge to improve their own performance.
10. *Psychological Control.* Skilled athletes can control their mental abilities during competition. This might include managing competitive stress by increasing or decreasing their arousal levels, mentally or visually rehearsing their skills, using positive self-talk, or applying strategies to increase focus, motivation, or confidence.

TRANSFER THIS

Recall the Coach Rodriguez scenario at the beginning of the chapter. It seems she might want to further reflect on the purpose of practice. First, it appears she might be practicing with the goal of performing well in practice. It's hard to blame her, as she is getting reinforced for organizing a well-run practice from administrators and parents. We encourage her to remember that the goal of practice is to learn and transfer, and sometimes learning is not directly observable during practice. Learning is best measured in retention and transfer tests, or in her case, in the games. Her team's "learning curve" shows a significant drop in performance on their transfer test (games), and it may be due to the way they practice.

Coach Rodriguez seems to be falling prey to some of the assumptions or beliefs that took her focus off the purpose of practice, particularly the tendencies to *look good in practice* and *perfect practice*. It seems her methods have players striving to demonstrate perfect techniques in practice, perhaps at the expense of athlete problem-solving and thinking skills. Her practices also seem to emphasize seeing *immediate results* of practice efforts. Long-term learning often requires time and patience. Finally, it appears *coach control* is primarily with the coach rather than shared with the players. Given her coach-centered practice structure, they may have grown dependent on her to detect and correct their performance errors. Perhaps some of her team's "unforced" game errors are due to this dependence.

The purpose of practice includes developing different skill types, and her emphasis is on technical skills, perhaps excluding the players learning tactical and mental skills. This might help explain some of the mental errors her players are making in competition. Volleyball also is considered "soft skill" dominant. It requires players to read unpredictable or open environments to solve problems and make rapid decisions. Her practice sessions align more with "hard skill" elements of making consistent or robotic movements in closed or predictable environments. We recommend she reflect on the "Top 10" list of important skill elements. For example, practice should develop skill elements such as anticipation (tactical), adaptability, and psychological control (mental). Development of these skills seems to be lacking in her tightly controlled, highly organized practice setting.

This chapter focused on coaches having a mind-set around the purpose of practice. As such, the items below are coach reflection questions or activities. The more you honestly reflect on them, the more you will be ready for the next chapters in this book.

Coaches, Transfer This

1. Reflect on the 10 things that take your focus off the purpose of practice. Identify a couple you can especially relate to, either from your past experiences or your own beliefs. Can they be modified to better align with the purpose of practice? How?
2. Some practice conditions facilitate good performance in practice but don't have the same impact on learning, or in the competition. Identify a potential "performance variable," or a practice condition or activity where athletes perform well and look good in practice but struggle to perform well in the game. Can this condition be modified for better learning? How?
3. All practice activities should be conducted for the purpose of answering the question "Will it transfer?" to the target task or context. This transfer can either be to a future practice activity or to the next competition. Identify some of your practice activities or conditions that you think transfer well and reflect on why or how they transfer well.
4. Do your practice sessions emphasize a balanced development in the three skill types of technical, tactical, and mental? Is your sport more hard- or soft-skill dominant? Share a practice activity that aligns with the nature of your sport (hard or soft) and seeks to develop abilities in all three skill types.
5. Reflect on the 10 skill elements most important for transfer of learning. Which of these elements do you effectively facilitate in your practices? Which of them would you like to explore further or emphasize more in practice? Why?

Coach Educators and Developers, Transfer This

1. Facilitate an open philosophical discussion about the purpose of practice at your level of competition. Seek consensus that regardless of athlete participation level, the purpose of practice is to facilitate transfer of learning forward.
2. Have coaches reflect on situations where they have witnessed a mismatch between athletes' performance in practice and their performance in competition. What are their explanations for this performance-learning distinction, or trade-off?

3. Facilitate a discussion of the importance of the different types of skill for performance. Ask coaches to provide examples where their athletes were less accomplished in certain types of skills (e.g., mental) and how that impacted the transfer of practice to the game. How could they have better developed these skills in practice?
4. Have coaches provide real-world examples of the "Top 10" elements that can take the focus off the purpose of practice. Debate and explore coach agreements and disagreements about the beliefs.
5. Explore and debate the "Top 10" skill elements with coaches. In what ways do coaches "teach" these skills in their practices? In what ways could they better incorporate them into their practices?

2

The Science of Transfer

Coach Johnson, a first-year hitting coach for a high school baseball team, was eager to learn about the science of hitting so that he could be a better coach. He hit (pun intended) the Internet hard and discovered the theory of "muscle memory." It was popular and something that seemed to make a lot of sense. He read about research that said good muscle memory was the result of hitters replicating the ideal swing pattern through thousands of repetitions (and that it took 10,000 hours to be an expert). So, batting practice in the preseason emphasized thousands of repetitions executing the "perfect" swing in the batting cage (tee work, soft-toss, and short-toss batting practice [BP]). He showed his players videos of the "best" swings among professional hitters and provided heavy amounts of instruction and feedback to change or fix their swing patterns. During preseason batting practice, his players' swings were looking beautiful, and they were making great contact. When the season started, his hitters struggled. At the halfway point in the season, his team had the lowest batting average in the league and was leading the league in strikeouts. He wondered what was going on, and he started to doubt the "science" of hitting.

Why a science chapter in a practice strategies book? Chapter 1 was a reflection on *why* we practice. The biggest reason stated was for the transfer of learning, so that coaches always ask the question, "Will it transfer?" We follow up now with, "*Why* will it transfer?" and, "Who says?" When coaches better understand why or how certain practice conditions may be better, their decision-making improves. They are more informed in designing and evaluating practice conditions. They trust their practice methods and are better able to communicate the *why* to their players. As a result, both coach and athlete are likely to get more out of practice.

This chapter provides (1) an overview of the transfer of learning and how it works, and (2) the key transfer of learning theories that most impact the design of practice conditions. We consolidated the most significant transfer of learning theories from the motor-learning, skill-acquisition, and expertise literature. Collectively, they represent the science behind the transfer of practice conditions, and they will transfer forward to support the remaining chapters of this book.

ABOUT TRANSFER OF LEARNING

Transfer of learning is defined as the influence of previous experiences on learning a new skill or on the performance of a skill in the *target context*. It rests on the premise that all new learning occurs against the backdrop of prior learning.[1] We identified in chapter 1 that the reason we practice a skill is to increase the likelihood of performing it in the target context, or to develop the capability to transfer the practice performance to the next skill or to a different environment. So, transfer is at the heart of learning in such a way that transfer and learning are essentially the same thing. In this way, we are always coaching and teaching for transfer for two primary reasons[2]:

1. *Advance the athlete to the next skill level.* The best coaches continue to provide opportunities for individualized skill development, regardless of skill level. Planning for transfer includes arranging the *sequence* and *complexity* of skills that athletes are practicing. Coaching is designing increasingly complex practice that fits an athlete's developmental level. A youth soccer coach might implement a stationary ball control drill before progressing to moving around a stationary defender and then to a moving defender. A college baseball coach might have a hitter hold on to a towel during a drill so that the front elbow stays connected and helps their swing. In both situations, coaches are relying on positive transfer of learning to advance the athlete to the next skill level.

2. *Evaluate the effectiveness of practice.* As discussed in chapter 1, the impact of practice should be evaluated *not* on how well the skill is performed in practice, but on how well the practiced skill is performed in the target context. For coaches, the test is most often performance in the competitive or game environment. Sometimes, however, the target context is how athletes perform in the next drill in practice. For example, did the basketball give-and-go drill transfer to the three-on-three scrimmage at the end of practice?

Direction and Amount of Transfer

All practice activities fall on a continuum of direction (positive to negative) and amount (zero to high) of transfer. A practice activity (transfer task) can produce *positive* transfer to the target task and could vary from low to high amounts. A practice activity can also generate *negative* transfer, which could also vary from low to high amounts, as seen in figure 2.1. A given practice activity (transfer task) falls on this continuum, and coaches can begin by plotting a drill or practice activity on this continuum.

Positive transfer facilitates performance on the target task. For example, practicing a gymnastic stunt in isolation (transfer task) might produce *high positive* transfer to the whole routine (target task). Practice of a figure-8 fast-break basketball drill (transfer task) might produce *low positive* transfer to a real-game fast break (target task), given both the similarities (passing skills) and differences (follow the pass and go behind the receiver) between the two tasks.

Negative transfer hinders performance on the target task. A beginning golfer with past experiences swinging a field hockey stick (transfer task) might yield

Transfer Direction

Negative	Zero	Positive

⬅――――――――――――――――――――――――――――➡

High	Low	Zero	Low	High

Transfer Amount

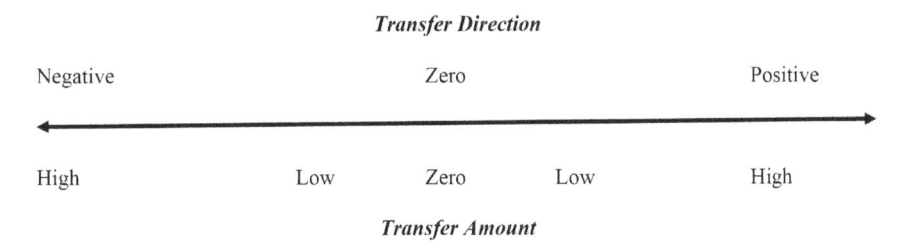

FIGURE 2.1
The continuum of transfer direction and amount of transfer. A practice activity can be placed on this continuum.

high negative transfer to the golf swing (target task) due to differences in grip, swing patterns, and speed, or a tennis player executing an overhead smash in badminton might experience *moderate negative* transfer due the wrist snap differences in the two skills. All practice activities fall somewhere on this continuum. To better design a practice activity with potential for high positive transfer, it's important to first determine the target task.

Distance of Transfer

Practice activities also fall on a continuum of transfer distance. Distance refers to how far forward coaches want to transfer their practice activity. How much separation is there between the transfer task and the target task? This has also been referred to as "transfer specificity," or how specific the transfer task is to the target task. Transfer distance is usually expressed in terms of near, moderate, or far transfer,[3] as shown in figure 2.2. A given practice activity falls on this distance continuum.

Near (Specific) Transfer

Coaches might plan activities that are near (specific) to the target task—that is, the transfer task is highly similar or identical to the demands of the target context. Near transfer typically involves a transfer task that is conducted at a point relatively close or near in time (e.g., same practice session or the next-day game). As well, near transfers typically involve the transfer between the *same* skill. For example, a swimmer practicing their event in a timed competitive task in the pool would be highly specific since it is almost identical and near to the actual race event. A long jumper might practice the approach (part practice) for several repetitions before practicing the whole long-jump skill. Transfer in these situations is usually high (amount) and positive (direction),

Transfer Distance

Near	Moderate	Far
Specific		General
Same Skill		Different Skills/Sport

FIGURE 2.2
The continuum of transfer distance. A practice activity can be placed on this continuum.

given the degree of specificity (or short distance) between the transfer and target task. It's worth noting here that many practice activities we consider to be near transfer may not actually be. A figure-8 basketball drill would *not* be considered near transfer if the target task is a five-on-five scrimmage (target task). They are relatively different, with some distance between the two activities. A modified three-on-two fast-break game with defenders is closer in similarity and distance to the five-on-five scrimmage and is a better example of near transfer. Coaches who attempt to simulate tomorrow's game (target task) with a game-like scrimmage (transfer task) are seeking near transfer. Though we make the case later, this might more often be moderate transfer.

Far (General) Transfer
On the other end of the continuum, far transfer situations are where the practice activity appears to have little to do with the target context. The transfer task is relatively dissimilar to, and distant in time from, the target task; the transfer task itself does not really look that "similar" to the target context. Far transfer emphasizes the improvement of more general underlying processes important to performance in the target context, such as fundamental movement patterns (e.g., running, jumping), anticipation and "court vision" (i.e., visually scanning the court), kinesthetic awareness, or pattern recognition. At the very end of the continuum, far transfer would involve the transfer between different skills. For example, a player's experience recognizing offensive patterns in soccer (transfer task) might facilitate positive far transfer to basketball game play (target context). A little closer in on the continuum, the swimmer practicing swimming at different distances in an open-water environment would be dissimilar to and far away from the target context of swimming a timed race in a pool. Transfer in these situations is generally not as high and positive as near-transfer situations.

Some coaches may recognize the concept of "donor" sports, in which two different sports are seen to hold value to success in the target sport, due to the "talent transfer" between the two sport(s).[4] For example, gymnastics has been considered a donor sport for diving, as it transfers body-control concepts and perceptual/psychological skills, such as attentional focus and concentration. Soccer may be considered a donor sport for basketball (or vice versa), given the transfer of perceptual, tactical, and decision-making skills. Far transfer provides an argument against the notion of early specialization in only one sport. Rather, it provides support for the diversification of sport experiences, as they provide transfer value in long-term athlete development.

Moderate Distance Transfer

Many practice conditions seek transfer from a moderate distance. In these situations, the transfer task is closer to the target task but "not all the way there."[5] For example, a soccer coach might use a small-sided soccer game (3 on 3), or a baseball coach might practice soft-toss hitting in a batting cage. These transfer tasks could be applied to the target context of the same skill later in practice, such as a soccer scrimmage or live batting practice (BP) on the field, respectively. They seek moderate distance transfer, as the target task is not the actual competition. Moderate transfer could also use a game or competition as the target context. In the examples above, the soccer scrimmage and the live BP on the field would be the transfer task and the target task is the actual game. Regardless, in all the examples above, the transfer task is moderately distant from the target task.

The goal of practice is to achieve high positive transfer, whether it be to the next practice activity (near) or to the competition (far). The "distance" perspective suggests that coaches are most often in the business of maximizing positive transfer from a moderate distance. It is unrealistic, in practice settings, to continually simulate the competitive game (i.e., near transfer). Real-world factors such as facilities, weather, player injuries, etc., make it either difficult or unwise to simulate identical competitive conditions. When the target task is the game or competition, many practice activities (e.g., modified drills, small games) are from a moderate distance. And we make the case later for positive transfer from a far distance.

THEORIES OF TRANSFER

Theories offer explanations for why transfer of learning occurs (or doesn't occur). Coaches with a better understanding of transfer theories will understand why some practice conditions yield more positive transfer than others. Hopefully, applying the theories will help coaches avoid the "copycat" approach to practice mentioned in chapter 1. We consolidated theories of research into four perspectives. All four offer explanations and predictions for the transfer of motor-skill learning; they provide the foundation transfer. They are presented in chronological order; that is, theories 1 and 2 have been around the longest, while theories 3 and 4 are newer and more contemporary. First, some notes about the four theories included in this chapter:

1. They are research-supported and replicated through a significant number of well-designed research studies. This means you can trust the theory as a valid and objective explanation, and less subject to personal bias, opinions, guesswork, or fads.
2. Each theory has boundaries, weaknesses, or areas that don't *fully* explain transfer of learning. They are not perfect, but they have stimulated much additional research.
3. One theory does not hold "the answer." Predicting positive transfer is the result of a combination or balance of theories. We should take the best from all of them. Good coaches absorb as much knowledge as they can; they embrace the idea that "knowledge is power."
4. They are practical; each can be applied in the real world. They are able to move out of a controlled lab and into the real world of coaching and practice. They help inform better practice (hence, this book!).

Transfer Theory 1: The Specificity of Transfer
Many years ago (2004), some of the best Major League Baseball (MLB) hitters stepped in to hit against one of the best fast-pitch softball pitchers, Olympian Jennie Finch. In an all-star exhibition event, she faced three MLB hitters, Albert Pujols, Mike Piazza, and Brian Giles. All three hitters struck out, never making contact with the ball! How could that be? Surely their bat speed and skill are good enough to hit a bigger, slower (68 mph) softball. The interpretation of their non-success lies in the negative transfer related to a conflicting stimulus-response situation. In the transfer task of hitting a softball pitch, the hitters executed a similar response (swing) but to a different stimulus (underhand softball pitch). The visual stimulus of a softball pitch is different. It perceptually rises from a lower release point (hip) and a non-elevated mound, and tracking or "seeing" a pitch from a distance of 17 fewer feet away requires a different visual strategy. No wonder Giles commented at the time, "Her fastball was the fastest thing I've ever seen from that distance. It rises and cuts at the same time." Pujols kept it simple, "I never want to experience that again."[6]

This theoretical perspective sought to predict transfer by analyzing the level of specificity needed between the practice activity and the target context. Does practice have to be highly similar (specific) to the target task? Can transfer occur when the practice activity is less similar (more general) to the target context? Research in this area offers support for both similarity-based transfer (specificity) and principles-based transfer (general).

Similarity-Based Transfer
Strength and conditioning coaches tell us that the *specificity of training* principle is paramount. The athlete's conditioning activities must match the energy system (e.g., anaerobic) and muscle types (e.g., fast twitch) that are demanded in the game. Similarly, the most traditional explanation of transfer of learning contends that positive transfer is due to the match between the transfer task (practice activity) and the target context (game environment). This explanation served as the starting point for most other theories. Thorndike's original theory (1914) of "identical elements" suggests that the more characteristics that are similar between two skills, the greater the transfer.[7] These characteristics, or elements, can be general (e.g., goal of the skill) or specific (e.g., downward wrist snap at release). A variation of this perspective analyzes the stimulus and response elements (S-R) of the transfer task and the target task. If the two tasks share an identical stimulus (S) (e.g., a rolling ball) and an identical response (R) (e.g., the kicking movement), then high positive transfer would be predicted. Tasks that share less similar or conflicting stimulus and response elements would yield low or negative transfer. This S-R relationship might help explain, for example, the negative transfer seen between hitting a baseball pitch and a fast-pitch softball (as shown above). While the two skills have a similar response (R) in the bat swing, the stimulus (S) element is distinctly different.

The similarity-based model more recently moved to identifying the specific areas that need to match for positive transfer to occur between the transfer and the target tasks. Elements that have been identified include (1) movement patterns (e.g., gymnastics kipping motion), (2) strategic elements (e.g., defensive positioning strategies), (3) conceptual elements (e.g., soccer offside rule), and (4) perceptual elements (e.g., visually scanning the field).[8]

An interesting area of research related to specificity is *transfer-appropriate processing*.[9] This perspective asks, "Does the practice activity require similar problem-solving processes as the target task?" It suggests that positive transfer occurs due to similarity of the cognitive processes required by the transfer task and the target skill. For example, if the two tasks involve rapid decision-making and a high degree of attention shifting, then positive transfer would be more likely. The theory suggests coaches should analyze for the mental-processing similarities between practice and the target context. For example, while shooting 10 free throws in a row at the end of a basketball practice is very similar in the movement elements (techniques) in shooting free throws in a game, the "processing" required in the game is very different. In the game context, the player must shift attention from the previous play, process current fatigue level, manage distractions from a variety of sources, manage the stress of only one or two (sometimes three) opportunities (vs. 10), and plan for the next defensive alignment. The 10 free-throw practice activity would not transfer well to the game due to the dissimilar type of problem-solving used in the practice task (not transfer appropriate). Similarly, serious golf instructors lament the practice of playing golf with a "mulligan." Getting a do-over after a bad shot removes the processing of stress and focus needed in the real competition and is not transfer appropriate. Coaches can do much to design practice for more transfer-appropriate processing.

Regardless of what elements are included in the specificity perspective, the premise is simple: Practice activities should be as similar as possible to the target context. For most coaches, this supports the idea of making practice conditions as game-like as possible. However, science shows it is not that simple, and there is value in practice activities that are less specific, targeting more general elements of transfer.

Principles-Based Transfer
Science also supports that transfer of learning occurs through the understanding of more general underlying principles, rules, concepts, or laws related to the practice task (and later applied to the target context).[10] It might explain why a soccer coach uses a zone tag game as a warm-up activity so that the general concept of spacing would transfer to a drill later in practice. These far-transfer principles are used to support practice design strategies such as sequencing sports of similar classifications. For example, the youth sport director or teacher might sequence together the "invasion" sports of soccer and lacrosse, given their similarities in guarding territory principles or

offensive spacing rules. A local youth softball coach once described how she plays competitive games of kickball early in the preseason. While it wasn't specific to softball, the principles learned in kickball helped her players apply softball game concepts and strategies, such as advancing runners, getting outs, and base running.

The theory might also explain the positive transfer of common movement principles across different sports, such as the learned principles of force production in boxing transferring to baseball hitting/swing. Athletes might also transfer perceptual concepts or principles from a variety of practice experiences, such as applying the visual search of the opponent's body cues to both tennis and soccer for enhanced anticipation. The principles-based perspective supports the concept that positive transfer can occur between relatively *dissimilar* skills (less specificity), if the underlying principles between the transfer and the target task are similar. As mentioned above, far transfer of more underlying movement principles or general elements contributes to athlete development and supports the notion of diversification—participating in a variety of different sports at a young age.

Transfer Theory 2: Motor Programs and Schemas
Ever wonder how the elite 100-meter hurdlers seem so perfectly automated and rhythmic when they stride over the hurdles in a race? Some interesting evidence suggests a generalized motor program (GMP) might be given some credit for this.[11] *Experimenters tested the relative timing of college hurdlers' strides when performed under several different parameters or performance conditions. The kinematics of the highly skilled hurdlers' strides were measured while racing in four different conditions: (1) normal race, at full speed, (2) shortened hurdle distance, at full speed with the hurdles set 1 meter closer together, (3) slow motion, running the race as slow as possible, and (4) simulation, where the hurdles were removed and runners simulated running the race. Their results clearly showed that the timing structure of the hurdle stride remained remarkably stable in the skilled subjects despite considerable variations in the hurdle condition. Regardless of the parameter that changed (speed, hurdle distance, hurdle/no hurdle, jump height), each stride kept its own temporal identity, and they could not be mistaken for another one. There is an explanation for the automated rhythm we see in a race. And the explanation (a GMP) allowed the hurdler to positively transfer their internal timing and rhythm to a variety of different conditions.*

We separate this theory into two different perspectives. Both are based on the original schema theory from the 1970s, and both have implications for transfer of learning.[12]

Generalized Motor Program (GMP)
A popular term used in sport is that of "muscle memory." The GMP theory offers some explanation for skilled athletes that seem to produce movements that are very similar and consistent no matter the situation or context. These movement patterns are very predictable and seem to look the same way all the time; as well they are automatic and nonconscious movements that many coaches covet. The theory suggests that certain elements of a well-learned movement pattern transfer forward, from one activity to the next. These elements are called *relative timing* and *relative force*, and they constitute the GMP, or an internal timing and rhythm for an athlete's movement pattern.[13] With practice, this internal rhythm gets "wired in" and stored relatively permanently in long-term memory and in the central nervous system as a "solution" for executing a skill. The GMP provides the consistent rhythm and timing of similar-looking movement patterns. A separate GMP would exist for fundamental movements such as the bat swing, the overhand throwing motion, or the kicking motion. It also might provide the rhythm or timing of a swimmer's crawl stroke or the sprinter's hurdle action.

The important point of the GMP theory is that the internal rhythm and timing of a movement pattern does not change across different performance situations. The GMP constitutes an athlete's "signature" of his or her movement. An athlete transfers the GMP to a variety of performance situations. For example, a softball infielder has a GMP for the overhand throwing motion; she would use the same internal rhythm and timing for all her throws, regardless of whether she throws from third base, second base, or "in the hole." And the softball player would use the same GMP for different skills that use the same similar overhand throwing motion, such as serving a tennis ball or volleyball (see figure 2.3). It may go without saying that developing a good GMP is essential for skilled performance.

It should be noted that although the GMP provides a transferable range of stability across different contexts and skills, there are situations when performing outside the GMP would hurt performance. A tennis player who *really* slows down her forehand stroke for a drop shot or a baseball pitcher

FIGURE 2.3
The same GMP would be used to help control the movement pattern for each of the different sport skills.

who *really* slows down his arm motion to throw a changeup are likely to use a timing and rhythm that is outside of their GMP. As such, the control of that skill would suffer. It might help explain the common "Wow, my timing is off" comment heard from softball or baseball players trying to hit a wiffleball in their first few attempts. The swing with the very light bat requires a different internal timing and rhythm (outside their learned GMP).

Schemas (Movement Relationships)
Schema theory contends that once an athlete is equipped with a hard-wired and transferable GMP, then the focus of practice shifts to learning how to modify it to meet the demands of the sport. Through practice, the athlete learns the more specific parameters to use with their GMP (termed "parameterized" in the theory).[14] Parameters are modifiable things like the overall speed, size, direction, force of the movement, or using different muscles.

Examples are numerous. While using the same GMP, the soccer player executes goal kicks of different distances, forces, and angles; or the baseball outfielder executes throws to second base from different positions in the field but still maintains the same GMP. In this perspective, the athlete is *subconsciously* learning the *relationships* between key aspects (parameters) of the skill. These relationships are called schemas and stored in long-term memory. For example, the soccer player attempting a shot on goal "abstracts" the relationship between (1) the amount of force generated on the shot, (2) the outcome of the shot, and (3) the feeling they got after the shot. The player learns this relationship and transfers it to future attempts. Continued repetitions strengthen the "schema" for the skill. A schema develops because of accumulated repetitions and experiences within a given GMP.

Getting more specific, repetitions provide an opportunity to better learn relationships that will increase skill and better guide, or transfer to, future attempts. The theory says that after each repetition, athletes briefly and unconsciously abstract four important sources of information. These sources include (1) the initial environmental conditions (e.g., distance from target), (2) the movement parameters (e.g., force), (3) the sensory feedback received (e.g., feeling of the movement), and (4) the outcome of the movement (e.g., short or long). Figure 2.4 shows the four elements abstracted to form the memory representation of a skill.[15]

Schemas are offered as an explanation for how athletes can detect the problem on a repetition and correct it for successful performance in the next trial. With practice, for example, the basketball player more often makes the second free throw after a missed first attempt. The do-over effect is in part due to a strong schema enabling the player to detect and modify the relationship between the movement parameter (e.g., knee bend) and shot outcome (e.g., short or long). Through practice, they have developed a schema for the free throw, and they are able to apply it to the next shot. In addition, the schema theory is an explanation for athletes who execute a skill successfully,

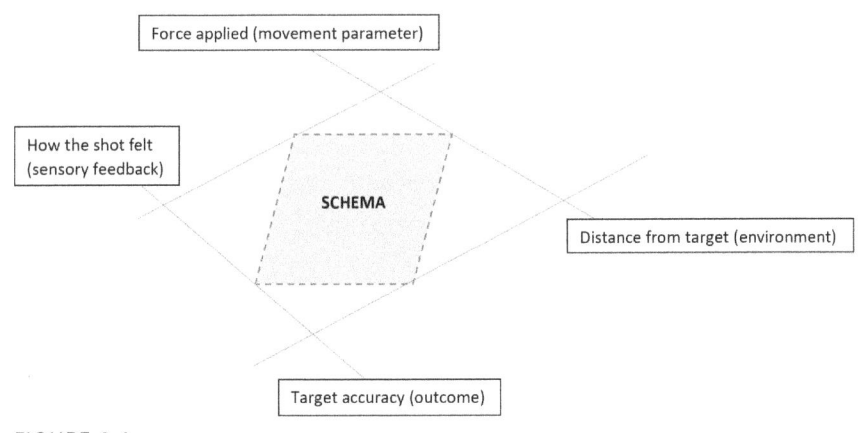

FIGURE 2.4
Schema representation of the elements abstracted from each practice repetition. The schema is stored in long-term memory, updated with continued practice, and transferred to future attempts. (Adapted from Kerr, "Getting into the Scheme of Things")

even if they haven't specifically practiced it before. For example, the soccer player might execute a successful goal kick from a body position, speed, and field location that they have not practiced before. They relied on a strong schema and transferred it forward to successfully execute the skill.

From the schema perspective, how you practice will impact the strength of your schema. As we discuss later (chapter 7), the quality, type, and number of repetitions are important to update and strengthen schemas. Repetitions that strategically change or vary the (a) initial conditions or (b) movement parameters have been shown to better strengthen schemas; they transfer better to a variety of performance conditions.

Transfer Theory 3: Cognitive Effort[16]
In a 2006 study, 38 surgical residents took a series of four short lessons in microsurgery: how to reattach tiny vessels.[17] Each lesson included some instruction followed by some practice. Half the docs completed the "normal" training: all four lessons in a normal, one-day-long intensive training. The other half completed the same lessons spaced out with a week's interval between them. In a test given a month after their last session, those who completed the spaced-out lessons a week apart outperformed their colleagues in all areas, including time to complete the surgery, number of hand movements, and success in reattaching vessels in live rats. Perhaps scarier was the finding that several of the surgeons who completed the training sessions in the normal one-day-long lessons damaged the rats' vessels beyond repair and were unable to finish their surgeries! The explanation was that the spacing of practice sessions, though more effortful and less convenient, built stronger long-term memories through processes related to memory consolidation and retrieval (and less forgetting). The medical school since reevaluated their normal instructional procedures. Good thing!

The previous theory suggested that subconscious, long-term memory mechanisms are important to transfer of learning (motor programs and schema). In contrast, this theory emphasizes the importance of the memory systems that require *conscious* awareness. It emphasizes that learning physical skills is a *cognitive* process and transfer depends largely on how skills are rehearsed and encoded into memory.

Memory: Rehearsal and Retrieval
This perspective uses common memory models to describe the ability to store and retrieve information so practice can be remembered and transferred later. Several elements of the memory system are likely familiar to coaches, such as the role of the *sensory memory, working memory,* and *long-term memory*. Figure 2.5 shows the common multistore or working memory model that has applications for the transfer of learning.[18]

To transfer learning, athletes must effectively use their memory systems. For example, it's important that athletes selectively attend to skill elements in *sensory memory* (e.g., the defender's hips) and connect it, in their *working memory*, with their *long-term memory* of the skill (how and what pass to make). The cognitive effort theory suggests coaches should focus on intentional strategies that improve the *storage strength* and *retrieval strength* of their athletes' memory systems.[19] For example, repetitions with effective demonstrations, cues, and analogies help encode or store a skill in long-term memory, and help the athlete retrieve the skill from memory later or in a different context. Performance in competition depends on how athletes developed their working memory in practice, or how well practice improved (a) their attention to the important skill elements, (b) the transfer of knowledge to long-term memory, and (c) the retrieval of information from their long-term memory.

Cognition: The Mental Work
Essential to this theory is the study of *forgetting* and its impact on learning. Concepts such as decay and interference are related to forgetting. While decay is the effect of time on the memory systems, interference is how other factors impact the rehearsal and retrieval processes. These factors might

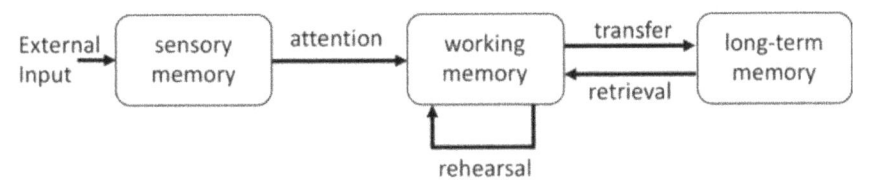

FIGURE 2.5
Traditional multistore memory model. Practice conditions that strengthen the memory systems are a key aspect of cognitive effort theory. (Adapted from Baddeley, "Working Memory")

include fatigue, distractions, or competing memories. An interesting branch of cognitive effort theories includes those that clarify the role of forgetting in the transfer of learning. It contends that practice conditions that induce forgetting and/or interference during rehearsal are needed for learning; it generates better storage (for the long term) and retrieval (in the short term) of memories. Transfer of learning is increased with *more* mental work, or when cognition is more "effortful" or "difficult" during practice.

Several research areas have been offered to support the cognitive effort perspective. Two such hypotheses suggest that the "reloading" or "contextual interference" that occurs with repetitions that are spaced with time or between other activities require the re-creating of memories, motor programs, or movement solutions more often. The result is greater retention and transfer of learning.[20] For example, executing repetitions of the bunting skill at random moments during a baseball practice is more effortful for the athletes' working memory, compared to a more traditional practice session of 20 consecutive bunting repetitions. A related concept is the "desirable difficulties" view that practice manipulations appearing to be difficult during training can be desirable for long-term retention and transfer because they strengthen encoding and retrieval processes.[21]

The cognitive effort perspective refutes the traditional practice emphasis on rote repetition to memorize skills (more muscle memory). It suggests that repetitions where athletes are on "autopilot" during practice often produce "pretty" practice performances that don't transfer well to the game. To the contrary, repetitions high in cognitive effort may produce "ugly" practice performances but better transfer. Check out Trevor Ragan's website of interesting resources supporting the concept of "training ugly" to enhance learning.[22]

Transfer Theory 4: Ecological Dynamics
Dick Fosbury used his new flop technique on the high jump to win the gold medal with a then Olympic record of 7 feet, 4.25 inches in the 1968 Olympics. If you don't believe it, take a look: https://www.youtube.com/watch?v=CZsH46Ek2ao. All accepted techniques at the time were facedown movements, either straddling or rolling over the bar. His new head-first, face-up flop of the back over the bar was a radical change in technique. The traditional interpretation is he cognitively discovered his technique based on his knowledge of mechanics. However,

some theorists argue differently.[23] *At that time, there was a change in the high jump equipment: the sand and sawdust pits were replaced with the high-density foam mats we see today. His motivation to explore new techniques was driven by a change in the constraints of the task, rather than by his own research. Had the mats not changed to allow a softer landing, he never would have explored better movement solutions. This "constraints" interpretation is reinforced by a second, unheard-of, 16-year-old jumper (Debbie Brill), who, at the same time, adopted her new technique called the "Brill Bend." Fosbury and Brill had never met and trained in different locations. But the change in the mat (task constraint) encouraged her creative solution as well. Brill was quoted as saying, "There was no way anybody was going to land on their back in sand or sawdust. But when I saw the foam mat for the first time, I decided to try something completely different." Brill honed her own unique technique, guided by a curiosity about how to jump higher with a foam mat landing. Her coach didn't try and change Debbie's unusual technique; he just dubbed it the "Brill Bend" and let her jump away. Luckily for both athletes, their coaches welcomed creativity and the exploration of new techniques. Sometimes, creative new techniques are not cognitive strategies, but rather the athlete searching for a solution to satisfy the constraints of a task, whatever those constraints might be. So, coaches, manipulate those constraints and encourage your athletes to do the same!*

In contrast to the first three theories, this one contends that there is simply too much unpredictability and variation in sport for it all to be controlled by learned memories, cognition, or "hard-wired" motor programs. Ecological dynamics suggest information from and interactions with the *environment* are most important and largely ignored in the other theories.[24] Movement skills often emerge because of the dynamic interaction between variables related to the athlete, the skill, and the environment. We subdivide the theory into two main concepts since each has different implications for transfer.

"Constraint" Interactions
An athlete's observed skill is viewed as a temporary "movement solution" that is determined by the interaction of three *constraints* involved at the time of skill execution. The movement we observe is not the result of a learned motor program, but rather the result of a process of "self-organization"

around these constraints. The constraints that interact to elicit the observed skill or movement are[25]:

1. the *individual* (learner)
2. the *task*
3. the *environment*

For example, the basketball player's execution of a low crossover dribble (movement solution) in a drill is the result of the interaction between the player's hand size (individual), the ball's diameter (task), and the location of the stationary cones (environment). As discussed later, an important part of this perspective is manipulating the constraints so that the athlete adopts a more skillful movement solution. In the practice environment, constraints are the boundaries that impact performance, or all the factors that can influence skill acquisition and performance (either to limit or enable).

Interesting evidence in support of this self-organization is the science that measures coordination patterns in skillful athletes executing repetitive movements such as the golf swing and tennis serve. While their outcome is accurate and consistent (shot accuracy), and their movement looks very consistent to the naked eye, there is a high amount of internal *variability* between each of their repetitions and between other skillful performers. In consecutive repetitions of the same swing, there is *not* a replication of an identical pattern of coordination. Rather, the variability in movement and the body's ability to self-organize a different solution for each repetition are essential for skillful performance. This was originally termed "repetition without repetition." Similar results are found comparing the swing patterns of different golfers. There is no one identical (and ideal) coordination pattern that all golfers use.[26] Each golfer has discovered their own movement solution based on the interaction of their constraints.

The notion that interacting constraints shape skillful movement has also led to the development of related frameworks, such as Nonlinear Pedagogy (NLP)[27] and the Constraints-Led Approach (CLA).[28] Both approaches suggest the coach's role is to identify and manipulate the key constraints in practice that shape athletes' behaviors and facilitates discovery of more skillful movement solutions. In this perspective, the coach's role changes to that of a more learner-centered, hands-off facilitator of skill development. Instructional methods are often indirect, as opposed to traditional direct methods. For example, rather than directly providing the "correct" instructional cues and feedback, the coach would manipulate the practice environment, which forces the athlete to search for better movements and behaviors. Considerable research shows that replacing direct instruction with a systematic manipulation of task and/or environmental constraints (e.g., goal heights, boundary distances, rule modifications, and equipment scaling) can improve athletes' movement patterns and decision-making during game play.[29] Other coach-friendly approaches applying this theory include the games-based approach (GBA) or Teaching Games for Understanding (TGfU).[30] They emphasize modifying the constraints of game play so that athletes *discover* game-like solutions that are more transferable to the real game or competition (see chapter 9).

Perception-Action Coupling
Perception-action is the concept that an athlete's action is essentially coupled with the information they perceive in the environment.[31] An action is regulated by the information available in the environment, and actions then regulate the perception of environmental information. Building on the concept of self-organization, it proposes this perception-action connection is an unconscious process that dictates the movement an athlete will produce. An example of this might be in the volleyball serve. The initiation of the timing and coordination between the hip and serving arm in striking the volleyball (action) becomes connected (coupled) to the peak height of the ball toss (perception of environment).[32] With practice, athletes develop and rely on strong couplings to perform. Importantly, the elements of perception and the elements of the action are *inseparable*. So, we should not practice them separately. In the volleyball serve example above, the player should limit the practice of the toss by itself (perception) because it's connected to the movement (action). As another example, the information available to the soccer athlete when dribbling around cones (perception) is coupled with the movement solution, or dribbling techniques (action), he or she must generate to be successful. In this case, the player's dribbling solutions are coupled with the static environment (cones don't move). This coupling is different than the one required in the game. The movement solution that emerges in a dynamic environment (moving defenders and

teammates) will be different than what was practiced. You might say that with the cone dribble drill, they are practicing the wrong perception-action coupling, and it's less likely to transfer to the game.

Several practice approaches have emerged from the perception-action concept. One is the Representative Learning Design (RLD),[33] which emphasizes simulating the necessary *sources* of the contextual or perceptual information of the competitive environment (i.e., making a task or practice more "representative"). RLD holds that a practice environment rich with varied and dynamic sources of information will encourage the athlete to explore the "perceptual motor workspace" to develop *adaptive* movement solutions more likely to be used in competition. Practice should be representative of the coupling that occurs in the game. Since games require the athlete to search for the relevant sources of information to create an action that works, then so should practice. Coaches should determine the informational characteristics within the competitive environment (e.g., incoming ball flight information, speed, spin in tennis) and consider how that interacts with the action characteristics (e.g., court positioning in tennis) in the game. For example, in tennis, ball flight information and the opponent's on-court position are cited as key information for performers to act on. As such, a representative practice task would require that both the ball flight and opponent's court positioning are simulated closely so that the athletes can explore and generate solutions that would benefit them during a rally.

The perception-action perspective predicts poor transfer of practice situations that are not representative of the target context. For example, in hitting off pitching machines or returning serves against a ball machine, the action (timing and coordination of the swing or return) is coupled with the environmental information from the machine (e.g., release points, ball spins). Research has shown a different action (timing and coordination) emerges from the players when the ball comes from the pitcher's hand or server's racket.[34] So, machine-based practice is not representative and results in a different coupling than the game requires. For coaches, the key to transfer is to (1) assess the "representativeness" of practice drills, and (2) keep the game-like perception and action coupled in practice activities. We encourage coaches to check out Rob Gray's *Perception and Action Podcast*,[35] which shares interesting elements of science supporting practice conditions that "keep 'em coupled."

TRANSFER THIS

Remember the Coach Johnson scenario at the beginning of the chapter? He read about one popular theory, and he trusted the exaggerated claims or opinions of "experts," or the logic of a currently hot practice fad. He trusted part of one theory (GMP/muscle memory) to guide his practice methods. Since his practice methods were limited, so too was the potential for transfer of learning. For Coach Johnson, implementing practice methods that align with a combination of theoretical elements likely would have helped him design practice to increase transfer of learning. We recommend he review the theory elements of transfer-appropriate processing and ecological dynamics to start. For example, per ecological dynamics, the skill of hitting has natural variability and requires a high level of adaptability, and the action of the swing must be solved in connection with the game-like perception of the pitch. Coaches should embrace the science behind the transfer of learning and use various parts of the different theories that fit with their coaching philosophy and their real-world experiences. Remember, no one theory holds the answer, but collectively, they offer explanations and predictions of when positive transfer will or will not occur. These theories should help coaches answer *why* they are doing certain drills or practice activities. The remainder of this book uses these foundational theories to support recommended practice conditions. Using a scientific foundation will help to recommend the practice methods provided in the remaining chapters with a sense of trust and confidence.

Coaches, Transfer This

1. Try this exercise to evaluate practice activities using the transfer continuums of direction (positive or negative), amount (high or low), and distance (near or far):

    - Identify a commonly used practice activity (transfer task).
    - Next, identify your target task.
    - Then, plot your transfer task on the continuum of direction.
    - Next, plot your transfer task on the distance continuum.
    - Evaluate your practice activity? Will it transfer? Why or why not?

2. Which of the theories do you think are most predictive of positive transfer? Why? Do you see value in all the theories to evaluate your practice for transfer?

3. When you find drills in books or on the Internet, use the theories (more than one) to evaluate their value to your situation. Sometimes they may look or sound good but not transfer well.
4. Clearly identify your target task(s) for your practice activities. It may not always be the game or competition. Sometimes it will be the next drill or activity. You are more likely to design transferable practice activities if you know your target task (see the distance continuum).
5. Embrace the power of far transfer in developing athletes' skills. You might use "different" activities or sports to promote transfer and athletes' development.

Coach Educators and Developers, Transfer This
1. Provide a variety of resources, (e.g., books, websites, podcasts) to your coaches that are research supported and emphasize theory-to-practice (e.g., this book!).
2. Encourage your coaches to attend theory-to-practice coaching and teaching conferences or workshops. There is value in both sport-specific and "general" coaching workshops.
3. Endorse the benefits of far transfer from a long-term athlete development perspective. For example, encourage coaches to diversify young athletes' sport experiences, participating in different activities or sports rather than a single sport.
4. Since there is no secret or one best theory, there is no "best" way to achieve transfer. Encourage coaches to explore and adopt practice conditions that are supported not only by several theories but also by their own personalities and coaching philosophies.
5. Ask your coaches to evaluate some of their current practice activities against the theories (more than one). What theory elements are they already using in practice, and which elements could be further explored?

3

The Foundation for Transfer

One of our student athletes, a hurdler on the college track team, shared a powerful memory of her first-year track coach during her senior year of high school. She was a talented hurdler in high school and was getting attention from college coaches. She recalled her high school coach approaching her one practice and telling her he didn't really understand the hurdling event and that it was a weakness in his coaching. He asked her how she was feeling about her development, and if she had any ideas on how he could help her improve. She thought about it and said something like, "Maybe bring in a college hurdler to work with me or something." Two practices later, guess who showed up to practice—her coach had located and recruited a former college hurdler to donate his time and expertise in practice. She commented, "That's when I knew my coach had my back. I practiced harder after that."

The transfer of practice to the competition starts long before the practice drill or activity. As mentioned in chapter 2, the transfer of learning is a long-term process that takes time and patience, and the conditions need to be right to facilitate transfer. To use a gardening analogy, transfer "grows" better when the soil is fertilized and prepared ahead of time. This chapter is about coaches building a foundation (soil) that better allows transfer of learning to take root. With this foundation, the practice methods discussed in the rest of the book become more effective.

THE ATHLETE-CENTERED COACH

Learning is more likely when the coach is *athlete centered*. National and international standards of coaching cite athlete-centered coaching as the number-one characteristic of quality coaching.[1] So, what does an athlete-centered coach look like?

A Teacher First

Essential to being athlete centered is for coaches to view themselves primarily as teachers. Wade Gilbert and others have adapted the famous Pyramid of Success by legendary coach John Wooden.[2] The original pyramid depicted the desirable athlete characteristics, and the modified Pyramid of Teaching Success in Sport (PoTSS) organizes 15 coaching characteristics (athlete centered) into five levels (see figure 3.1). Note that "Teacher" is at the apex of the

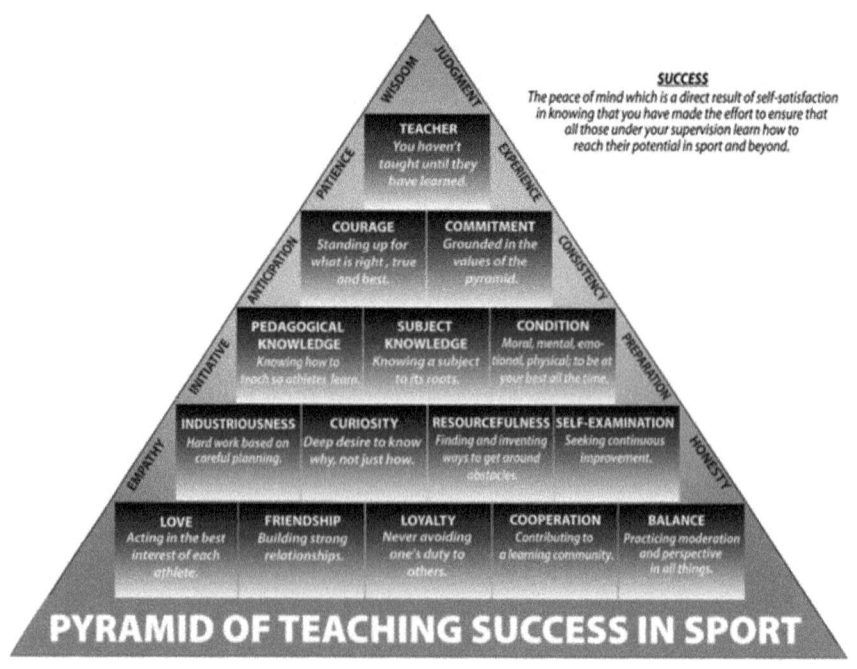

PYRAMID OF TEACHING SUCCESS IN SPORT

SUCCESS
The peace of mind which is a direct result of self-satisfaction in knowing that you have made the effort to ensure that all those under your supervision learn how to reach their potential in sport and beyond.

TEACHER — You haven't taught until they have learned.

COURAGE — Standing up for what is right, true and best.
COMMITMENT — Grounded in the values of the pyramid.

PEDAGOGICAL KNOWLEDGE — Knowing how to teach so athletes learn.
SUBJECT KNOWLEDGE — Knowing a subject to its roots.
CONDITION — Moral, mental, emotional, physical; to be at your best all the time.

INDUSTRIOUSNESS — Hard work based on careful planning.
CURIOSITY — Deep desire to know why, not just how.
RESOURCEFULNESS — Finding and inventing ways to get around obstacles.
SELF-EXAMINATION — Seeking continuous improvement.

LOVE — Acting in the best interest of each athlete.
FRIENDSHIP — Building strong relationships.
LOYALTY — Never avoiding one's duty to others.
COOPERATION — Contributing to a learning community.
BALANCE — Practicing moderation and perspective in all things.

Side labels: WISDOM, JUDGMENT, PATIENCE, EXPERIENCE, ANTICIPATION, CONSISTENCY, INITIATIVE, PREPARATION, EMPATHY, HONESTY

FIGURE 3.1
The Pyramid of Teaching Success in Sport. As a foundation for the transfer of learning, the coach is a teacher first, as shown at the top of the pyramid. Note: The Pyramid of Teaching Success in Sport © (graphic and contents) is copyrighted and owned by BeLikeCoach, Inc. (BeLikeCoach.com) and is free for public use, copying, and distribution by individuals and organizations dedicated to improving learning, teaching, sport, and youth development.

PoTSS; great coaches think of themselves first as *teachers*. Hence, the oft-used Wooden quote (repeated often in this book) is at the top of the pyramid, "*You haven't taught until they have learned.*"

A Cooperative Coaching Style

There are several styles of coaching documented in literature. To name a few, styles may include *command/coach centered, submissive/laissez-faire,* and *cooperative*. The cooperative style of coaching is viewed as the one most athlete centered.[3] These coaches view coaching as a partnership with their athletes. They typically share some decision-making with their athletes. They find the right balance between directing athletes and letting athletes direct themselves in the common and shared goal of achieving success. Cooperative-style coaches will design practices that include less direct instruction, and they provide opportunities for questioning, problem-solving, and self-discovery among their athletes. They nurture more of what transfers to performance, including being able to cope with pressure, adapting to changing situations, exhibiting discipline, and maintaining concentration.[4] This style shows high levels of caring, shared ownership, and trust in athletes, which improves communication and motivation in athletes. Cooperative-style coaches, for example, might share some control over the practice environment and invite input from their athletes.

Long-Term Development

According to the *National Standards for Sport Coaches*,[5] coaches should plan for "long-term athlete development with the intent to develop athletic potential and enhance physical literacy." Athlete-centered coaches generally take a long-term view of athlete development, compared to a more short-term view that seeks more immediate success. A coach with a long-term development view embraces the development of "athletic potential" at younger ages. Rather than encouraging athletes to specialize year-round in their one sport at an early age, they recognize the value of diversifying or *sampling* a variety of sports, activities, and movements in off-seasons or throughout the year. They see the value of multisport participation in developing a strong foundation or base of general athletic skills. Scientific and anecdotal evidence supports the recommendation that young athletes should develop a wide variety of physical, perceptual, and competitive experiences. These learning experiences enable *positive* and *far transfer* of general principles and concepts of movement to their sport(s) and beyond. It is also seen to improve athlete resilience and the ability to handle increased training and competition demands of higher-level, single-sport participation.[6] Consider the far transfer of past experiences in the sport sampling examples below[7]:

> Playing basketball had a significant impact on the way I play the game of soccer. In basketball I was a power forward and I would go up and rebound the ball. So learning the timing of your jump, learning the trajectory of the ball coming off the rim, all those things play a massive role. (Soccer Olympian Abby Wambach)

> My trick question to young campers is always, "How do you learn the concepts of team offense in lacrosse or team defense in lacrosse in the off-season, when you are not playing with your team?" The answer is by playing basketball, by playing ice hockey, and by playing soccer and those other team games, because many of those principles are exactly the same. Probably 95 percent [of our players] are multisport athletes. It's always a bit strange to me if somebody is not playing other sports in high school. (Dom Starsia, four-time national championship lacrosse coach, University of Virginia)

For young athletes, there is a strong attraction to specializing in one sport. The explosion of year-round "travel" teams and competitions and privatized training opportunities make specialization easier than ever. While this may lead to quicker improvement and more immediate success, athlete-centered coaches realize it may not be in the best long-term interest of the athlete.

The long-term development view would also apply to coaching during a single season. Skill acquisition and athlete performance are developmental processes made up of continual and sequential improvements throughout the season. The coach may experience lower levels of athlete performance early in the season, but winning at the end of the season is often due to higher amounts of development and learning at the beginning of the season. For example, building off chapter 1 (purpose of practice), the coach would value different types of practice during a season that promote enjoyment of the sport. They could balance play, purposeful practice, competition, and maintenance activities, perhaps including unstructured peer-led play activities within practice. In general, the coach with a long-term development perspective understands that the constant focus to win in the short term often undercuts athlete development and their ability to win in the long-term. This is counterintuitive, but true for most coaches reading this book. Doing things that make it less likely a coach will win now is a big ask, but the athlete-centered coach is willing to go there to increase learning, far transfer, and later success.

A CULTURE OF COMMUNICATION

Perhaps the most important element of coaching success is that of effective communication. Former Boston Celtics coach Red Auerbach understood the importance of communication in his quote, "It's not what you tell them—it's what they hear."[8] Communication is a foundation for almost all aspects of coaching, such as trust and relationship-building. It allows coaches to better send and for athletes to better receive messages (i.e., instruction and feedback). It's a foundation that increases the potential for the transfer of learning.

The Fundamental Communication Skills

There are some fundamental communication skills that serve as guidelines for sending effective verbal and nonverbal messages. We offer a "Top 10" of the most important.[9]

1. *Be Credible.* This is the degree to which athletes trust what you say. Be both knowledgeable and honest about your knowledge. Use the cooperative style of coaching and be open, friendly, and empathetic. Model the behaviors you encourage of your athletes.
2. *Be Honest.* Be truthful about your perceptions of athlete skills and behaviors. Do it in a way that empowers the athlete to self-improve. Gauge your level of honesty to protect the athlete's self-esteem. Honestly evaluate the *behavior*, not the *athlete*. "That was a wrong decision, Tamara" is better than "What's wrong with you, Tamara?"
3. *Be Positive.* Sticks and stones break bones, and words DO hurt as well. Emphasize praise and intrinsic rewards over punishment and criticism to manage behaviors. Embrace the power of encouragement and an attitude of acceptance and mutual respect. Avoid sarcasm (e.g., "Nice job, butter fingers") and anger with your message.
4. *Be Consistent.* Be true to your word and follow through with what you say or promise you will do. Establish a clear and positive environment early,

including expectations, rules, and consequences. Be consistent, communicating and enforcing rules and consequences equally, without playing "favorites." Consistently use the positive approach and avoid speaking derogatorily of athletes in front of others. Be consistent with what you preach and what you do. Preaching emotional control from your athletes but throwing a temper tantrum at game officials is not consistent.

5. *Be a Good Listener.* First, seek to understand. Employ active listening skills, attend to athletes' total communication, and use nonverbal actions to confirm you understand (e.g., eye contact, nodding). Be empathetic and open to athlete concerns. Athletes feel accepted and worthwhile when they feel they are listened to. If you consistently fail to listen, athletes will stop talking and ultimately stop listening to you.

6. *Do the Nonverbal.* Nonverbal messages make up much of what you communicate to athletes. They can reinforce or contradict your verbal communication or your message. Modeling is powerful, and what you do and how you look is sometimes more powerful than *what* you say. Evaluate your own body motions and positions, facial expressions, voice characteristics, touching behaviors, and physical appearance. Verbal and nonverbal messages should be congruent. Making negative body gestures while you tell your athlete it's okay to make an error is contradictory.

7. *Be Direct.* Don't assume players know what you are thinking; tell them directly. Avoid telling all the players something, hoping it will reach the intended player later. Indirect messages get distorted and misinterpreted (remember the childhood "telephone" game?). Own your messages instead of relying on others (e.g., use "*I* think you need to . . ." rather than "the *team* feels you need to . . .").

8. *Seek Two-Way Communication.* Communicate a culture where athlete input and questions are valued. Instead of delivering all the messages yourself, question athletes often and engage in shared discussions related to their skill development. We hope you notice this to be an element threaded throughout this book.

9. *Monitor Electronic Communications.* Social media and instant messaging have become a major force in society and can have large impacts (positive and negative) on coach–athlete communication. Coaches should follow best practices when using social media and electronic communications, such as the guidelines offered by Robert Weinberg and Daniel Gould.[10]

10. *Do Self-Assessments.* Given the importance of communication, we encourage coaches to self-check their communication skills using instruments such as the "16 Guidelines for Sending Effective Messages"[11] or by recording and observing yourself on videotape. Self-assessments are most useful both in the preseason and during the season itself for coaches to evaluate and improve their fundamental communication skills.

A Common Language[12]

For groups of coaches and athletes, developing and sharing a common language can provide a foundation to enhance both communication and the transfer of learning. A common language consists of identifying, naming, and phrasing (in advance) the most important skills and drills so that all players can better remember, recognize, retrieve, and transfer what they are learning. It's a simplified and standardized language that is unique to the team or the coach/athlete. We provide an example of a common language below:

> Coach Stevens: "Talk about it!"
>
> When watching preseason scrimmages of a high school basketball team, one of the authors noticed (his son played) that Coach Stevens constantly yelled, "Talk about it!" to his players when they were playing man-to-man defense. The coach yelled it so often so that the dad/author was compelled to count the number of times he said it during one of the scrimmages . . . 24 times the coach yelled, "Talk about it!" to his team during the scrimmage. At the end of the season, the author still heard the phrase on occasion, so he counted again in the last game of the year. Coach Stevens shouted, "Talk about it!" 4 times in that game, quite a bit less than 24 times at the start of the season!

The phrase was part of a common language consistently used by the coaches and players throughout the season. The phrase meant complex concepts of handling offensive screens while playing man-to-man defense (taught early in the season). At the end of the year, "talk about it" cued players to look for and anticipate screens by talking earlier, louder, and more often. The language helped players select the best techniques to get past the screens (e.g., step over or go under) and to coordinate their action with their teammates. Late in the season, the players seemed to react to the phrase automatically with little distraction.

Note: A common language is *not* a motivational slogan (e.g., "All-in" or "Commitment"). Rather, it serves a specific purpose to increase transfer of learning. We highlight below *why* a common language is a foundation for transfer.

Encoded Learning

A common language provides a foundation for instruction and learning *during* practice. It consists of often-repeated and shortened phrases or words that convey more complicated concepts related to a skill. Concepts are taught within the phrase, and they get encoded in athletes' memory as part of the phrase. When these phrases are used consistently, the athletes' working memory of the skill is improved; it becomes better encoded and retrieved.[13] When the phrase is used, information is familiar (not new), so there is less demand on attention and memory. During practice, the phrase can be used to remind players quickly and effectively of what they've practiced in the past (i.e., transfer of learning). It can be used to cue athletes' attention before a drill starts or to fix errors during the drill. Common phrases can also be used to reinforce or frame instruction and questioning during practice. For example, when Coach Stevens notices players struggling with defensive communication, he can use the phrase to ask good questions about the topic of managing offensive screens: "When I say, 'Talk about it,' what do I expect to hear? What are your choices? What is the on-ball defender listening for? How do you move before talking? After talking? What techniques are most effective?" All these details get grouped and stored in athletes' memory under the topic of "talk about it." The coach can correct errors faster and players can quickly recall solutions.

Game Transfer

A common language also provides a foundation for *in-game coaching* and the transfer of practice concepts to the game. During live competition, coaches are advised to only deliver information that is familiar (not new) to athletes, so as to not overload their attention and memory and detract from performance. Common phrases can be used in the game to cue players to use well-learned concepts and improve performance without distracting them from the game. And since these phrases are encoded with lots of details, they are likely to be effective to improve performance. At the end of the season, it seems Coach Stevens's players used the common language to quickly adjust performance during the game with minimal distraction. When cued, they transferred what they had learned, and Coach Stevens was able to "teach" effectively during the game.

Culture Building

A shared language can be used to help build "culture" for the team or organization. Strong companies often create phrases and terminology to develop an identity, and they use them for internal and external communication, marketing, and branding.[14] Similarly, coaches can use a standardized vocabulary and terms to encode a unique and inclusive culture in their team. A shared language fosters communication with one another, rather than just with the group leader (remember two-way communication), and it facilitates a sense of belonging for players on the team. Coaches are encouraged to use the shared vocabulary outside of practice to keep the conversation going, such as during meals, on the bus, or in the locker room. As well, coaches should encourage players to use the vocabulary often. Consider the example below from a soccer coach who created two common phrases to help shape the culture of his team:

> We have two sayings that we use so much, the players now use them, "Next play" and "Aggressive mistakes." The first we use after an action where we see a player or team hanging their heads over a mistake or upset about something that just happened. You can't change it; move on and focus on the next one. The second is something we use going into an exercise, small game, or match to remind the player to go for it, take risks, make impact[ful] plays. If you aren't making mistakes, you are playing it safe and not making impactful plays, and consequently not stretching yourselves to be better.[15]

Both coaches and players used the phrases regularly to focus one another on what was valued most. The culture of the team is encoded in the language, and it spreads easily among players and teammates.

Developing the Common Language

The best way to develop a shared vocabulary is to (1) identify the core skills and concepts most important to learn, and (2) build a vocabulary list of terms and phrases for the concepts.[16] For example, below is a partial vocabulary list for basketball:

Core Skills: Man-to-man team defensive movement and communication (half court).

Key Terms and Phrases: "Talk about it," "Seek the level," "Get out and get down."

It may take a considerable amount of time and energy to develop an effective common language. Some coaches spend many hours collaborating with assistant coaches to build a list of the words and phrases they will adopt for the season. Once phrases are adopted, coaches should clearly teach the meaning of the phrases and consistently refer to them when instructing, providing feedback, or asking questions. They should monitor the language to ensure players understand and use it correctly. Phrases need to be used repeatedly and consistently among all coaches and players. Since it takes time for a shared language to "take root," the coach will need to apply patience and the long-term development perspective. Recall that Coach Stevens's "talk about it" phrase became more effective as the season wore on. He didn't need to use much at the end of the season, but when he did, it was evident players had learned and transferred what to do and how to do it.

AN INDIVIDUALIZED APPROACH

I treat all athletes the same no matter who they are.

The sentiment to treat athletes fairly is appreciated. However, treating them the *same* is ill-advised as it generally depresses learning and achievement.[17] Most coaches would agree that a one-size-fits-all approach is not very effective for the design of practice activities. Each athlete approaches and experiences the learning process in unique ways. The coach's role is to create the conditions for *each* athlete to learn from practice. While this can be difficult for larger teams and limited coaches, it begins by knowing the athlete as completely as possible. The coach should consider the different profiles of individual athletes and what each athlete "brings to the table."

Prior Knowledge and Experiences

Learning occurs best when new knowledge is connected to existing knowledge and skills. This is part of teaching for transfer. Remember, transfer of learning is the impact of *past* experiences on the attempt to learn a new skill. All athletes bring diverse views and knowledge from their past experiences participating in and/or observing sport. Their transferred experiences shape how they approach learning and instruction. An athlete's prior knowledge can either accelerate or hinder the learning process, so it's important to connect an athlete's past experiences to their current practice conditions. A soccer coach might connect with an athlete's past experiences in basketball when teaching soccer concepts, so they positively transfer learned concepts such as passing lanes and spacing. Sometimes athletes need to avoid negative transfer. They might transfer misconceptions that need to be corrected when learning new skills. For example, a novice volleyball player with past experiences in tennis may incorrectly assume a high degree of force is needed in executing a forearm pass. Or athletes might transfer incorrect movement techniques that interfere with the current skill. For example, an athlete with past experiences in badminton might execute an incorrect "wrist snap" on an overhead smash in tennis.

Making more connections to past experiences helps most in the beginning stages of learning as athletes seek to "get the idea" of the skill. As well, it helps advance athletes from a beginner knowing *what* to do to a more advanced level of *how and when* to do it. For example, teaching analogies that create images or feelings of past experiences have been shown to be impactful for learning.[18] To teach a soft landing, "Imagine you are landing in a puddle and trying to make it ripple, not splash," or, "Land as if in a room where a baby just fell asleep; don't wake the baby." We discuss analogies more in chapter 4 on designing practice.

There are numerous ways to gauge athletes' prior knowledge and experiences. Besides getting to know the athletes and their past experiences, coaches might conduct more formal self-assessments to build on transferred experiences and gauge appropriate starting points for teaching new skills or concepts. For example, a basketball coach might survey players about their past experiences before teaching team defense concepts. An example of a completed "athlete background self-assessment" is provided below.

Rate your level of experience with *basketball defenses* using the following scale (1–5):

1 = have never seen this

2 = have never used this, but have seen others use this

3 = have used this or similar in another sport or activity

4 = have used this some in practice

5 = have used this in competition

Athlete: Chris	Rating	Comments:
Full-court man-to-man press	3	Used some when I played soccer
Half-court man-to-man press	5	Used in my rec league basketball
2–3 half-court zone	5	Used in rec league basketball
1–3–1 half-court zone	1	
Half-court zone press	2	Other team used on us last year
Full-court zone press	1	

For this athlete (Chris), there is potential for both positive and negative transfer in half-court zone and man defenses, and likely zero transfer in zone-press defenses. We recommend background assessments be administered in the preseason, or they could also be done at the end of a practice to "prime" athlete attention for the next practice.[19]

Individual Differences

Along with considering athletes' prior experiences, coaches have the challenge to recognize the individual factors that make each athlete unique and different. Athletes have a "toolbox" in the form of abilities, interests, intelligences, and mind-sets that impact learning and achievement. These are a blend of genetic, environmental, and cultural factors that shape an athlete's current and potential achievement.

Motor, Physical, and Perceptual Differences
These factors will shape how an athlete moves and the rate/amount of skill acquisition. While these genetic factors cannot really be changed with practice,

they should be planned for and integrated into practice conditions to increase learning. Individual differences to look for might include, for example:

- Body type, limb lengths
- Vision, reaction time, anticipation
- Joint flexibility and strength
- Balance, coordination
- Speed, quickness, agility

Recognizing individual motor and physical differences aligns with the importance of athletes exploring their own "ideal" movement solution, rather than conforming to the one perfect technique (see chapters 1 and 2). Coaches should encourage the process of exploration and creativity, adopting movement patterns and techniques that fit with the individual's constraints. For example, rather than requiring all baseball players to take the "uppercut swing" for the ideal "launch angle," the coach might allow athletes to discover their "best" swing pattern that aligns with their own center of gravity, strength, and limb length (creating individualized launch angles). When coaches reflect on individual constraints, they are more likely to *modify* practice conditions that better *match* the individual athlete. For example, a coach might reduce the speed or increase the size of balls or objects that better match an athlete's reaction time and visual abilities. We discuss accommodating motor and physical constraints later in the book.

Learning, Cognitive, and Intelligence Differences
These factors shape how an athlete *learns* and how they develop their knowledge structure of skills. Most coaches have experienced how some athletes seem to "get" instructions or feedback immediately, while for others it takes awhile, and how some athletes develop a "sense" of the skill or game, while others struggle.

Learning Modes and Preferences. One way to conceptualize this is to recognize that individuals have unique and different preferences for absorbing and learning new information. Research-supported learner preferences (sometimes called learning modes) that have been identified, to name a few, include the kinesthetic mode (prefers learning by moving, doing, touching, feeling, and trying things out first), the visual mode (prefers learning by watching, observing others, and gathering information visually), the analytical mode (prefers learning by understanding the theory, principles, concepts, and strategies behind things), the listening mode (prefers learning by focusing on verbal descriptions, sounds, or rhythms), or the practical mode (prefers applying things to the real world and immediately trying out new concepts).[20] The coach who appreciates individualized learning modes is more likely to use a variety of instructional methods that play to multiple modes of learning and different athlete preferences. For example, in addition to providing verbal descriptions (listening) and demonstrations (visual) for skill instruction, the coach might use other methods such as discovery learning (kinesthetic or practical) or if–then questioning that align with other modes and preferences (kinesthetic and analytical) of different athletes. A second important point about learning modes is that athlete preferences are fluid rather than a fixed genetic trait that can't be changed or modified. Research shows that individuals' learner preferences change based on developmental (e.g., age, maturity) and environmental (e.g., culture, family) factors, and the nature of the content being taught (e.g., geometry is a visual subject).[21] For example, an athlete might prefer visual modes of learning (e.g., demonstrations) in the early learning of a new movement pattern but more analytical modes when learning different game concepts. Coaches can set the stage for increased transfer by teaching from and encouraging athletes to use a variety of learning modes (not just one).

Cognitive Differences. Science has also identified two cognitive differences important for transfer of learning[22]:

1. *High vs. Low Structure-Building.* This is the creation of coherent "mental maps" when learning new information. High structure-builders learn new material better than low structure-builders by building a more coherent model of new information. Low structure-builders have difficulty setting aside irrelevant information and struggle to condense concepts into an overall structure for transfer to future learning.
2. *Rule vs. Example Learning.* Rule learners tend to abstract the underlying principles or "rules" that differentiate the examples being studied. When presented with a new problem later, they apply the rules for an appropriate solution. Example learners tend to memorize the examples rather than the

underlying principles. Later, when a new solution is needed, they lack the grasp of the underlying rules, so they connect it to other examples, which are sometimes irrelevant.

Most interesting is the notion that high structure-builders and rule learners are more successful transferring their learning to unfamiliar situations than are low structure-builders and example learners.[23] And the evidence supports that these important cognitive abilities can be improved with practice. For example, when example learners are asked to compare two different concepts at once rather than one at a time, they improve in their ability to extract underlying rules (they become more of a rule learner).

Intelligence Differences. Science has dismissed the notion of a general, fixed intelligence (i.e., IQ) trait. The current view is that individuals have *different kinds* of intelligence, and they can be modified by a variety of factors. According to research, the kinds of intelligence are[24]:

- *Analytical intelligence*—the ability to do problem-solving tasks, such as in tests.
- *Creative intelligence*—the ability to synthesize and apply existing knowledge to deal with new or unusual situations.
- *Practical intelligence*—the ability to adapt to different settings and understand and do what needs to be done in a specific setting (i.e., street smarts).

Athletes draw on these intelligences differently. For example, an athlete with a higher level of creative intelligence might show more transfer of learning to novel skills or sport situations, and athletes with higher analytical intelligence might figure out a skill solution faster than others. Important to coaches is the notion that these intelligences are impacted by the athletes' environment and culture. For example, if an athlete grew up in an environment that emphasized practical skills, they come with higher practical intelligence, often at the expense of the other kinds of intelligence. The good news is that the evidence shows they can "catch up" in other intelligences. With practice, training, and experience, athletes can develop a "successful intelligence" for their skill or activity. Finally, the evidence shows that when instruction matches a learner's dominant intelligence ability, they tend to learn better.

The most important point about learning, cognitive, and intelligence differences is that they are not *fixed*. Rather, they can be developed and nurtured with instruction, experiences, and environmental changes. As we discuss later in this chapter, this *growth* mind-set is an essential foundation for learning.

Growth and Development

Matching coaching with athletes' developmental levels is an important foundation for transfer. Growth and development factors make it particularly difficult to adopt the one-size-fits-all approach. Below are some key aspects important for transfer.

First, we know that chronological age is not the best predictor of maturity. Two 16-year-old athletes may have very different physical, motor, or cognitive ages. And we know the early maturing athlete typically has a performance advantage over his/her later maturing teammate. This holds true especially with physical/anatomical maturity. Research indicates that the best predictor of success in many youth sports (e.g., baseball, track, football) is not motor *skill* differences, but rather anatomical age differences.[25] It's easy for coaches to focus on an athlete's current status and lose sight of the fact that their motor and cognitive constraints are growing and changing, all at different rates. The "abilities" they see this year may not be at the same level next year or even next month! This is especially true with the perceptual (e.g., visual) and motor (e.g., balance) abilities. The role of these abilities changes as athletes develop and as they gain skill. For example, a beginning volleyball player with a high level of coordination supports success in early practice, but in later practice their average level of explosive strength may not support the same level of success. Predicting athletes' ultimate level of achievement based on their early success is not supported by science.[26]

Second, understanding developmental differences will help coaches avoid "self-fulfilling prophecies" about individual athletes. They will resist labeling early or late maturing athletes that show promise, and they will resist the tendency to provide more attention to the "natural" athletes. They will avoid fulfilling their prophecies about which athletes are going to be special (or not). For the coach, this can be difficult. Athletes who "get it" more quickly may be easier to teach; they improve faster and often make us feel like better coaches. Research supports many coaches provide more instruction to the athletes they perceive to be more skilled or to have more "potential." This imbalance occurs even when coaches report they provide instruction equally.[27]

Finally, understanding developmental differences will help coaches promote a *mastery* coaching climate.[28] These practice conditions provide young athletes the opportunity to develop their skills relative to their own developmental level. Rather than comparing their success to other athletes, they should seek mastery of skills relative to their own past performances and amount of improvement. For young athletes who are very developmentally different and are developing at drastically different rates and amounts, this climate becomes increasingly important for creating a culture of learning, which is an essential foundation for transfer.

A CULTURE OF LEARNING

A culture of learning is our final foundational element to grow the transfer of learning. What is a culture of learning? It's practice sessions where all participants are hyper-focused on the process of self-improvement, seemingly unaware of how they look in the process. Players and coaches are on the same page, showing high levels of communication and support. All athletes are trying new things, taking risks, and solving problems together with a lot of trial and error. It's obvious that improvement is most important, regardless of athletes' different skill levels. The learning culture builds on the previous foundational elements, and coaches can do much to nurture the learning culture.

A "Safe" Environment

"Psychological safety" has been identified as a predictor for learning and team achievement.[29] It's when athletes feel safe to ask questions, speak up, take risks, seek feedback, and try new things. When this happens, athletes are more open to learning and practice, and will generally learn more and transfer more of what they practice. In a safe environment, athletes don't avoid making mistakes. Instead, they report, discuss, and get to the bottom of them. When athletes speak up and ask questions, they are more likely to experience learning moments, innovative solutions. Since sport is about learning and solving problems, coaches should create a safe environment for these activities. But how? A three-part approach for creating a safe environment is summarized below.[30]

Frame the sport as a learning problem. Give athletes a rationale for speaking up—sport requires both uncertainty and an interdependence of members and coaches to solve problems together. If the goal is to grow and achieve, then reinforce that struggle and share ownership of the process. Consider framing with a group orientation prior to the season, such as having your team read a common culture-building book together and sharing the important messages.

Invite athlete engagement. Be proactive in asking athletes genuine questions that seek feedback from them. Ask open-ended questions that provide opportunities for athletes to share ideas, observations, or solutions, such as, "Do you have any thoughts about breaking the press?" To help invite engagement, acknowledge you don't have all the answers, such as, "I may be missing something here; I need to hear from my players about this."

Monitor your responses. If a mistake happens or when you receive the requested input, how do you respond? Asking for honest feedback then ignoring it or getting defensive when you receive it doesn't help create a safe environment. Your responses (both verbal and nonverbal) can either help nurture or suppress a safe learning environment.

We should note some misconceptions associated with the "safe" environment. First, it's *not* about giving "fake praise" during practice to avoid athlete discomfort. A safe environment is more about the freedom for team members to give and receive honest and candid feedback to solve problems and get better. Rather than athletes playing it safe to keep their spot or protect their self-esteem, they add value to their team by taking calculated risks and stretching to improve. Second, creating and maintaining a safe environment is not a top-down coach directive. It's more of a "side-to-side" safety, with teammates holding one another accountable for feeling safe enough to "fail" in the process of learning.

A big part of psychological safety is the ability to learn from mistakes or failures. We like the Malcom Forbes quote, "Failure is success if we learn from it."[31] The role of failure in learning is often reinforced from high achievers in the real world, such as in the well-known quote from Michael Jordan:

> I've missed more than 9,000 shots in my career. I've lost almost 300 games. Twenty-six times, I've been trusted to take the game winning shot and missed. I've failed over and over and over again in my life. And that is why I succeed.[32]

In his book *In Praise of Failure*, Mark Anshel advocates for *positive failure*.[33] He advocates those mistakes and errors are necessary short-term experiences, and if used to improve your next performance, then, well, they really are not failures! From this perspective, failure is an important element for the transfer of learning. The coach's job is to create a "fail safely" climate that improves the probability of future success. Learning from failure is not automatic. For athletes to positively transfer their failure experiences, the coach needs to provide the necessary information to the athlete, including:

1. What caused the error(s)?
2. Was the failure within your control or out of your control?
3. What, specifically, do you need to do differently to make it more successful next time?
4. Were there any aspects of the failure that were positive and can be transferred forward?

To create the positive failure environment, the coach should strategically use encouragement, praising athletes for taking the "good" risks to get better. Coaches can also model the important role of failure. Local first-year high school baseball coach Cameron Schildt modeled positive failure before the start of his inaugural season as a varsity coach when he said, "I'm excited, but I've kind of tackled it head on. I'm not afraid to fail, and I think because my players see that quality in me, they're not afraid to fail as well."[34]

Coach Modeling

To establish any culture, the desired behaviors should be modeled by its leaders. Modeling is a powerful way to shape behaviors; by nature, we imitate others. Coaches can improve the learning culture by demonstrating the type of learner they would like to see in their athletes. Consider the perspective of Karch Karaly, head coach of the USA Women's National Volleyball Team: "Everyone who works with our athletes is good at modeling being learners. There's always stuff to be learned. And if we model that, it can help with mindset of our athletes." Coach Karaly is widely known to ask any observers of their practices, "What do you see out there that we can be doing better?" and he regularly ends conversations with his players by asking, "How can I be better for you?"[35]

Coaches should model that improving skills is the goal. It is a constant process that requires feedback, input, and risks. By asking for feedback, the coach becomes vulnerable, taking the risk that the input may be uncomfortable or unpleasant to hear.

Mind-Set

And finally, coaches can help create a learning culture by viewing learning from the "mind-set" perspective.[36] In general, whether individuals have more of a "growth" or "fixed" mind-set is a predictor of learning and achievement. The growth mind-set is the belief that skills are built (not born), and you are capable of learning and growing, while the fixed mind-set is the belief that skills are born and relatively set; you are limited by genetics and abilities. These beliefs elicit certain behaviors in athletes that are important for learning. Key distinctions between the two mind-sets are highlighted below:

Growth Mind-Set	*Fixed Mind-Set*
Failure is an opportunity to grow.	Failure is the limit of my abilities.
I can learn to do anything I want.	I'm either good at it or I'm not.
Challenges help me grow.	I don't like to be challenged.
I like to try new things.	I stick to what I know.
Feedback is good.	Feedback is criticism and doesn't help.
When I get frustrated, I try harder.	When I'm frustrated, I give up.
My effort and attitude determine my success.	My potential is predetermined.

The growth mind-set perspective facilitates the mental skills that coaches value most. Most coaches embrace athletes who give high amounts of effort to improve, and they value when athletes are more receptive to their instruction and feedback. The growth mind-set, with its focus on mastering skills and overcoming challenges, also facilitates desirable athlete skills such as *mental toughness* and *competitiveness*. An important question is whether athletes are born with their mind-set and their related mental skills or if they can be developed and improved. In the spirit of the growth mind-set, yes, coaches can do much to influence (and change) their athletes' beliefs! It starts by embracing and implementing aspects of the culture of learning discussed earlier (e.g., psychological safety). Below, we offer some examples of more specific strategies to promote the growth mind-set[37]:

- Reduce praise of talent and outcomes; increase praise on effort. For example, replace "Way to be a winner today" with "Your practice on your serve really showed today. Nice job."
- Make "yet" a large part of your vocabulary. Shift the athlete from believing "I can't do it" to "I can't do it yet."
- Share popular, real-life stories of the value of failures. Failures help inspire successes (e.g., Michael Jordan quote).
- Avoid the all-too-easy, quick ability labels. Replace "He is slow footed" with process-focused phrases such as "I can see the improvement on your work to stay low and keep your feet moving on defense."
- Use more process-related challenge goals (vs. outcome or winning) for some practice drills. For example, "Let's see if we can improve to six consecutive passes in this drill."

The development and transfer of desirable mental skills, such as determination, grit, competitiveness, and stick-to-itiveness, can be facilitated in practice environments that promote and develop the growth mind-set in athletes.

TRANSFER THIS

Let's return to our high school hurdler. It seems her coach is off to a good start to building a foundation for the transfer of learning. He facilitated two-way and credible communication, shared in decision-making, and sincerely listened to his athlete. These are markers of an athlete-centered coach using a cooperative coaching style. He showed an individualized approach, getting to know her needs, and treated her differently by finding instruction that matched her skills, experiences, and goals. He used strong communication skills (see "The Fundamental Communication Skills" section) to establish mutual trust, credibility, and relationship-building efforts. Further, it seems her coach was working on a culture of learning when he modeled vulnerability and the willingness to learn, rather than having all the answers. It could be an indication he has a psychologically safe environment that encourages risk-taking, failure, feedback, and the value of learning to learn. Keep it up, Coach!

Coaches, Transfer This

1. Transfer of learning grows when the conditions are right. It is a long-term developmental process. There is no "quick fix" for the transfer of practice to the competition. It's built over time and is more likely to occur when you have built a solid foundation for learning.
2. Transfer is more likely to occur when you are *athlete centered*, take a *long-term development* perspective, and use a *cooperative coaching style*. Do you coach this way?
3. Individualize your approach. While being fair, treat them differently, considering each athlete's past experiences, individual differences, and developmental levels. Realize they develop at different rates and amounts, and avoid labeling or making predictions of athletes based on their early success.
4. Do you have a *common language* established for your team or athlete(s)? Take the time to build and develop a common language of phrases and words that becomes part of your communication and culture for everyone on your team. It will facilitate transfer both within practice and to the competition.
5. Build, reinforce, and model a safe culture of learning, one that values the role of risk-taking, mistakes, errors, and feedback in practice. Reinforce that "getting better" is the goal, and regardless of genetics, we can all improve (coaches *and* athletes).

Coach Educators and Developers, Transfer This

1. Facilitate open discussions about the elements of coaching that foster positive athlete development. For example: *How and why do some coaches consistently maximize the development of their players while others seem to consistently have players who decline or don't reach their potential?* Connect the discussion to the content of this chapter.
2. Have coaches reflect on the elements of the Pyramid of Teaching Success in Sport (PoTSS). What elements are they strong in? Which ones need more focus? How do the coaches align with the top of the pyramid and the definition of success?
3. Ask coaches to reflect on the following statement: *Athletes don't care how much you know until they know how much you care.* Do they agree? How

does this relate to the foundation for transfer of learning? Encourage coaches to give examples and applications.
4. Identify and share some phrases or words that coaches have used to establish a *common language* among players and team. Evaluate why/how they are effective or ways they can be improved to facilitate transfer.
5. Conduct or facilitate self-assessments of coaches in foundational elements. For example, videotape coaches during practice and monitor types of verbal and nonverbal communication messages or record the frequency of feedback statements that praise ability vs. effort. Provide some written assessments for coaches to self-assess on areas such as communication or mind-sets. Many simple assessments can easily be found on the Internet.

4

Designing Practice for Transfer

Mrs. Thomas, a high school athletic director, is a self-proclaimed "gadget junkie." She spends hours searching the Internet and catalogs to find great tools that her coaches can use in practice to increase athlete performance. Last year, she was dismayed when two of her coaches rejected products that she bought for them. One product was the popular training aid "speed-agility-quickness ladder." Her track coach said she did not like this device for increasing a runner's speed. A second product was the "dribble goggles" that prevent players from looking at the ball while dribbling. Her basketball coach said he liked other drills to teach players to look up. They told her to save her money and to include them before she buys products next time.

Conducting quality practice sessions begins with effective planning and design. This chapter identifies important practice design concepts that apply specifically to the transfer of learning. As we plan to increase transfer of learning, we reemphasize there is no quick fix or "perfect" practice activity for practice conditions to transfer to the competitive environment. Transfer of learning is most often a cumulative effect resulting from sequential and well-designed learning experiences.

DESIGN FOR "OPTIMAL CHALLENGES"
Parents may recognize this:

> When one of this book's author's two sons were eight and nine years old, they went through a phase of trying to jump and touch things out of their reach. When they went into a store, they would look for doorways or hanging objects to jump and touch. They competed. But the competition with the sibling was not as strong as the one one of the sons had with himself if he ever found a doorway that was 2 inches out of his reach on the first jump. Fifteen jumps and 10 minutes later, he would rejoin Dad in the store. He stayed with Dad if he touched the doorway easily. He stayed with Dad if the doorway was 5 inches out of his reach. And since both boys were different heights, rarely did both boys stay with Dad. One seemed to find a challenge while the other was disinterested. The lesson was clear . . . if you want to engage a child, give them a challenge just beyond their reach.

Athlete motivation and learning are enhanced when athletes are challenged to perform just above their current level of skill. To achieve this, practice should adapt to match athletes' levels of expertise. An athlete who is under-challenged or struggles too much in a drill may be a result of the coach misreading the athlete's level of readiness relative to the difficulty of the task. To optimally challenge athletes, we consider two science-supported concepts (with analogies).

The "Sweet Spot"
One way to conceive of the athlete-challenge match is to consider the *motivational* effects of practice conditions. To establish a *sweet spot* for motivation, we use Mihaly Csikszentmihalyi's original "flow" concept that athletes experience when they have a perfect balance between their skill level and the level of task difficulty.[1] Flow refers to the experience of being in the optimal state of mind and body when performing. Athletes "in the zone" would experience complete concentration, ease of movement, complete control, and transformation of time (e.g., game slowing down) and perception (e.g., objects appearing larger). A requirement for experiencing flow is the ideal match between an athlete's current skill level and the difficulty of the task. When the challenge is matched to athlete skill level, motivation and anxiety levels are optimal for performance

DESIGNING PRACTICE FOR TRANSFER

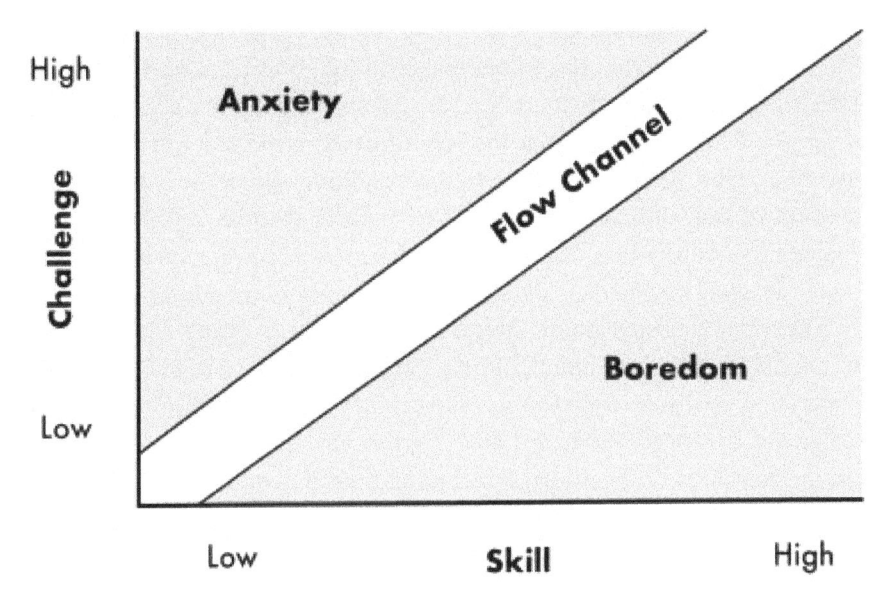

A two-axis diagram with "Challenge" (Low to High) on the vertical axis and "Skill" (Low to High) on the horizontal axis. A diagonal "Flow Channel" band runs from the lower-left to the upper-right. Above the channel is labeled "Anxiety"; below it is labeled "Boredom".

FIGURE 4.1
The original "flow" concept showing the "sweet spot" of athlete enjoyment and intrinsic motivation. (Adapted from Csikszentmihalyi, *Flow*)

and enjoyment. As seen in figure 4.1, mismatches between challenge and skill result in conditions of anxiety (task too challenging) or boredom (task too easy).[2] In this sweet spot, athletes are more likely to get "lost" in the activity, connect with the love of the sport, and intrinsically enjoy practice or performing. In the parent example above, the boys were likely in their sweet spot when they were "lost" in their jumps, with no clue where Dad went.

What can the coach do to facilitate the motivational sweet spot? It largely depends on the athletes' beliefs or expectancies about their ability to complete a practice activity with some success. Athletes need to feel competent and confident in their ability to learn something new. Expected success is essential to the athlete learning, and practice activities, even if difficult and challenging, should facilitate *positive* athlete expectancies.[3] Coaches might consider, for example, starting and ending practice sessions with challenging yet attainable practice drills or modified games (see chapters 8 and 9). They might start practice sessions with activities that have high success rates and add complexity or difficulty later in the practice session.

The "Goldilocks Principle"

The second way to conceive of optimal challenge is to consider the *learning* effects of practice tasks that are too easy, too hard, or "just right." The *challenge point hypothesis* looks at the role of practice difficulty in motor-skill learning.[4] How difficult should practice conditions be; what is the optimal amount of task difficulty? Grounded in transfer theories 2 (schemas) and 3 (cognitive effort) (see chapter 2), the framework for the challenge point hypothesis seeks to predict "optimal challenge points" for athlete learning.

The term "challenge point" suggests that learning in practice is a function of two things: (1) the amount and type of the *new information* or degree of uncertainty available to the learner, and (2) the *functional task difficulty* of the skill being practiced. What and how much is new information is dependent on the readiness of the athletes, including their individual differences, skill levels, and past experiences. For learning to occur, the new information must be matched with the individual athlete. This is called *functional task difficulty*, or the task's actual or perceived difficulty in relation to the athlete and the conditions of practice (e.g., stationary or moving). Learning is limited if there is too little or too much new information and is optimized when the available information aligns with the athlete's readiness to absorb it.

Individual athletes have optimal challenge points, or an optimal task difficulty to maximize potential for learning. For beginners, activities low in functional task difficulty provide the available new information needed for the learning effect. Dribbling a basketball around a stationary cone might provide the new information needed to maximize learning. However, a novice shooting jump shots over moving defenders likely provides too much new information for learning. For more skilled athletes, practice activities higher in task difficulty are more likely to provide the new information needed to learn. Dribbling a basketball through live defenders using three different techniques might provide the optimal challenge point for higher-skilled players. Before moving on, let's summarize the two main points of the challenge point hypothesis that are most relevant for transfer:

1. *For learning to occur there must be new information.* Practice conditions need to provide new information or uncertainty; performing well in practice often suggests that no new information is being provided, so nothing

is being learned. The optimal challenge point for learning is not the same one needed for immediate performance. Recall the performance-learning trade-off from chapter 1.
2. *For learning to occur an optimal amount of information and difficulty is needed.* The optimal amount differs as a function of athlete skill level and the difficulty of the task to be learned. Learning is slowed when there is too little or too much information relative to athlete readiness. Coaches need to modify task difficulty by increasing or decreasing the availability of new information. Simple skills need an increase in information and difficulty; complex skills need a decrease in information and difficulty.

The coach's challenge is to design "optimal" practice conditions for motivation and learning by managing practice difficulty and challenge. While it may sound easy, creating optimal challenge is often hard to achieve on a consistent basis. For example, some coaches are effective at managing difficulty for beginning-level athletes. They may be good at designing drills that break skills down or simplify them so less-skilled athletes show improvement (e.g., hitting tees, cone dribble, 2-line layup drills). However, it's often harder to design drills that optimally challenge athletes as they become more skillful. For athletes to keep advancing and learning, practice activities need to provide *new* information or difficulty. Conducting practice activities that are relatively simple and encourage mastery of the fundamental skills is a worthy goal, but those practices may not provide the optimal challenge for learning. As well, practice activities that overly focus on increasing difficulty with high amounts of complex new information may not provide the optimal challenge.

Creating "optimal challenge" conditions that manage the difficulty of practice conditions and provide new information to athletes at their level of readiness is a big task, but in many ways the transfer of learning depends on it. Strategies for managing optimal challenge conditions are addressed next.

DESIGN AROUND PRACTICE GOALS

To design practice for optimal challenge, we apply the practice design framework presented by Nicola Hodges and Keith Lohse,[5] who identified three "types" of practice, or practice goals, to manage the challenge point:

Goal 1: Practice-to-Learn (PTL)

Goal 2: Practice-to-Transfer (PTT)

Goal 3: Practice-to-Maintain (PTM)

Practice-to-Learn (PTL)

This type of practice emphasizes learning by increasing challenges and creating new information, making performance increasingly difficult for athletes. Drills and practice repetitions add new challenges, variations, or elements of uncertainty. Here, coaches design activities that are moderate to high in functional task difficulty. The coach is designing the "overload" to bring about long-term learning. PTL activities are designed to produce high levels of thinking and problem-solving in athletes, in ways that learning becomes *more* effortful. The coach avoids "easy" practice activities, such as rote repetitions of the same skill. Just like we would avoid cramming for a test (memorizing) because it is mostly forgotten the next day, PTL activities avoid easy repetitions because they don't provide the new information needed for learning.

Given the difficulty of these activities, athletes might struggle to perform well. Recall the case we made earlier about the distinction between performance and learning (chapter 2), where often the best long-term learning occurs at the expense of good practice performance. This type of practice requires both coaches and athletes to be comfortable sacrificing performance in practice to maximize learning. Coaches can help athletes recognize and appreciate the distinction between practicing for performance and just practicing. Since PTL activities produce more errors and mistakes, the coach might reduce the emphasis on performance outcomes, and reward desirable behaviors or improvements in the process (e.g., strategies or techniques). This is easier to do if the coach has fostered a safe learning culture with a growth and positive failure mind-set (see chapter 3).

It's important to note that PTL activities do *not* seek to simulate or mimic the specific elements of competition. Rather, the focus is on the cognitive effort needed for long-term learning. However, this PTL practice is still very important for transfer, as game performance depends on the athletes' levels of learning. These activities often produce *moderate* or *far transfer* of more *general* game skills or principles. For example, conducting challenging drills that require a shift in attentional focus and fast memory retrieval can transfer to game performance, where similar processes are required.

Practice-to-Transfer (PTT)

Practice activities for this goal require the *simulation* of the elements of competition or the game. They are designed to mimic the difficulties or challenges found in the competition. PTT activities seek *near* transfer to the game, given the high degree of similarity of the practice task to the target task (game). They attempt to re-create and/or replicate elements of the game and focus on the athletes' specific situational understanding rather than generalized processes. Often, the focus is on tactical skills (e.g., what to do when), but may also include mental, emotional, and environmental factors (e.g., anxiety, noise, distractions, playing surface). As well, PTT activities might replicate the specific perceptual and cognitive processes (e.g., game speed, opponent positions, rapid decisions, visual focus) or physiological demands of the competition (e.g., fatigue and rest periods). PTT shifts the emphasis from long-term learning to successful performances in game-like conditions. There is the expectation of positive outcomes, performing with fewer mistakes. This is, after all, what is required in the game. These activities also are designed to change from week to week, as the upcoming opponent and/or competitive challenges change.

The simulation of game-like elements is not an all-or-none proposition. A "full" simulation requires high levels of specificity in all skill elements related to the game (e.g., perceptual, mental, tactical, technical) and in all environmental elements (e.g., crowd noise). Full simulations may *not* be the best strategy for a few reasons. First, it may not be realistic to simulate key aspects of the competitive environment. For example, it's hard to simulate the skill, size, strength, or strategies of the opponent, or the weather conditions or field surfaces of tomorrow's game. Even game-like scrimmages rarely achieve full simulation of the upcoming competition. Second, the frequent simulation of competitive conditions in practice carries inherent physical and psychological risks such as athlete injuries, overtraining, or loss of athlete confidence. Third, true simulations of the competitive environment run the risk of creating difficulties that exceed athlete readiness and the optimal challenge point. So, coaches should be deliberate and strategic in designing PTT activities. The target task might not be the *whole* competitive environment or game, but only parts of it. For example, for the practice session before tomorrow's game, the coach might design a practice activity that simulates decision-making at game speeds, but not activities that simulate the physical demands of the competition (e.g., rest intervals and fatigue). Or, instead of the traditional scrimmage, the coach might design modified games (e.g., small-sided game) to simulate targeted game-like elements (e.g., rest intervals).

Practice-to-Maintain (PTM)
Practice activities for this goal seek to reinforce the essential skills of the sport, establish "automaticity" for certain technical and tactical skills, and enhance mental skills such as confidence and motivation. The core movements, techniques, and sequences should be repeated, mastered, and "second nature" for athletes in their sport. They are often the predictable movements and patterns that athletes and teams should be able to execute with little attention or conscious awareness. Generally, they emphasize the technical skills players rely on in competition (e.g., serving motion), but they can also include tactical skills that should be "reflexive" in athletes (e.g., recognition of cues to pass, defensive movement in response to ball movement). PTM activities might be done daily to ensure consistent execution of key skills. PTM conditions enhance athlete motivation and confidence, as they provide athletes opportunities to experience success at their level of readiness. Remember, expected success and feelings of competence are not only important for athlete motivation but also for learning.[6] PTM activities are also a way to maximize athletes' strengths to accommodate their weaknesses. It's important to give athletes opportunities to further demonstrate their strengths. It further increases athlete enjoyment and motivation and transfers well to competition.[7]

PTM activities are low to moderate in functional difficulty, providing low amounts of new information. As well, they are low in simulation and similarity (e.g., lower anxiety levels, different perceptual information). However, they are important for transfer. They seek to reinforce learned skills, so they are "overlearned" as deep memories. This overlearning allows athletes to be more creative problem solvers later in practice or in competition. With automaticity, athletes have reduced loads on memory and attentional capacity, and can allocate more attention to important perceptual and game elements

Table 4.1. Summary of practice goals, with key characteristics and practice examples.

Practice Goal	Characteristics	Practice Examples
Learn (PTL)	Long-term learning Cognitively difficult; demands on attention and memory; high levels of problem-solving Reduced success; mistakes and errors	Random, unpredictable repetitions Distort skill or game elements, e.g., overload defenders, block part of vision, complete task in faster-than-normal time
Transfer (PTT)	Competition simulation and specificity Tactical and mental skills Higher success; fewer mistakes and errors	Opponent simulation, e.g., tomorrow's game Small-sided game simulating competition element(s), e.g., pressure and spacing
Maintain (PTM)	Reinforces automaticity and "reflexive" nature of movements and behaviors Builds feelings of competence, confidence, and motivation High success; demonstrates strengths	Consecutive repetitions of a skill, e.g., get in 500 shots Independent practice of athlete strengths, e.g., work on favorite shot

such as opponent position, ball movement, or teammate communication. Table 4.1 provides a comparison of the three practice goals with practice examples for each goal.

A Balanced Practice Design

The value of this framework is in designing the appropriate *balance* of practice activities. A balanced approach is more likely to provide optimal challenge for learning, motivation, and ultimately transfer. Coaches might start by identifying goals that are overemphasized or underrepresented in their practice planning. For example, practice sessions consisting of all PTL activities may provide too much difficulty (and anxiety) and suppress athlete motivation. Balancing with more PTM activities might help with designing optimal challenge. As well, an overemphasis on PTM activities might provide too little challenge and suppress athlete learning and transfer. There also may be reasons why coaches might design practice with a *purposeful imbalance* among practice goals. They might prioritize certain practice goals at different points in the season. For example:

1. More PTM activities the day before a game to increase athlete confidence and motivation.
2. More PTT activities later in the season to better prepare for opponents.
3. More PTL activities early in the season to increase athlete thinking, problem-solving, and learning as a foundation for performance later in the season.

A second strategy in balancing goals is to design practice activities that combine the objectives of the different practice goals. For example, when conducting PTL drills, coaches might progressively add elements of specificity that mimic (PTT) the game (e.g., add game-like rest times between shots). High school baseball coach Cameron Schildt provided an example of practice that combines the PTL and PTT practice goals:

> I try to make practice harder than the games . . . so that players are used to being in those uncomfortable situations and learning from those moments of struggle . . . that is where I believe transfer occurs . . . and that is where I step in, stop practice, and teach them how to think and what to do. They will be more prepared when we must score or make a play in the game.[8]

Finally, as mentioned earlier, transfer of learning is a cumulative and developmental process. The success of the PTT goal depends on the achievement of the other two practice goals. For PTT simulations to be more effective, athletes need to consistently perform the prerequisite technical, tactical, and mental skills. This may be an area where transfer breaks down. If athletes are not "ready" for PTT activities, then they will be less effective. To address this, coaches should progressively add PTT activities as they get closer to competition, and as players gain skill and readiness.

MANIPULATE PRACTICE "CONSTRAINTS"
One way to manage difficulty in practice and increase learning is to design learning conditions by modifying the practice environment. The coach can be a "learning designer" who controls the elements or "constraints" of the practice session through more indirect (vs. direct) methods. Significant support for this approach comes from theories related to ecological dynamics

(transfer theory 4, see chapter 2), specifically in the areas of the *constraints-led approach*, *nonlinear pedagogy*, and *representative learning design*.

Constraints are the "ingredients" of a practice activity or the "interacting sources of information" available to the athlete.[9] Recall from the science (chapter 2) that constraints are related to (1) the individual (athlete), (2) the task, and (3) the environment. The coach considers how changing the constraints can create opportunities for players to discover solutions to movement problems that will advance their skill. For example, rather than verbally instructing players on how to move more without the ball, the coach might change the number of players in a drill (task) so they are encouraged to explore and adopt strategies. In this approach, coaches are encouraged to "prescribe a task, not the solution." In other words, even though coaches might know of optimal solutions, they strategically provide athletes with a problem to solve or goal to achieve while minimizing the details about how to solve or achieve it.[10]

Implementing Practice Constraints

How should a coach design the manipulation of practice constraints to shape learning? The "constraints-led approach" recommends coaches begin by identifying all the possible constraints that can influence performance in their sport.[11] This first step would build a list of all possible constraints of the skill or sport under the three headings—individual, task, and environment. Using field hockey as an example, individual (athlete) constraints might include factors such as power, speed, fatigue, and body type. Task constraints might include factors such as boundaries (size and shape), goals (size, orientation), players (numbers), and start positions (player and ball feed). Environment constraints might include factors such as turf characteristics and climate. Second, the coach should clearly identify the intent of the practice activity, or the target skill, concept, or behavior they want to see in their athlete(s). This *target behavior* frames the practice task and gives it purpose and intentionality. Target behaviors (or intentions) are aligned with an athlete's level of readiness and are focused on the process of the skill rather than the outcome. They should prevent athletes from "going through the motions during a practice activity." Third, coaches should shape practice by *manipulating the constraints* that would likely elicit the target behavior. These are generally related to the task and/or the environment. To help identify the key task constraints to manipulate, a useful approach is applying the STEPS[12] process, which suggests a simple and effective way to identify types of practice constraints to manipulate.

Space: make zones or boundaries bigger, smaller, different shapes, different goal locations or directions

Task: modify rules, limit teams, change positions, change task goals, alter accuracy requirements

Equipment: use different ball or equipment sizes, weights, shapes, and feel

People: change numbers or positioning of players, match or mismatch partners or teams

Speed: change the intensity and speed of a drill or game or the time to complete a task

Let's provide a research-to-practice example of an equipment manipulation (E) that elicited target behaviors or intentions:

> A study sought to improve puck control, skate speeds, and shooting skills (target behaviors) of less-skilled hockey players by manipulating the weight/mass of the hockey puck (equipment constraint manipulation). They found that using a lighter-than-regulation puck elicited faster skate times and better puck control in a game-like, timed obstacle course; it also elicited increased shooting accuracy after skating as fast as possible from the center line. The equipment modification, compared to the regulation puck, elicited improved performance in skills important to hockey competition (skate speed, puck control, and shot accuracy).[13]

There has been considerable research using constraint manipulations. Table 4.2 highlights more research-to-practice examples that identified a target behavior(s) and manipulated specific constraints to elicit the target behavior(s) and increase learning.[14] There are some important considerations for designing practice constraints, and we provide them next.

Athlete Readiness

Constraint manipulations should always be designed based on athlete readiness and their individual constraints. For example, making a space larger to elicit

Table 4.2. Research-supported examples of STEPS constraint manipulations. The bottom portion is for coaches to identify their own target behavior and manipulation.

Target Behavior or Practice Intent	Practice Constraint(s) Manipulated
Use the backhand stroke more often rather than running around the ball to hit the forehand stroke (tennis).	(**S**pace) Move court centerline and recovery box 5 ft. to the right. Perform drills and matches moving back to the new recovery box after each shot.
Change a hurdle motion from "jumping" over the hurdle to "running" over the hurdle (track).	(**T**ask) Put marker on track placed closely after hurdle to encourage snap down and vertical landing.
Keep forearm connected to the body early in the pitching delivery (prevent the "forearm flyout") of the arm separating too early (baseball).	(**E**quipment) Pitch while holding a playground/connection ball below the pitching arm. It must roll toward the plate, not to the side, after pitch delivery.
Improve the team's ability to exploit and execute counterattack opportunities (field hockey).	(**P**eople) Overload more attacking players (3 v. 1) to explore more pass-receive solutions with success.
Increase visual scanning of field to improve anticipation and decision-making in dribbling and passing (soccer).	(**S**peed) No clock or time kept on larger field with low compression ball to slow play down and encourage head up and looking ahead.

Target Behavior or Practice Intent	Practice (Constraint) Manipulation (circle one)	How Manipulated to Elicit Target Behavior
	Space, Task, Equipment, People, Speed	

more movement off the ball might yield too much fatigue in younger athletes with shorter legs and less-developed cardiovascular systems. As well, changes in equipment (e.g., implement weights or target sizes) may not match the developmental level of young athletes (e.g., visual system, strength, balance).

Keep Perception-Action Coupled. The manipulation of task constraints is not the same as simplifying the task to increase success. Coaches should be careful that when they manipulate task constraints, they don't "de-couple" the information in the environment (perception) from the movement required (action). Remember, for transfer to occur, practice should replicate the perception-action coupling of the competition as often as possible. For example, changing constraints to dribble a soccer ball around stationary cones and on an artificial surface might oversimplify the skill. The movement solution (skill) practiced in this environment is very different than the one needed in the competition. Solving the problem of dribbling around moving defenders and bumpy surfaces is very different than the one for dribbling around cones on a smooth surface. Consider the earlier research example of hockey puck manipulation. The researchers were careful to keep the perceptual environment game-like when they changed the constraint (hockey puck).

Avoid "Over-Constraining."[15] Some constraints might limit options or behaviors in ways that reduce game-like problem-solving. Athletes need to search for and identify their own solutions as much as possible. For example, consider the popular "two-touch only" drill when in possession of the soccer ball. It constrains the players by encouraging them to pass the ball early. But it might be overly prescriptive and force athletes to discover only one solution. It prevents the athlete from learning about when and why it is beneficial to make passes on the first or second touch, dribble the ball to create space, or slow play down by keeping possession. In this case, the constraint manipulation is not very game-like. We discuss games-based approaches more in chapter 9.

Be Clear about the Target Behavior (Intention). It's important to make sure the constraint manipulations clearly elicit the target behavior(s). This point is highlighted in the opening scenario of Mrs. Thomas, the athletic director who likes to buy popular gadgets or devices to increase learning and performance. Sometimes these practice manipulations may not elicit the desired behaviors. Her coaches sensed the devices didn't constrain practice to elicit their target behaviors. For the speed-agility-quickness ladder, if the intention is for the device to increase a runner's speed, the manipulation may only be partially effective. Top coaches have suggested that the movement patterns encouraged by the ladders work to slow down the athlete. They elicit lower knee lifts and reduced stride lengths in attempts to increase cadence.[16] For the dribble goggles, if the intention is to use this device to encourage athletes to look up by blocking the view of their hands and ball while they dribble, the device may only be partially effective. Game dribbling includes the visual information (or "optical flow") of the hands, ball, and ground while dribbling. This loss of specificity or game-like optical flow when using the goggles creates the potential for negative transfer.[17] In all practice activities, coaches should evaluate constraints relative to the intention or the target behavior they encourage.

Still Teaching
Even though constraint manipulation might be seen as indirect or "hands-off" instruction, it still requires the coach to be an active participant during practice. Manipulations are most effective when combined with *instructional methods* such as focusing athletes' attention to external cues, analogies, and questioning. We discuss this further in chapter 6. Also, coaches should carefully monitor the use of constraint manipulations. When they consistently observe the desired behavior or technique in their athletes, coaches should identify and manipulate new ones, so athletes continue their skill development.

The manipulation of practice constraints is a progressive teaching tool to guide athletes to more desirable behavior, skills, and actions. It may take considerable practice and patience for coaches to effectively implement the constraints-led approach, but as discussed in later chapters, it's worth the effort!

BUILD TOWARD TRANSFER
Practice activities are often an example of far transfer, as the transfer task (practice drill) is somewhat dissimilar and distant to the target task (game). Practice should progressively move toward moderate-near or moderate transfer since these conditions yield higher amounts of positive transfer. In this approach, practice is designed to build toward transfer, getting athletes closer to game-like conditions as they gain skill.

Building toward transfer is good teaching. Effective practice activities progress over time; they get more challenging and complex. Drills become more game-like as elements of challenge and difficulty are added. Isolating new concepts then integrating them with other skills and concepts builds on positive transfer. Practice advancements might include progressing from single movements to combination movements, slower to faster speeds, small groups to large groups, easy to hard drills, or predictable to chaotic conditions. Below are specific ways to help coaches build toward transfer.

Replace Purpose with "Objectives"[18]
Coaches typically have a *purpose* for using a certain practice activity. For example, a coach may say, "This passing drill works on player movement and looking for open teammates." The reason (purpose) for the drill is good, but it might not be targeted enough to monitor challenge and facilitate near transfer.

A practice *objective* is different. It is something that is *observable and measurable*. An objective defines what your athletes will be able to do by the end of the activity, and what the effective practice will look like. At the completion of the drill, you can more clearly see if players have learned what you have taught. To better frame a practice activity and provide a clear measure of success, consider this: "This passing drill requires the completion of five consecutive, accurate passes to teammates by using at least two off-the-ball movement techniques."

Practice objectives allow coaches to build off athletes' past performance and adjust practice for higher levels of achievement. Using our example, the objective can be moved upward so that the drill increases in focus and challenge. For example: "Now, can you complete six consecutive, accurate passes by showing me *three* different off-the-ball movements?"

Practice objectives provide a measure of athlete learning and readiness, and they help coaches design more sequential PTL activities. If athletes can't accomplish the practice objective, they may not have mastered (and transferred) the skills of passing and moving from earlier practice. Before athletes can transfer to the game, they need to master the important underlying skills. Designing drills with practice objectives provides a "metric" that helps both athletes and coaches build toward transfer, and we encourage coaches to use them as much as possible.

Design "Platform" Activities

One of the best methods of building toward transfer is using what Doug Lemov[19] calls a "platform." These are practice activities that introduce new information on a platform of a familiar structure. They provide a basic format of a drill that players learn to execute at a high level. Once the basic format and fundamental skills/concepts of the platform are mastered, the coaches build off the platform by adding in endless variations or extensions of new information, concepts, or complexities. Instead of introducing brand-new drills and concepts, adding skill variations builds on past concepts and produces near and positive transfer. Platforms allow coaches to manage difficulty, focus players, and combine the benefits of PTM and PTL practice. Platforms might be practiced every day and mastered (PTM goals), but the coach can easily add new concepts and challenges to increase learning (PTL goals) and get players closer to competition elements (transfer).

There are several examples of platform activities. Platforms work well with skill drills that involve small groups of players (e.g., small-sided games).

A great example is the common soccer training exercise "rondos." Rondos involve a group of four to five players playing "keep-away" from two players in the middle. This platform, or basic structure of the activity, remains while the coach can modify to practice endless variations that can improve both skill (e.g., passing and receiving) and perception (e.g., head up and eyes ahead, determine/anticipating space, judge weight of pass). Coaches can easily add more game-like variations, competitions, or simulations.[20] Another example would be the defensive "shell" drill commonly used in basketball. This drill positions players in a moving shell structure of four to five players (no offensive players) to isolate and practice team and individual movement of half-court man-to-man defense. Players can practice executing the shell drill with the addition of new information—certain offensive players, after a change of possession, off an in-bounds play, or with less than 10 seconds on the clock. These complexities add progressive challenges but in familiar conditions. Other examples might be the "Carolina" (3 on 2) drill in basketball, "box drills" in lacrosse, or "four-square" in tennis. Look them up!

Designing platforms can pay dividends for transfer of learning. We want to emphasize *why* platform activities are an ideal design. They enhance learning by balancing new or complex information with the familiarity of a well-learned practice structure. This accommodates limitations in athlete attention and memory, and athletes better absorb and remember new information. For the coach, platforms address limitations in valuable practice time. Consider the time and effort it takes to introduce and explain new drills. Then add the time athletes spend learning how to complete the drill (e.g., rules, logistics). Using a familiar activity or drill, coaches avoid long verbal descriptions and demonstrations. Athletes execute it right the first time (e.g., they know where to go and where to stand) and they can focus on learning the new concept rather than drill logistics. We encourage coaches to design high-quality platform-type drills or activities that can be extended and expanded easily with new challenges. Good practice activities get better with age the more they are used (rather than get boring).

Monitor Types of Practice

A common breakdown in the transfer of learning is conducting simulation-type (PTT) activities when athletes are not ready. As discussed earlier, one way to monitor this is to balance practice activities between the PTM, PTL, and PTT goals. Some coaches divide practice activities into *phases* and monitor them to build toward transfer.[21] For example, the basketball coach might divide and label their practice activities as follows:

Phase 1: Unopposed drills without defenders or "on air" drills (PTM).

Phase 2: Drills that manipulate "opposition" constraints. These push players to make certain movement solutions or decisions by using defenders strategically. For example, making a player use their nondominant hand by using a defender who forces it (PTL).

Phase 3: Small-sided games that simulate competitive advantages or disadvantages, such as two-on-two or three-on-four games (PTL or PTT).

Phase 4: Game-like full-speed drills with stoppages to simulate flow and transitions between offense and defense (PTT).

Coaches can design and monitor practice relative to how much time is spent in each *type* of practice (phases in this example) to achieve the practice goals. For example, phases 1 and 2 are PTM or PTL activities without the game-like cues and decision-making. When coaches are satisfied with athletes' practice of phase 1 and 2 drills, they can spend more time in phase 3 and 4 activities. However, spending too much time in phases 1 and 2 (at the expense of 3 and 4) might generate good practice performance, but not under game conditions of pressure and/or speed. Whatever labels coaches put on practice types (i.e., phases), it's important to plan different types of practice that build into transfer.

MAXIMIZE TIME ON TASK

The final strategy for practice design is to maximize the time athletes spend executing skills during practice. While this may sound obvious, in a typical practice session less-experienced coaches have (1) long lines, with athletes waiting their turn, (2) athletes standing and listening to excessive verbal instructions, or (3) poorly designed drills that are logistically complicated with long transition times. Sometimes the highest number of repetitions are performed by . . . the coach! Yes, the coach serves, spikes, and sets to his volleyball players while they stand in lines taking their turn executing the skills. Practice design should always permit athletes to get the maximum number of touches, repetitions, and engagement during practice. Throughout this book we stress that the *quality* of practice is essential for transfer of learning. However, maximizing the *quantity* of practice is important too, especially when practice times are limited for coaches and athletes (e.g., 2-hour sessions). We highlight next some areas coaches can maximize practice time for transfer of learning.

Rest and Downtime
While rest is necessary in many practice situations, coaches can do much to structure practice in ways that rest is "built in" to the practice schedule. We discuss methods in chapter 7 where *interleaved* and *spaced* repetitions not only increase learning but allow for rest time by executing "different" skills and movements. This avoids fatigue from using the same muscles and movements (consecutive repetitions of the same skill). During games players might rotate positions to avoid fatigue, or the coach might design sideline activities to better engage players while they are off the field. For example, while on the sideline, players might do light drills or activities with a partner, or they might actively evaluate teammate play during the game (e.g., using a game-play checklist).

Drill Design
Many drills are designed in ways that reduce the number of touches or contacts that players receive. The traditional two-line layup drill, for example, in basketball yields about three touches/layups per player in a 5-minute period. The eight-person circle drill of volleyball players, tasked to see how many times they can hit the ball before it touches the floor, will yield few contacts per player (perhaps more for the skilled players!). Drill and game design should consider group size and whether it affords opportunities for *all* players to get high numbers of touches. Coaches are encouraged to review the manipulation of *practice constraints* discussed earlier in this chapter to get ideas about how the environment can be modified to increase athlete participation. Static drills should be replaced by active game activities that encourage high participation, such as players (vs. the coach) initiating play and rotating to various positions. Consider too that drill design is best when its logistical and administrative elements are relatively simple. As discussed earlier, rather than spend valuable practice time explaining several new drills or moving from station to station,

consider designing and extending *platform* activities. This saves practice time from long sets of verbal instructions, demonstrations, and logistics.

Equipment and Facilities

The basketball coach might choose the two-line layup drill because he only has two basketballs and one goal. The volleyball coach may select the eight-person circle drill because she has only half the gym or a small practice space. Part of the challenge of coaching is to design practice so that the lack of equipment and facilities does not cause reduced time on task or fewer repetitions. One way to accomplish this is to look for equipment substitutions or alternatives. Playground balls (similar size and weight), for example, might substitute for soccer balls or volleyballs. Coaches can also modify the practice setting to allow more repetitions and practice time. Consider a research example:

> One study supported using a modified practice setting for the shot put (a practice setting with high wait times). Athletes who practiced half of their repetitions in a modified setting (into a hanging tarp in a gymnasium) learned the skill as well as athletes who performed all their repetitions in the real setting (open space).[22]

Though modified facilities or alternative equipment can effectively maximize time on task, we warn coaches that modifications should not change the underlying coordination of the movement. If players use different or ineffective techniques to kick a different ball, then transfer will be limited (potentially negative). In addition, coaches should consider the extent the modification changes the athletes' perception of the environment. Perhaps one reason athletes practicing the shot put learned equally well in the modified setting was that they *alternated* their modified practice repetitions with the natural (real) setting. Half of their practice repetitions were completed with competition-like perception-action coupling.

Technologies

An increasingly popular way to maximize time on task is to use technology that can substitute for real practice (e.g., on rainy days) or provide additional practice to improve the actual skill. Technologies might include simulators, virtual-reality glasses, or computer-based training programs to improve perceptual skills (e.g., pitch or serve recognition). They are most popular in the effort to increase athletes' perceptual or cognitive skills and are seen to be useful because they can be used outside of practice time to enhance performance. Technologies on the market include Neurotracker, stroboscopic glasses, Halo Sport, Fit Light, Sport Vision, Dynavision, Win Reality, and GameSense, to name a few.

Are these technologies useful for maximizing time on task and do they transfer to the real game? Well, yes and no. There is evidence that using certain technologies increases perceptual or cognitive skills and can generate near and moderate transfer. Using baseball/softball as an example, practicing pitch-recognition skills on a computer screen can improve pitch recognition in a posttest after the training (near). As well, pitch recognition practice on a computer screen can improve pitch recognition in an on-field posttest of hitters identifying pitches from a live pitcher (moderate). However, science has yet to establish that technology practice can transfer to the ability to get more hits in a game (far transfer).[23]

We recommend that if coaches use technology to substitute for real practice, they do so with a "trained eye." Its value depends on several factors. Since transfer depends on the similarity and specificity of the transfer task (see chapter 6), coaches should evaluate the "fidelity" of the technology. There is little evidence to support training with technologies that use non-sport-specific stimuli. For example, improving the general visual abilities of depth perception or tracking offers little positive transfer to the competition. There is some evidence that sport-specific anticipation can be improved with technology practice, but transfer to the real game has yet to be shown. There is also evidence that visual gaze training (e.g., "quiet eye") can produce far transfer to competition, but only for certain hard and self-paced skills (e.g., golf putting and target shooting). And there is some evidence that virtual-environment (VE) technologies can produce far transfer, but only if the simulation is "adaptive," or changes as the athlete's skill level improves.

Using technologies for practice often "can't hurt." They can be useful in increasing time on task or engaging athletes when time, equipment, and facilities are limited. They can improve mental skills such as athlete confidence, motivation, and interest. But we suggest coaches be more critical relative to transfer, and evaluate technologies based on their specificity. Science has come a long way, but it has yet to support the consistent use of technology for transfer of learning all the way to the game.[24]

TRANSFER THIS

Mrs. Thomas, our "gadget junkie" athletic director at the beginning of the chapter, failed to realize that the clear identification of a target behavior is key to designing practice conditions. As discussed earlier (manipulating practice constraints), her devices (speed-agility-quickness ladder and dribble goggles) artificially constrained the practice activity and may not have elicited the desired skills and behavior in the athletes. Her coaches reminded her that they are in the best position to manipulate practice constraints that create optimal challenges for their athletes, fit within their practice goals, and build toward transfer. Though Mrs. Thomas was well intentioned, designing practice for transfer is a result of sequential and well-designed learning experiences. Coaches are in the best position to evaluate practice tools (including current technologies) that positively transfer and maximize practice time. When shopping for practice gadgets, Mrs. Thomas should keep in mind the purpose of practice: Will it transfer?

Coaches, Transfer This

1. All athletes have an optimal challenge point, or an individual level of practice difficulty where they learn with high enjoyment and motivation. Practice should be designed around creating optimal challenges to all athletes at their individual levels.
2. Recognize and appreciate the difference between practice activities designed to learn (PTL), transfer (PTT), or maintain (PTM) athlete skills. These practice goals should be strategically balanced to support the athletes' optimal challenge and the coaches' objectives.
3. Practice design should include the strategic manipulation of practice conditions that elicit target behaviors. Coaches look to indirectly modify the constraints of the task and environment in ways that encourage successful execution of the target behaviors.
4. Design practice activities that are sequential and naturally progress in difficulty. Identify measurable practice objectives that can guide and monitor skill improvement. Design platform-type drills that build toward transfer,

and can easily be modified to create more difficulty, include game-like variations, or focus on key skills.
5. Identify and eliminate/reduce practice elements that decrease the amount of athlete repetitions, contacts/touches, decision-making, or interactions. Design activities and drills that increase athlete time on task. Strategically use equipment, facilities, and technologies that increase athlete engagement, practice, and enjoyment.

Coach Educators and Developers, Transfer This
1. Facilitate open discussions about the two science-supported concepts of the "sweet spot" and the "goldilocks principle." Have they had athletes' experience "flow" in practice or a game? If so, how did their practice conditions prepare athletes for that opportunity? How have they conducted practice with the optimal amount of difficulty? Have they experienced situations of designing too little or too much difficulty?
2. Have coaches identify examples of drills or activities they have used that align with the three practice goals (PTL, PTT, and PTM). Have they experienced conditions when their practice activities were imbalanced among the goals (either accidentally or intentionally)? If so, what was the impact or result of the imbalance?
3. Practice applying the STEPS approach to practice design. Ask coaches to brainstorm ways they could manipulate practice activities in each of the five areas of STEPS. Make sure they identify the target behavior or intention before they manipulate. Does the manipulation elicit the desired behavior(s)?
4. Share examples of "platform" activities coaches have used in practice with success. Why were they effective? If they haven't used platform activities, have them try designing one in their sport(s).
5. Explore and evaluate gadgets or technologies that coaches have used or seen. As of this writing, a popular technology getting a lot of attention on the market is the WIN Reality VR Baseball or Softball Trainer (https://winreality.com/win-reality-vr/). Does this technology effectively build toward transfer? Does it elicit the desired skills or behaviors, and will it facilitate positive transfer? Why or why not?

5

Practice Analysis for Transfer

Shane is a parent volunteer coach for a youth basketball team (ages 12–13). As he plans and conducts his practice sessions, he relies heavily on the drills he remembers from his time as a high school basketball player. One of his favorite drills was the full-court figure-8 drill. Shane uses this drill every practice for about 15 minutes. Initially, his players struggled with the drill. They didn't go the right speeds or were too far away from each other as they moved down the court; they passed the ball behind their teammates or they often forgot to pass and "go behind" their pass. But as the season continues, his players are getting good at the drill, and they look smooth, fast, and efficient. He feels happy about this, and parents comment on how much players have improved in the drill. He overheard one parent say, "Now if they would only just do that in the game!"

One view of transfer is that practice conditions should be as similar as possible to the competitive environment (chapter 1). Recall, however, from chapter 4 (practice design) that a *full* simulation of the competitive environment in practice is often not possible or advisable. Simulating *all* the elements of competition (e.g., opponent's size, game anxiety) is often unrealistic. Too much simulation can increase the potential for overtraining or injury and can misalign with athlete readiness (e.g., skill level, confidence). We suggested earlier that the simulation of game-like elements is not always an all-or-none endeavor. A preferred strategy might be the *partial* modification of practice drills, games, and activities to increase similarity to the competition (moderate and positive transfer). When doing drills for learning (practice-to-learn goals) or maintenance (practice-to-maintain goals), coaches can progressively add elements of specificity (e.g., time between repetitions) that make them more game-like and increase their transfer potential. To this end, coaches should analyze and design their drills to increase in similarity and get them closer to a full simulation (game-like conditions). This chapter provides a systematic approach for analyzing practice to increase the similarity between practice and the competition.

ELEMENTS OF SIMILARITY

The first theory in the science chapter (2) emphasized that the key to transfer is how similar practice is to the game (specificity). More specifically, principles of specificity and "identical elements" suggest the potential for positive transfer is dependent on the degree to which the *elements* of the practice task simulate the *elements* of the target task (the game). So, the focus should move to identifying and manipulating the specific practice elements coaches want to transfer forward. Below we summarize the most common elements of practice similarity.[1] These elements guide the transfer analysis of our practice drills or games.

1. *Movement Elements.* Is the movement pattern(s) and/or technique(s) used by the athlete in practice highly similar or identical to that used in the game? If so, what are the movement elements? If not, what movement elements are different? For example:

    - Does the track sprint-start drill use the same pattern, coordination, and arm movement used in the race?
    - Does the basketball block-out activity require the same leg and arm movements used in game block-outs?
    - Does the wall-spike volleyball drill use the same lower/upper body coordination and wrist snap as used in game spikes?

2. *Strategic and Conceptual Elements.* Does the practice activity require athletes to apply highly similar or identical concepts, strategies, or problem-solving as required in the game? If so, what are the elements? If not, what elements are different? For example:

- Does the field hockey passing drill use the same give-and-go and spacing concepts as the game requires?
- Does the three-on-three soccer keep-away drill require the athletes to solve the same problems (e.g., passing angles and directions) as in the game?
- Does the blocking dummy football drill require the same strategies as used in real game blocking?

3. *Perceptual Elements.* Does the practice activity require athletes to use their *senses* to *perceive* and interpret the environment the same way the game requires? If so, what are the perceptual elements? If not, what perceptual elements are different? For example:

    - Does the soccer dribble drill require athletes to look up and scan the field like they do in the game?
    - Does the coach-pitch batting practice (behind L screen) require the same visual search and pitch detection as it would against a game pitcher?
    - Does golf driving-range practice on an artificial surface provide the same "feel" (proprioceptive feedback) as hitting a golf ball in the fairway on a real course?

4. *Speed-Accuracy Elements.* Does the practice activity require highly similar or identical requirements of balancing speed, accuracy, and timing as would be required of the game? If so, what are the elements? If not, what elements are different? For example:

    - Does the softball target-throw drill require the athlete to balance both speed and accuracy as it would in the real game?
    - Does the part practice drill of approach-only (run but not jump) require the same trade-off of speed and accuracy as required in competition long jump?
    - Does the lacrosse goalie-movement drill require the same level of coincident timing (body-ball timing) as would be needed in the real game?

5. *Mental Elements.* Does the practice activity require the same psychological, mental, and emotional skills needed for success in the competition? If so, what are the elements? If not, what elements are different? For example:

    - Does the different-distance golf putt drill require the same level of concentration needed for putting in an actual golf match?

- Does the four-on-four modified football scrimmage require the linebackers to shift their focus of attention as would be required in the game?
- Does the shoot-20-free-throws drill at the end of practice simulate the anxiety and attention control needed when shooting free throws in a game?

SPECIFICITY-BASED TASK ANALYSIS (SIMILARITY)

Using the five elements of similarity above, we provide a *specificity-based task analysis* for coaches to assess how "game-like" their practice activities are, or how far away or close a practice activity might be to the elements of competition. Table 5.1 shows three sample practice activities—each practice activity is analyzed on the five elements of similarity. The higher the score, the more similar the practice activity is to the game. Elements with low scores indicate little specificity of the drill to the game. The total score reflects the overall "positive transfer potential" of the practice activity. The idea is to use the analysis to help coaches assess and modify specific elements of their practice

Table 5.1. Specificity-based task analysis. Analyze and rate the sample practice activities on the five elements of similarity. The target task is the game or competition.

Rate the Degree of Similarity of Practice Activity to Game Requirements (circle or write a number from 0 to 5):						
0 = No similarity to 5 = Identical						
Practice Activity (Examples)	Movement Elements	Strategic & Conceptual Elements	Perceptual Elements	Speed-Accuracy Elements	Mental Elements	Total Score
Full-Court Figure-8 Passing Drill (Pass and Go Behind)	0 1 2 3 4 5	0 1 2 3 4 5	0 1 2 3 4 5	0 1 2 3 4 5	0 1 2 3 4 5	/25
Pitching Machine Batting Practice	0 1 2 3 4 5	0 1 2 3 4 5	0 1 2 3 4 5	0 1 2 3 4 5	0 1 2 3 4 5	/25
3-on-3 Rapid-Score Small-Field Drill (Soccer)	0 1 2 3 4 5	0 1 2 3 4 5	0 1 2 3 4 5	0 1 2 3 4 5	0 1 2 3 4 5	/25

activities to make them more game-like and increase their transfer potential. Coaches, try your assessment first, before looking at our answers!

Our Ratings and Interpretations

Below are our ratings and interpretations of the practice activity samples. Your ratings may be different (and correct) depending on your interpretation of the activity and justification(s) of similarity. We discuss later how low-rated drills may be modified for increased positive transfer.

Full-court figure-8 passing drill. For the popular figure-8 passing drill in basketball, where players advance down the court by passing and going behind the player they pass to, there is little similarity to the fast break or to advancing the ball quickly down court in the game. Our ratings for each element are provided below:

Movement	Strategic & Conceptual	Perceptual	Speed-Accuracy	Mental	Total
3	1	2	4	3	*13 (out of 25)*

The strategic and conceptual element provides the most dissimilarity (score of 1). The concept of running behind the player you passed to is opposite of the typical game strategy of passing and filling open spaces or lanes as you advance down court. As well, there are few decisions to be made (e.g., pass/no pass) in the drill compared to the game. The closest element of similarity might be in speed-accuracy requirements (score of 4) that somewhat match those in the game. The drill requires a balance of speed, accuracy, and timing while moving, similar to the game. Movement and mental elements are analyzed for moderate similarity (each with a score of 3). For example, there are similar passing techniques as used in the game, but little similarity in fast-break dribbling techniques. Perceptual elements are mostly dissimilar (score of 2). Despite similarities in visual tracking of the ball, there is little in common with the visual field of the real environment, which has defenders, opponents, and the ball moving in different directions at different speeds.

Pitching machine batting practice (baseball/softball). This practice activity has a lower-than-expected similarity score as it is relatively nonspecific to game conditions. Our ratings for each element are provided below:

Movement	Strategic & Conceptual	Perceptual	Speed-Accuracy	Mental	Total
4	2	3	4	2	15 (out of 25)

The strategic and conceptual elements were rated low (score of 2) due to the complex decision-making, attention, and problem-solving required in the game compared to hitting off a predictable machine. For example, pitches in the game are of different types and speeds, requiring more decision-making and attention to elements such as pitch counts and game situations. As well, the longer, more complex between-pitch intervals in the game introduce different types of problem-solving and attention demands. The mental elements were also rated low on similarity (score of 2), primarily due to the dissimilarities in the management of anxiety, concentration, and attention. Game hitting requires the control of significantly higher levels of anxiety, arousal, and concentration. The perceptual elements received a moderate rating (score of 3). Though similar in visual tracking, there is a different visual search related to detecting pitch-release cues (out of a moving hand vs. from a stationary machine). Coaches are likely to use pitching machine practice to get more repetitions of the swing. As expected, both the speed-accuracy (e.g., trade-off and timing) and movement elements (e.g., swing techniques) are rated high in similarity (scores of 4). We didn't rate them a score of 5 because of the research showing that skilled hitters calibrate the timing or initiation of their movements and swing with the visual detection of the pitch release.[2] And this calibration is different when hitting off a pitching machine. We might have been generous rating them a 4!

The three-on-three rapid-score soccer drill is rated highest in overall similarity with the most potential, of our three examples, for game transfer. Our ratings for each element are provided below:

Movement	Strategic & Conceptual	Perceptual	Speed-Accuracy	Mental	Total
4	3	3	3	4	17 (out of 25)

The practice activity has the most similarity in the movement skills (score of 4) of dribbling, passing, ball control, and shooting. The drill required the players to execute the same movements and techniques as they would in a game, though the smaller field changes their techniques of ball control and speed of passing. As well, there is high similarity in the mental elements (score of 4), as the drill creates similar game-like conditions of pressure and anxiety that need to be managed. The drill simulates some game strategy and concepts (score of 3) such as spacing and moving, but the limitation of three players and the rapid-score rule facilitate different decision-making than a game requires. As well, there is moderate similarity in the perceptual elements (score of 3). The different goal locations, fewer players, and the high speed of the drill change the visual scanning of the players compared to the game. Too, speed and accuracy elements were rated moderate (score of 3), as the drill requires ball control at consistently high speeds, while game-like ball control requires a blend of different speeds and more control of both speed and accuracy.

Implementing the Task Analysis

We offer a few important points about using the task analysis. First, *know the purpose* of the practice activity and how it aligns with one or more of your practice goals. Often, a practice activity is *not* designed to be game-like, for clear and obvious reasons. In many cases, a practice activity may be done to achieve the goals of learning (PTL) or maintenance (PTM) rather than for transfer (PTT). In this case, we encourage coaches to design the activities with the level of challenge that promotes learning and/or maintenance (see chapter 4). However, when athletes are ready, we encourage coaches to strategically add elements of specificity that can facilitate transfer goals.

Second, coaches can use the specificity-based task analysis to *modify the constraints* of the drill to achieve higher similarity. How can you change the drill to be more game-like? Start with the elements that received low similarity ratings. For example, in the three-on-three rapid-score small-field soccer drill above, the coach might rearrange the goals so that directional advancement of the ball for scoring mimics that of the game (higher perceptual elements rating). For the pitching machine practice, the hitting coach might create pressure scenarios during machine batting practice that better simulate game-like anxiety, or they might mimic between-pitch times and distractions that simulate concentration and attentional control (higher mental elements rating). Coaches might frequently and unpredictably change machine pitch speeds, types, or locations that more resemble game-like decision-making (higher strategic and conceptual elements rating). We note that few practice activities will yield a perfect total score (25). Outside of a full simulation, the goal is to modify practice so that it gets closer in specificity (and transfers) to the target task.

Third, coaches might apply the specificity-based task analysis using a *different target task* (not the game). The coach might seek increased similarity between the practice drill to a more advanced drill or activity (target task). In this way, players are progressively moving closer to game-like conditions. For example, in the low-rated figure-8 passing basketball drill, the target task might be a modified fast-break game which maintains spacing and requires players to score a basket. The coach uses the task analysis to increase similarity of the drill to the modified fast-break game (a higher strategic and conceptual rating). Alternatively, the coach might decide to eliminate the figure-8 drill from practice altogether because of its negative transfer, or its lack of transfer to the game or to the next practice activity. If not eliminated, perhaps it could be more useful as a *fun* warm-up or cool-down activity.

To summarize, the specificity-based task analysis can be useful to coaches for two primary reasons. First, it can help coaches clarify the purpose of practice activities, to align with one or more practice goals more clearly (practice to learn, maintain, or transfer). Second, the task analysis can help coaches evaluate and modify practice activities to better align with the purpose of practice: Will it transfer?

PRINCIPLES-BASED TASK ANALYSIS (GENERAL)

Recall in our science chapter (2) the concept of *far transfer* and the science supporting *principles-based transfer*. These are situations where the practice activity is very different than the target task, but still may yield positive transfer of learning. In these cases, the practice activity is relatively dissimilar to, and distant (far) from the target task. Conditions of far transfer rely on principles-based transfer, or the development of more general underlying processes important to performance in the game or competition. These might include processes such as visual search, pattern recognition, postural control, anticipation, or interpreting kinesthetic feedback. Often, these learned principles involve the *inter-task* transfer between different skills. For example, a player's experience recognizing offensive patterns in soccer (transfer task) may transfer positively to basketball game play (target task).

There is value in seeking positive transfer from practice conditions that are less specific and distant to the competition. There are two reasons for this. First, remember that being an *athlete-centered* coach encourages and facilitates the well-rounded development of athletes (see chapter 3). This sometimes means breaking training up with fun and enjoyable activities outside the "grind" of purposeful practice. For example, the popular basketball shooting elimination game of "knock out" has little transfer value to competition, but it can be an entertaining warm-up or cool-down activity done for fun or social reasons. Second, the athlete-centered coach values the role of *diversification* in more than one sport rather than specializing in one sport year-round. There is support for the concept of "donor" sports. These are other sports or skills that hold transfer value to achievement in a "primary" sport or skill.[3] Researchers have noted, for example, a "talent transfer" between the donor sport of gymnastics and the primary sport of diving. This makes sense when you consider the similarities in a variety of movement elements (e.g., body control, tight mid-air rotations) and mental elements (e.g., focused concentration). There is also evidence supporting the fact that individuals with extensive participation in a variety of nonspecific sporting activities develop transferable donor skills in perceptual and strategic/conceptual elements such as proprioceptive acuity (i.e., kinesthetic awareness) and a "game sense" (i.e., court vision).[4]

Since far transfer has been shown to have significant value in the long-term development of athletes, it's useful for coaches to conduct a *principles-based task analysis* for far transfer. This analysis assesses the similarities of different donor activities to a target activity or sport. The analysis should help identify the value of different practice activities based on their similar elements and their potential for transfer. For example, a coach may use a nonspecific and fun tag game for a warm-up activity because it facilitates a similar type of down-court visual scanning as the game requires (perceptual element). The goal is to determine a clear purpose or intent for using donor activities to facilitate transfer.

Two different principles-based task analyses are provided in table 5.2. For the first analysis, the target activity/sport is soccer. One donor activity is

Table 5.2. Principles-based task analysis (general). Ratings are provided for two donor activities on the five elements of similarity. For the first two donor activities, the target activity is soccer, and ratings were provided by the authors. For the second two donor activities, the target activity is softball, and coaches are encouraged to provide their own ratings.

Rate the Degree of Similarity of the Donor Activity to Target Activity (circle or write number from 0 to 5):						
0 = No similarity to 5 = Identical						
Target Sport or Activity: Soccer						
Donor Activity (Examples)	Movement Elements	Strategic & Conceptual Elements	Perceptual Elements	Speed-Accuracy Elements	Mental Elements	Total
Parkour (participation outside of practice)	0 1 2 3 4 5 4	0 1 2 3 4 5 1	0 1 2 3 4 5 4	0 1 2 3 4 5 1	0 1 2 3 4 5 2	/25 12
Capture the Flag Game (warm-up activity)	0 1 2 3 4 5 3	0 1 2 3 4 5 4	0 1 2 3 4 5 3	0 1 2 3 4 5 1	0 1 2 3 4 5 3	/25 14
Target Sport or Activity: Softball						
Donor Activity (Examples)	Movement Elements	Strategic & Conceptual Elements	Perceptual Elements	Speed-Accuracy Elements	Mental Elements	Total
Tennis (participation outside of practice in off-season)	0 1 2 3 4 5	0 1 2 3 4 5	0 1 2 3 4 5	0 1 2 3 4 5	0 1 2 3 4 5	/25
Kickball Games (preseason activity during practice)	0 1 2 3 4 5	0 1 2 3 4 5	0 1 2 3 4 5	0 1 2 3 4 5	0 1 2 3 4 5	/25

outside of practice time (parkour) and the other is a warm-up activity within a practice session (capture the flag). Again, each practice activity is analyzed on the five elements of similarity. Remember, the higher the score, the more similar the practice activity is to the target skill or sport, and elements with low scores indicate little similarity. We use the same rating scale (0–5), though we recognize there will be less overall similarity (and lower scores) in these activities, so our ratings of similarity are more liberal. The total score reflects the overall "positive transfer potential" of the donor activity. The idea is for coaches to identify the general principles from different activities that are more like their target task. Coaches can then manipulate or design donor activities that have more potential for positive transfer. For this analysis, we provide our rating first, followed by our interpretation of the ratings.

Interpretation of Ratings (First Analysis)

Parkour. Using the above task analysis, the soccer coach may like the far-transfer value of players participating in a different sport or activity outside of practice, such as Parkour challenge courses. These are challenge courses (at gyms, parks, and other facilities) where participants "attempt to get from point A to point B in the most fluid way possible, without assisting equipment and in the fastest and most efficient way possible. . . . It involves seeing one's environment in a new way, envisioning the potential for navigating by movement around, across, through, and over its features."[5] Movements include a variety of fundamental movement techniques like jumps, somersaults, rolling, climbing, vaulting, running and stopping, and moving over and around a variety of obstacles and challenges. Ratings were highest in the movement and perceptual elements (scores of 4). Similarities to the target sport of soccer include elements such as sidestep maneuvers, accelerations, quick stops (movement elements), and quick visual scanning of the environment, judging distances and time to contact with objects, and space/gap detection (perceptual elements). There is little similarity (transfer potential) in the other elements of the donor activity (scores of 1 or 2).

Capture the Flag. As well, soccer coaches may recognize the value of participating in different activities within the same practice session. For example, the classic team game of capture the flag can offer far transfer to soccer. The objective is to steal the other team's flag and take it to their own base. "Enemy players can be 'tagged' by players in their home territory and, depending on the rules, they may be out of the game, become members of the opposite team, sent back to their own territory, or frozen in place ('in jail') until freed by a member of their own team."[6] The strategic and conceptual category was rated most similar (score of 4). Similar skills to soccer play might include deception, observation, anticipation, spacing, and zone protection. Several elements were rated as moderately similar (scores of 3). Similar movement elements include speed, dodging, and acceleration, while the capture the flag elements of effective player communication and allocation of attention to help the team are similar mental elements. Finally, players with their eyes up to detect offensive and defensive positions and running lanes while listening to teammate cues are similar perceptual elements used in the game of soccer.

The second analysis in table 5.2 is for coaches to try on their own using the following scenario: Two local softball coaches reported benefits of their players participating in different activities (other than softball). One coach has her players play tennis matches in the off-season. The other coach has her players play kickball games during practice sessions in the preseason. Using the principles-based task analysis, rate the activities to determine the transfer value of the two donor activities to the target sport of softball. Which elements are more likely to transfer positively to the target activity of softball? Why?

ENVIRONMENT-BASED TASK ANALYSIS

A key element of the ecological dynamics theory (transfer theory 4 in chapter 2) is the similarity of the perception-action coupling. Is the practice environment similar enough to the game so that game-like movement solutions emerge in practice? Any practice that separates or de-couples the athlete's game-like *perception* of the *environment* from the athlete's *movement solution* will not be specific enough to optimize transfer. The guiding principle for specificity from this perspective is that what learners are seeing, hearing, and feeling in the practice environment should mimic the game environment.[7] This perspective argues that specificity comes down to one essential element: the highly specific relationship between the information in the environment and the athletes' movement. This relationship should be practiced; this is what transfers. The emphasis shifts from practicing the *action* (movement) to practicing the *interaction* between the environment and the movement.[8]

From this perspective, coaches should survey practice environments to ensure that the information available to athletes in the practice environment is the same as that available in the competition. As a result of this match, the movement solutions athletes develop in practice will be the ones used in competition; more positive transfer will occur. For example, a player who practices shooting with moving defenders (environment) will generate movement solutions that are very similar to the ones needed in competition (similar environment). Since the player is practicing game-like movement solutions, positive transfer is more likely.

The perception-action coupling concept challenges some of the more traditional coaching methods. One recommendation is to avoid practice drills or activities that employ overly artificial practice environments. For example, dribbling around cones in soccer or basketball provides "fake" information that is not available in the game. Ball handling is driven by information from the environment. In a game, you use information from the defender's postures and movements relative to other things around you (e.g., boundaries) to guide your action (e.g., what, how, and when to dribble or pick up). A cone is an abstract environmental cue that is irrelevant; no decision-making or problem-solving is required of the athlete. When coaches are frustrated that their basketball players don't look up to scan the court while dribbling in a game, recall their practice drills where they dribbled around cones. And then recall who placed those cones on the ground in the first place! Athletes need real-life environmental cues in practice if they are going to develop skills for transfer to the game.

A second recommendation is to avoid oversimplifying the practice environment. While simplifying skill practice can be effective for learning, care should be taken not to take it too far out of its environmental context. Doing so runs the risk of de-coupling the game-like perception action. As an example of this, one research study found that the dry-land practice of divers jumping into a foam pit produced differences in step length, board depression, and jump height of divers when compared to practice in the real aquatic setting.[9] Since the movement elements of the approach and takeoff (force) were different, transfer from the dry-land environment to the aquatic training environment was limited. The rationale for dry-land training is to provide repetitions that isolate and focus on key parts of the skill. However, the environmental change in dry-land practice compelled athletes to use movement patterns that were less functional and different than those used in competition. While practice in simplified or alternative environments can be useful, we encourage coaches to use it sparingly, as such conditions may not simulate the perception-action coupling of the competition.

Representative Learning Design (RLD)
The idea is to create or modify practice drills and activities that are more "representative" of the game environment. While it may sound like a simple concept, it can be difficult to implement. Like the task analyses in the first

part of our chapter, we recommend starting by assessing the task representativeness of practice activities. The representative learning design (RLD) framework assesses the degree to which practice tasks simulate key aspects of specific performance environments (i.e., competition). Recently, researchers developed and validated a practical tool that tennis coaches can use to assess the representativeness of their tennis practice drills. The tool is proposed for use in assessing and enhancing practice design in tennis to increase the coupling between information in the environment and movement, and to maximize the potential for transfer to competition. We encourage interested coaches to access the actual validated instrument in the research study.[10] For our coaches, we provide a modified version of the assessment tool in table 5.3 and apply the analysis to a popular basketball shooting drill (spot shots). Ten elements of the practice task are rated on a representative scale of 1 (not at all) to 5 (certainly). The total representativeness score reflects the level of similarity in the information available to the athlete between the practice task and the game. We provide our analysis in table 5.3 and an interpretation of our ratings below. See if you agree!

Interpretation of Ratings

The practice activity is not very representative of the competitive environment (score of 16 out of 40). Shooting in this practice drill is often de-coupled from the information available during the game. For example, in the game environment, players must detect locations of other players and teammates in the game so they can move to different areas to receive passes and take shots. Passes come from all angles in the game based on movements of the environment. The game also requires players to explore the environment so they can shoot from different locations randomly (e.g., a shot from baseline, next shot from the wing) and vary their movements before taking shots (e.g., off a screen, from baseline, or a rotation). As well, they are required to use changing environmental information to execute shot variations in the game (e.g., quicker release, higher jump). There is little exploration of game-like movement solutions and actions in this practice drill.

Basketball coaches could use this assessment to modify the drill and enhance the transfer potential of it. They could manipulate the environment in one or more of the 10 representative elements. Coaches, pause for a moment

Table 5.3. Environment-based task analysis. Using the representative learning design (RLD) approach, the basketball drill (30-second spot shot) is rated on how much the 10 elements of the practice task/environment are representative of the competition.

Practice Activity: 30-Second Spot Shot Drill (Basketball)	
Players work in partners. One player shoots (makes) as many shots as possible in 30 seconds from a designated spot (e.g., the wing) on the court. Partner rebounds and passes the ball back to the shooter as quickly as possible. Players rotate and repeat from five different spots on the court. Continue until both players have taken shots at the five different spots on the court.	
Rate each item 1–5 on the following representativeness scale:	
1　　　　　　　　*2*　　　　　　　*3*　　　　　　　*4*　　　　　　　*5* *Not at All*　　　　　　　　　　*Could Be Better*　　　　　　　　　　*Certainly*	
Representativeness *Does the Practice Task and the Environment:*	*Rating*
1. Possess a goal similar to the type of goal required in competition?	2
2. Use constraints (e.g., rules, boundaries, equipment, instructions, restrictions) that encourage the transfer of movements or skills to the competition?	1
3. Encourage variation *between* shots similar to what is expected during competition?	1
4. Encourage variation *within* the same shots similar to what is expected during competition?	1
5. Pass or feed the ball to the player in a manner similar to what is expected in competition?	2
6. Require the player to execute the skill and move (before and after execution) in a manner similar to what is required during competition?	1
7. Encourage players to use their vision and scan of environment similar to what is required during competition?	2
8. Encourage decision-making similar to what is expected during competition?	2
9. Elicit emotions similar to those (e.g., intensity, stress, focus) experienced during competition?	2
10. Encourage players to use psychological skills (e.g., attention, concentration, memory) similar to those used during the competition?	2
Total Representativeness Score	**16/40**

here: *How could you modify this drill to increase transfer?* Here are three possible modifications (with the representative element number):

1. The coach might require players to take one shot at a time from a spot, rotating shots from the five different spots so the between-shot element is more similar (3).
2. The coach might add in other moving players (offensive or defensive) in the drill so that shooters must visually search and scan the court in ways similar to the game (7).
3. The coach may plan more than one ball-feed location, so the shooter must move differently to receive the pass, as the game requires (6).

We encourage coaches to analyze the transfer potential of practice activities based on the principles of specificity and representativeness. Coaches can use the task analyses to modify existing practice activities or design new ones in ways that increase game-like practice conditions. We caution coaches that building into practice the realism of game environments often increases difficulty and challenge to the athlete. Adding too much difficulty to practice can negatively impact learning, so the coach is encouraged to manage the "optimal" amount (see chapter 4). Practice should become progressively and increasingly specific and representative of the competitive environment.

TRANSFER THIS
Recall Shane, the volunteer basketball coach at the beginning of the chapter. If he were to apply the specificity-based or environment-based task analysis to his figure-8 drill, he would have identified several elements that were not like an actual basketball game. We rated his drill earlier in this chapter, and it scored a 13 (out of 25). Specifically, the strategies and concepts of the drill (e.g., filling lanes, going behind teammates) are very dissimilar and likely yield negative transfer (recall chapter 2, science). As such, the transfer value of the drill is low, perhaps explaining the parent comment, "Now if they would only just do that in the game!" Instead, it seems the drill should inspire parents to say, "We never want to do that in a game!" We would advise Shane to modify his drill to include more game-like elements, using the task analysis, or he might make the drill a fun 5-minute warm-up activity (vs. 15 minutes). If he modifies elements of the drill to make it more game-like, players may struggle

more in the drill during practice, but we encourage Shane to revisit the purpose of practice (see chapter 1) and the notion of the performance-learning trade-off. Finally, rather than accepting traditional, familiar, or popular drills, we encourage Shane to select and evaluate drills with the mind-set of "Will it transfer?" The task analyses in this chapter helps him answer this question.

Coaches, Transfer This
1. When selecting, designing, or modifying practice activities and drills, use the transfer task analyses to help answer the question: "Will it transfer?"
2. To assess the transfer value of a practice activity or drill, apply it to the five elements of similarity. The elements inform coaches of the strengths and weaknesses of a practice activity.
3. Use the elements of similarity to manipulate practice activities. Change practice constraints that increase similarity in the low-rated elements or target specific elements to align with practice objectives (e.g., increase anxiety control).
4. Consider the transfer value of nonspecific "donor" activities. Apply the task analysis to increase the transfer value of warm-up activities, fun games, or different sports/activities.
5. Consider the "representativeness" of practice activities. In the practice environment, are athlete perceptions and their connected movement solutions similar to what they would experience in the competition? Assess this using representativeness tools, such as the sample in this chapter, or develop some to use in your sport.

Coach Educators and Developers, Transfer This
This is a perfect opportunity for coaches to evaluate and reflect on the transfer value of practice drills or activities.

1. Have coaches provide some of their own drills for a specificity-based task analysis (perhaps their favorite ones). Have more than one coach conduct an analysis for comparison and debate. Are the drills reaffirmed or should they be reassessed for transfer?
2. In advance, provide coaches with some well-known or popular practice drills or activities to analyze and discuss (perhaps from the Internet).

3. Ask coaches to speculate on the far transfer value of different sports or activities, then apply the principles-based task analyses to see which elements might positively transfer.
4. After specific or general task analyses are completed, see if coaches can modify/manipulate elements of the practice activity so that ratings would be higher.
5. Using the practice representativeness assessment sample provided, explore how coaches might adapt and apply it to measure the representativeness of their own practice activities. See if they can design a similar assessment for a drill in their sport. Perhaps access the validated RPAT tool (see note 13) and have coaches discuss and adapt it (like we did).

6

Skill Instruction That Transfers

Coach Beeston gave a short "roll-out speech" (instructions) before starting practice. Below is an excerpt of his speech:

> The main thing from tonight's session . . . it's going to require intensity from both a physical and mental standpoint. I'm going to be asking you questions throughout—just to check for understanding. Don't shout out the answer. That's a big important thing because I want you to think about the answers you are giving. If you know the answer and I go like that [raises hand], raise your hand. If you don't know the answer, that's OK. We'll work through it, we'll problem-solve together. Sometimes I might call on you even if your hand isn't raised, OK, because the game requires you to be switched on at all times, so I am going to be calling on guys at times to make sure the focus is still there, alright, so we're locked in from the first minute to the last minute.[1]

The focus of this chapter is to explore elements of instruction that can help narrow the gap between what is taught and what is learned (and transferred). Recall the John Wooden quote from earlier, "You haven't taught until they have learned." We begin this chapter by suggesting what the goal of instruction should be: *Create the independent, adaptable, and problem-solving athlete.* We want athletes to perform their practiced skills in the competition *independently*, without having to rely on outside instruction. And we want our athletes to think and *solve problems* on the fly, *adapting* movements and decision-making to the ever-changing demands of the performance environment.

There is some irony in the notion that achieving the goal of instruction (above) may depend on the coach providing less (vs. more) instruction and using more *indirect* (vs. direct) methods. Recall from chapter 3 (foundations) that the cooperative style of coaching shifts the traditional coach-centered and coach-led view of practice to the more contemporary athlete-centered view. This is where the coach, instead of providing high amounts of explicit and direct instruction to athletes, uses a variety of indirect methods that increase athlete decision-making and problem-solving during practice, reducing the amount of direct instruction. As discussed in chapter 1, a traditional view of coaching is that the coach holds the knowledge, information, and template needed for players to learn and improve their skill(s), and that players absorb coaches' knowledge and depend on their instructions to learn skills—they need more instruction to maximize learning. In short, *more* coach-led instruction is better. Because tradition is so strong, it's easy for coaches to fall into the trap of over-coaching or providing too much of a good thing (instructions).

The perils of over-coaching were addressed early in the wildly popular 1974 book by Tim Gallwey, *The Inner Game of Tennis*.[2] He questioned the role of too much instruction: "Verbal instruction [actually] decreased the probability of the desired correction occurring. . . . Images are better than words, showing is better than telling, and too much instruction is worse than none."

While higher amounts of direct instruction hold value in certain situations, such as teaching high-risk skills (football tackling, gymnastics, archery), a growing body of evidence supports that athletes often learn better when they receive less instruction using more indirect and athlete-centered methods.[3] Good instruction also recognizes that young athletes are limited in attending to, storing, and retrieving information (i.e., attention and memory). We discuss four areas of instruction that can help coaches "do more with less" and create the independent, adaptable, and problem-solving athlete.

INSTRUCT BY MANAGING ATHLETE ATTENTION

Attention is an essential aspect of receiving instructions that will be learned, remembered, and transferred. It is a limited mental resource. Theories support the notion that attention is a "pool of cognitive effort" that individuals learn to allocate to meet the demands of a task.[4] Athletes must manage their attentional resource so they can (a) commit the key elements of instruction to memory, and (b) retrieve the key elements of instruction when needed in competition. It starts with capturing and focusing athlete attention.

Capture the Attention

Learning from instructions begins with the athlete "paying attention." It's easy for instruction to be half attended to by athletes; distractions and attention wandering are commonplace during instruction. Transfer of learning is enhanced if coaches can create an instructional environment that captures athletes' attention. There are two essential methods for capturing athletes' attention, described below.

Relevance of the Information

Attention and memory are enhanced when the athlete views the information as meaningful or relevant.[5] One of the more powerful ways to increase relevance and capture athlete attention is by using the individual names of athletes and *personalizing* instruction when possible, such as, "Carly, since you have longer arms, you might position yourself farther back on this defense."

Another way to increase the relevance of instruction is by making *connections* to athletes' prior knowledge and experience. Athletes get greater meaning from instructions if they relate them to a previous experience. Remember, athletes bring their past experiences with them, and connecting those experiences to current instruction makes it more relevant, captures attention, and facilitates learning: "Mike, do you remember the important hand placement from our flip-turn drill? Yes, let's apply that same placement but with a higher level of force in this drill."

Directing attention to how the current skill is different than past skills can reduce the potential for negative transfer that sometimes occurs from past experiences. Pointing out similarities and differences of both past and current skills is an attention-directing instructional strategy that has been shown to increase learning:[6] "Susan, how are your elbows for the overhead set different from the forearm pass? Right! Remember, your elbows do the opposite of what they did with the forearm pass—they flare out not in."

Another way to increase relevance is to *prompt* athletes to reflect on the importance of upcoming practice activities. We know a local soccer coach who prompts her athletes during warm-ups or practice breaks to reflect on what they want to get out of an upcoming practice drill. Something like: "When we come back from water break, be ready to tell me the keys to success in our shellbox drill, especially when we speed it up to game speed." Before instruction, players quickly share their reflections about the relevance of the next practice activity. The coach reports players seem to pay more attention to her instructions this way, and she often modifies her planned instructions and/or activity based on athlete responses.

Finally, instructions are more relevant when coaches can clearly communicate the *why* of the activity. Coaches should not assume their athletes will automatically see the relevance of their instructions. For example, the basketball player who wonders, *How is this going to help my shot?* may not see relevance until the coach points out: "This technique will help you get more good shots off by speeding up your release." We strongly encourage coaches to communicate the *why* during skill instruction as much as possible.

Quantity of the Information
Attention capacity has limits. A coach providing large amounts of information can easily overload athletes' attention capacity. The overwhelming sentiment for instruction is to keep it "short and simple." Attention demands are particularly high for individuals with a lower working memory capacity. We can expect that beginners will have difficulty paying attention to more than one or two items at a time. The common view of "paralysis by analysis" is when coaches overload athletes with too much information. As a result, the athlete will focus attention on too many things or on the wrong things. They are less likely to retain and transfer the instructions. Verbal instructions should present the minimum amount of information necessary to communicate what an athlete needs to do. In general, "less is better" with respect to verbal instructions.[7]

Coaches should seek to instruct in ways that leave space in an athlete's attention capacity. This can be accomplished several ways, including:

1. Providing verbal instructions on part(s) of a complex skill rather than the whole skill
2. Frequently interspersing short (e.g., 10–15 seconds) verbal instructions with physical practice

3. Rather than new drills, use drills or activities that are similar and familiar to athletes, ones that can be extended with short bouts of instruction (see "Design 'Platform' Activities" in chapter 4.
4. Use familiar concepts and language that connect information and simplify instruction (see "A Common Language" in chapter 3).
5. Use visual demonstrations (discussed later) to limit or complement short verbal instructions, especially when the skill is new, complex, or difficult.
6. Avoid giving instruction while athletes are engaged in game play. It typically exceeds athletes' attentional capacity, and the allocation of attention to instruction usually sacrifices athletes' attention to the game. Instead, pull athletes aside or instruct during breaks in play, when there are fewer competing distractions.

Focus the Attention

After capturing athletes' attention, instructions should focus on the most important skill elements. We highlight two important areas of focusing athletes' attention.

Practice Shifting Attention

Athletes can manage limited attention by effectively shifting their attention within the changing performance situations. A popular conception of attention shifting is that during performance, athletes' attention is allocated along a continuum of two main dimensions[8]:

1. *Internal* (attending to own thoughts and feelings) to *external* (attending to outside or environmental cues
2. *Narrow* (attending to very few things) to *broad* (attending to many things)

Performance is sometimes explained by how athletes shift their attention within these dimensions. For example, athletes who "see" the whole floor with good anticipation likely shifted their attention as needed to a broader and external focus, while athletes who "miss" key cues (e.g., defender's position) may not have shifted from their more internal or narrow attentional focus. As well, attention shifting is related to athlete anxiety. Optimal anxiety levels facilitate effective attention shifting, while anxiety levels too high or too low can impair shifting. For example, a nervous lacrosse player fails to see an open teammate in front of the goal in the game (the one she sees all the time in practice). Under pressure, focus of attention may have shifted from broad to narrow (she focused only on the defender) or from external to internal (she focused on her tension and nervousness).

When possible, instructions should encourage athletes to effectively *control* or *shift* their attention. Athletes who practice controlling their attention can better manage both attention and anxiety in game conditions. Instructions should direct athlete attention to game-relevant cues and the correct feelings associated with them.[9] As well, they should encourage athletes to shift and control their attention for different situations:

"Cam, between batters, where is your focus?" (game situation, what to do if ball hit to me)

"What are/should you be feeling?" (alert, poised)

"OK, Cam, when you get ready to deliver the pitch, where is your focus?" (catcher's mitt)

"What and how should you be feeling at this point?" (confident, relaxed)

Direct Attention to the External
A second area of attention-focusing instruction further distinguishes between internal and external attention. When teaching a skill, should a coach focus athletes' attention on (a) their own body or limb movements (*internal focus*), or (b) away from the skill, on the movement outcome or an environmental element (*external focus*)? Below are examples contrasting the two attention-focus types. Notice the difference may seem subtle, but clearly athletes' attention can be differentially focused on internal versus external elements.

Skill: *Volleyball serve*

- Internal focus: Just before ball contact, shift your weight from the back to the front leg.
- External focus: Just before ball contact, shift your weight toward the target.

Skill: *Front crawl stroke*

- Internal focus: Pull your hand back.
- External focus: Pull the water back.

Skill: *Sprint start (race)*

- Internal focus: Fully extend your leg as you leave the blocks.
- External focus: Push hard against the block behind you.

Research indicates a clear difference in learning and performance in athletes using an internal vs. external focus.[10] An internal focus is preferred and more prevalent in coaches' instructions. Some studies show over 90 percent of coach instructions are related to an internal focus (e.g., body movements). But which focus is best for learning? Despite the strong tendency to direct athlete attentional focus internally, a very large body of research has found that instructions promoting an *external focus* generate better practice performance and also better learning (transfer and retention tests). The learning benefit of external-focused instruction is robust and consistent. The superiority of an external focus has been found in a variety of motor skills such as swinging a golf club, shooting a basketball, serving a volleyball, passing in soccer, throwing a dart, striking a tennis ball, balancing on a platform, and jumping.[11] It appears the common practice of instructing athletes to focus their conscious attention on their own body movements should be replaced by more instructions that induce an external focus, whereby the learners' attention is directed to the *effects* or *outcomes* of their movements.

Perhaps most relevant to transfer of learning is *why* the external focus effect is so strong. One perspective is that when learners adopt an internal focus—focusing on the arm movement in a volleyball serve, for example—they are *constraining* the motor system by consciously attempting to control the action.[12] This disrupts the natural flow and coordination of the movement. In contrast, attending to the desired path of the ball (external focus) promotes the use of more automatic, nonconscious processes while solving the movement problem. Ecological dynamics and perception-action coupling (transfer theory 4) suggest that a nonconscious perception of the important environmental information (external focus) is essential. While an internal focus may oppress and constrain joint motion, an external focus frees up the movement pathways in ways that allow the body to adapt to the changing environmental demands. Consider this analogy:

> An internal focus is like riding a one-speed beach cruiser bicycle on a mountain bike trail. It is constrained to act one way regardless of trail changes. The external focus is like riding a dual-suspension multi-speed mountain bike that is free to quickly adapt to changes in the trail. Which bike would you rather have on the mountain bike trail?[13]

Athletes who adopt an external focus are also more resilient to the stress, anxiety, and pressure of the competitive environment.[14] Most coaches have had athletes who "choked" under pressure, or at least experienced performance losses in times of stress or pressure. Consider an example of stress-induced thoughts going through the athlete's mind: *OK, I gotta make this shot for my team; if I miss we may lose. Remember, keep my elbow in, bend my knees, don't leave it short.*

Stress conditions trigger internal thoughts, and athletes tend to shift their attention to an internal monitoring of their movements. A shift to internal control can "de-automatize" automatic movements and can be detrimental to performance. An external focus can keep attention away from internal thoughts and maintain the automaticity of movements.[15] Athletes who have practiced with an emphasis on internal thoughts (e.g., *elbow in*) will more readily shift to an internal focus in times of stress; that's how they practiced. In contrast, athletes who have learned and practiced skills by shifting to an external focus are more likely to maintain the benefits (automatic, nonconscious processes) of an external focus during competition.

Let's finish with a couple of caveats for the external focus recommendation. First, the focus of attention should be directed to what athletes *want* to occur, not on what they *don't want* to happen. This ironic effect is the research-supported tendency of learners to perform actions they are intentionally trying to avoid.[16] For example, the soccer instruction, "Shoot into the open space," yields better performance compared to the instruction of, "Don't shoot within reach of the keeper." The notion is that "evading the keeper" instructions generate a subtle bias *toward* what you are trying to avoid (directing vision toward the keeper) and *away* from the most important information you should use (looking toward the open space).

Second, there remains instructional value in internally focused attention. There is evidence that beginners just starting to learn skills might benefit from an internal focus of attention to important technique elements, since their efforts are more consciously controlled in the early stages of practice. As well, there is evidence suggesting that when learning skills more "kinesthetic" (body awareness) in nature (e.g., gymnastics skills), athletes benefit from using instruction using an internal focus.[17]

We point to the distinction between instruction and cueing made by Nick Winkelman in his book, *The Language of Coaching*. If coaches need to direct athletes' attention to internal skill elements (e.g., "Feel your back arch"), they should do it during preliminary explanations and instructions. But when athletes get ready to perform a repetition, they should use an externally focused cue. For example, the basketball coach might discuss the importance of hand and elbow position in a ball-handling drill, but when the drill starts, the dribbler's attention is directed to one external cue, such as "Drive the ball through the floor." Put another way, internal language is good for *describing* the *what* of the movement, and external language is good for *coaching* the *how* of the movement.[18]

INSTRUCT WITH CUES AND ANALOGIES

Transfer of learning is enhanced with the effective use of verbal cues and analogies. The emphasis here is on the benefits of using fewer words (verbal cues) and more implicit instructions (analogies and metaphors).

Verbal Cues

A verbal cue is a word or concise phrase that focuses the learner's attention or prompts a movement (e.g., *bend knees*), movement sequence (e.g., *pull, kick, glide*), or environmental element (e.g., *see the ball*).[19] Like any coaching method, its effectiveness is not automatic, and some key factors determine verbal cues' effectiveness.

One Thought at a Time

Cues should consist of one, two, or only a few words. They should accommodate limitations in working memory and attention. While the cue itself may contain a few words, it represents the one prioritized thought that a coach believes will improve execution the most, and it's the final idea that should be put in an athlete's mind before they move. Winkelman suggests the externally focused cue should follow the "rule of one": "One rep, one cue, one focus."[20] Coaches might deliver more detailed, internally focused instruction prior to the cue, but they provide the athlete with one filtered external cue just before the repetition. For example, after instruction about the importance of leg and arm position to generate more force, the pitching coach might provide (and repeat as needed) the one external cue: "Explode toward home plate."

Focus the Content
Good cues depend on *what* they contain. Cues are better when they:

1. are *externally* focused
2. are *vivid* and excite imagery
3. accurately *represent the key skill* component(s)

Using one of Winkelman's examples, let's first take a pretest to see if we can pick out the best content for a verbal cue.

Question: A track coach instructs her athlete about the role of hip extension at takeoff and its importance for jump height. After instruction, the coach delivers the one cue, immediately before the athlete executes the jump. Which cue below is the best one for the coach to provide?

Cue A: Focus on driving through your legs.

Cue B: Focus on blasting through your hips.

Cue C: Focus on exploding toward the ceiling.

Cue D: Focus on jumping as high as you can.

Answer: Applying our three criteria, we can dismiss *Cue A* and *Cue B*, as they are internally focused since "driving legs" and "blasting hips" are actions within the body. The remaining *Cue C* and *Cue D* are somewhat equitable in accuracy; both will likely elicit full hip extension in the repetition. Our best answer is *Cue C*, as "exploding" and "toward the ceiling" are more vivid words that excite imagery about the movement. It's more attention-focusing and memory-enhancing than *Cue D* ("Jump as high as you can").

Winkelman further recommends constructing cues based on the three characteristics of *distance, direction,* and *description* (3D):

Distance: How close or how far away should the athlete externally focus, for example, on the racket or on the target?

Direction: Which way should the athlete focus, for example, toward, away, or through something?

Description: How should the movement be performed (action verb), for example, push, explode, or drive?

A good cue will include each of the 3D elements. Let's use our previous example (*Cue C* above) to show the three Ds:

"Focus on exploding toward the ceiling."

"Focus on *exploding* [description] *toward* [direction] the *ceiling* [distance]."

Let's take a second pretest on the 3D content of a verbal cue.

Question: Underline and label the words that give the direction, distance, and description in the cue example below:

"Focus on driving your shoulder through their hip pocket." (football tackle)

Answer: If you underlined *driving* (description), *through* (direction), and *pocket* (distance), then you got it right! Notice that compared to our first example, the distance became closer or more proximal to the athlete (*ceiling* vs. *pocket*). The direction of focus changed (*toward* vs. *through*). And the action verb describing the movement changed (*driving* vs. *exploding*).

With respect to the *distance* element of the cue, some interesting research suggests using it depends on factors such as athlete skill level and type of sport played (implement vs. non-implement sports). In general, more experienced athletes benefit from more distal or faraway cues (e.g., the target or finish line), while less experienced athletes benefit more from cues that are more proximal or closer to them (e.g., the racket or opponent's hip).[21] In short, the content of your instructional cues matters!

Analogies and Metaphors

Sometimes instructional cues are effectively delivered as analogies or metaphors. Analogies can effectively transfer past experiences and knowledge to help make better sense of a new situation. "Absorb the landing like mountain bike shocks" transfers a familiar image and feeling to help an athlete (with mountain bike experience) perform the current skill. Analogies are external and implicit verbal cues that are stronger in *description*. They can create familiar metaphors that are more memorable than verbal cues. Using our previous cue of "exploding toward the ceiling" the coach might instead use the analogy of "explode off the ground like a rocket at blastoff."

For analogies to be effective, they should adhere to the principles of *familiarity* and *similarity*.[22] For familiarity, the analogy or metaphor must access athletes' past experiences. The "mountain bike shocks" example above would be ineffective if athletes had never ridden a mountain bike. The "rocket at blastoff" metaphor likely generates familiar images in most athletes' minds. For *similarity*, the analogy and the movement must have something in common. In both of our examples, the metaphor aligns with the essential rules or relevant features of the desired movement. As well, the analogies are generally more effective when the coach is familiar with the concepts and they fit with the coach's personality. For example, a coach with more familiarity, passion, experience, and love of snow skiing may replace "like mountain bike shocks" with "like a mogul skier." And familiar non-sport cues can also be effective, such as, "Catch the ball like an egg you don't want to break."

In Support of Analogy/Metaphor Instructions

Research supporting analogy or metaphor instructions usually compares practice conditions that are identical, with the only difference being whether athletes receive traditional (explicit) verbal instructions or analogies or metaphors (implicit). Below are examples contrasting traditional explicit instructions with *analogy* or *metaphor* instructions.[23]

Skill: *Golf putt*

- Traditional instructions: Slow your arms on the backswing and accelerate them on the forward swing.
- Analogy/metaphor instructions (implicit): Move the clubhead like the pendulum swing-like motion of a grandfather clock.

Skill: *Darts*

- Traditional instructions (explicit): Throw by slowly extending the arm and quickly flicking the wrist.
- Analogy/metaphor instructions (implicit): Throw the dart as if you were throwing a crumpled-up piece of paper into a wastebasket located just behind the dartboard.

Research often shows that analogy or metaphor instructions can be more effective for learning movement skills when compared to traditional (explicit) instructions.[24] They can be effective learning tools for a few reasons. They help manage athlete limitations in working memory and attention capacity. Analogies can generate stronger memory of the skill element(s) and they take up less space in athletes' attention capacity (so they can attend to other important things!). A convincing line of support for analogies or metaphors is somewhat analogous (sorry) to the benefits seen with external cues: they can help athletes become more immune to performance losses when they are under pressure or stress (i.e., choking). Studies show that on transfer tests, subjects that practiced with analogy instructions outperform those that received traditional instructions. The transfer tests required subjects to perform the practiced skill(s) under "pressure" or "stress" conditions, such as performing with new distractions, being evaluated by an expert, or the risk of losing money.[25]

In summary, using verbal cues, analogies, and externally focused instruction are effective ways to deliver skill information to increase the transfer of learning. Instructing with fewer words can be challenging. Like any instructional skill, it takes some planning and practice. Planning for them and including them on practice plans increases the likelihood they will get used in practice. Conducting self-evaluations (e.g., video record yourself) of the types, amounts, and quality of verbal instructions and cues is a good place to start.

INSTRUCT WITH QUESTIONS

Coaches who are athlete centered and embrace the culture of learning and communication (chapter 3) may naturally use questioning as an instructional method. Compared to direct and explicit instruction, questioning can better engage athletes in the learning process, enhance memory, and enhance learning.[26] The goal of questioning is to create an environment where athletes show up to practice expecting to be mentally engaged; they are attentive and alert, ready to solve their own problems and make their own decisions. Questioning can help develop the type of *thinking* and problem-solving in athletes that transfers well to competition. Good questioning depends on *what* to ask (question types) and *how* to ask (questioning methods).

Question Types

Different types of questions can achieve different objectives. While there is no one *best* type of question to ask, a question should have a clear purpose. Table 6.1 provides the five different types of questions, each with a clear purpose and examples.[27]

We encourage coaches to be intentional about their types of questions. Asking more questions is a good start, but it's most effective when coaches know *why* they are asking the question (its purpose). A question with no purpose reduces its impact on learning and transfer. For example, simple, rhetorical, or yes/no questions may be better used as reminders or advice. There is little energy, thinking, and engagement involved to answer questions when the answer is obvious, such as, "Should we sprint full speed or half speed to the base?" These questions run counter to the purpose of questioning. Questioning is most effective when there is a clear purpose and when questions are asked to stimulate thinking, recall, or problem-solving.

Questioning Methods

Coaches have likely tried questioning that didn't work. Ineffective questioning can reduce practice time or interrupt the flow of practice. Good questioning takes some planning and practice on the part of the coach. Doug Lemov provides some effective methods in his book *The Coach's Guide to Teaching*. We build on some of these below.

Set the Stage

To begin, return to this chapter's opening scenario. Coach Beeston set the stage for effective questioning and player engagement at the start of the drill/practice. It can be viewed in its entirety at https://www.coachsguidetoteaching.com/. He gave an introductory set of instructions that clearly communicated

Table 6.1. Five different question types, each with a clear purpose and examples. Coaches add their own examples for number 3.

Question Type	Purpose	Examples
Knowledge Building	Encourage stronger memory by forcing retrieval of learned or practiced concepts, skills, or terms. Use easy-to-ask, frequently asked recall questions.	1. What are our two principles of setting the screen? 2. What do we call this box-out technique? 3.
Discovery	Enhance memory by getting athletes to seek general solutions to problems. Use with new concepts to encourage attention to possible solutions in the future.	1. What ways can we attack this zone? 2. What defensive positions can we use for this attack? 3.
Environment	Encourage athletes to search the environment for the most important information. Shape perception to improve anticipation, decision-making, and discovering best movement solutions.	1. Where were you looking when the ball was passed? 2. What will tell you where the dribbler is going? 3.
Check for Understanding	Determine if instruction was effective and if athletes understand. Get feedback about gaps in understanding and memory to improve instruction.	1. What did we say was the most important thing about bat position? 2. What were the two things to watch for against this zone? 3.
Decision-Making	Encourage athletes to quickly solve problems based on their perception of the environment, existing knowledge, and their own skills, strengths, and abilities. Ask more advanced and situation-specific questions that build off the other questions and are essential for transfer.	1. In this situation, what are your best pitch choices? 2. In this formation, what are our two options to defend? 3.

the type of participation and thinking he expected from his players, including the expectations for engagement and how questions will be used. This set up a safe, nonjudgmental learning environment and provided the "why" for using questions and expecting engagement. Such a method primes athletes for increased attention, thinking, and problem-solving later in practice.

Be Targeted and Specific

Coaches should avoid cursory or insincere questions that don't stimulate athlete thinking. For example, the all-too-common questions asked after giving instructions, "Everybody got it?" "Understand?" or "Make sense?" can be verbal habits that don't generate much response and do little to assess real understanding. They sometimes condition athletes to "tune out" the coach's questions. Questions should be more targeted and specific, for example: "What two things do we want to do when defending this move, Fisher?" or "Good, and what did we say to do if the dribbler gets past us, Marcus? Great, let's try it."

Build on Questions

Questions should match athletes' skill levels. A popular method is to ask a series of questions that build on one another and lead to the eventual discovery of the intended concept. As each question is answered, the coach either reinforces the response or redirects the athlete. Once the correct answer has been given, the coach asks the next question in the sequence. In the example below, the soccer player discovers solutions gradually and develops a better understanding of *why* certain techniques are better:

> "What is the goal of the defenders here?"
>
> "Yes, what are ways we can protect the ball from them?"
>
> "OK, what parts of the foot best keep the ball close?"

Use Hand Raising

Although it sounds basic, requiring an athlete to raise their hand to answer a question is essential for effective questioning. Recall from Coach Beeston's roll-out speech:

> Don't shout out the answer. . . . I want you to think about the answers you are giving. If you know the answer and I go like that [raises hand], raise your hand. If you don't know the answer, that's OK, we'll work through it, we'll problem-solve together.

A quick response called out verbally runs the risk of being a shallow answer rather than encouraging deeper problem-solving. Besides encouraging quality of thinking, the hand raise allows the coach to distribute answers more equitably across all teammates to increase engagement and athletes listening to one another. The coach can choose to ignore the hand of the athlete who always answers and ask athletes who answer less. This is one way the coach can reinforce a culture where all athletes feel valued, not just the "smart" or skilled ones. Finally, hand raising provides feedback to the coach. Only a couple hands being raised might mean a lack of understanding, or disconnected athletes. The few athletes that raise their hands understand, but what about the others? Several hands being raised likely means a high level of understanding and buy-in to the problem-solving environment.

Show Me
To harness the power of an image (next section below), we recommend coaches use a questioning technique where they physically demonstrate what was instructed. Other players can watch and learn from the line of questioning. For example:

> "What were our two most important elements of the bat position for the bunt?"
>
> "*Show me* what that looks like, Gus."
>
> "OK, Gus. Tommy, what do you think about Gus's bat position?"

Use Cold Calls
In addition to hand raising, it's also important to use *cold calls* to facilitate thinking. This is asking any player to answer at any time, not waiting on a hand to be raised. Of course, this method is best used with developmentally and age-appropriate athletes. While calling on the same few players who consistently answer questions can break the silence and move practice along, it fails to engage the other athletes and provides an incomplete check for understanding. Are all players thinking, and do they all understand the concept(s)? Recall again, from the roll-out speech:

> Sometimes I might call on you even if your hand isn't raised, OK, because the game requires you to be switched on at all times, so I am going to be calling on guys at times to make sure the focus is still there, alright, so we're locked in from the first minute to the last minute.

A related technique is to use *follow-on cold calls* to encourage athletes to listen to each other, and increase engagement and communication, for example: "I like that answer. Can you think of another technique that might work, Alayna?" And an extended method is to move cold calls to partners or small groups. Such an approach relieves the cold call pressure on an individual athlete and promotes team-wide thinking and engagement: "What's our best approach on defense here? Turn and talk to your partner and I'll be looking for some good answers in 30 seconds."

An interesting extension of questioning is when players practice a skill with the *expectation* that they will be teaching it to others. Research supports that when athletes practice a skill expecting to teach it, they learn it better.[28] This aligns with a method used by college basketball coach Greg Neeley[29]:

> When we instruct using game film, we sometimes split into groups and each group has to interpret a part of the game film and share it with the team. This allows the players to take ownership, and if they are going to teach it, they definitely have to know it.

Use Wait Times

The examples above apply the technique of *wait time*. Wait time encourages deeper thinking and problem-solving. It gives players some time to think through answers. It's important for players to understand that the first answer or idea they come up with may not always be the best. As much as logistically possible, the coach should try and wait for answers and draw out more thinking by moving to other players.

> "Greg, give me a little more on why you think that is the best technique to use."
>
> "Julius, elaborate a bit more on why Greg's technique might be the best."

Be Strategic

When possible, questioning should be in context and situation-specific. As well, questions can be used to help support coaches' objectives and goals. As an example, we provide another excerpt from college basketball coach Greg Neeley:

If we are going to trap ball screens in our next game, I'll explain to them why we are doing it. We'll practice that in preparation for the game and after practice, I'll ask a few guys questions such as: "Do you feel good about trapping ball screens against this team?" "Do you understand why we're trapping this team?" We will strategically choose which guys we ask these questions to. It may be the guys who seem to be a bit more skeptical when we break from our normal scheme, or it may be the guys who are going to be most involved in the action. Even more, it may be the guys who have the most influence in our locker room. We're trying to create ownership in the game plan instead of having a coach-dictated game plan.[30]

Coach Neeley strategically employs questioning after practice, targeted at certain players, and for specific purposes. With planning, coaches can use questioning to not only increase learning but to help achieve larger coaching objectives.

INSTRUCT WITH DEMONSTRATIONS

Demonstration is a widely used instructional method. Visual images are an important aid for working memory (encoding and retrieval), and to communicate a lot of information in a short amount of time. Several factors are important for using demonstrations to increase transfer of learning. Some recommendations are obvious and practical. For example, athletes should be positioned so they can see the key elements of the demonstration. Do group formations, viewing angles, or distractions allow athletes to see the knee angle of the model? As well, athletes' attention should be focused and directed to the purpose of the demonstration (or the key elements). Pre-cueing athletes in advance of the demonstration (not during) and focusing attention to *one or two elements* (not several) of the skill (e.g., "Watch the wrist snap at release") are sound methods for demonstrations. Since demonstrations are key for transfer of learning, more research-supported factors are provided below.

What the Athlete "Gets" from the Demonstration

Science provides two different perspectives of how athletes learn from demonstrations. These two views help us design more effective demonstrations. The *cognitive view* is that athletes remember and store images as a memory and as a reference to help with future practice. This "observational learning" requires quality demonstrations that athletes can store and retrieve in memory, and demonstrations should facilitate the cognitive processes of attention, retention, reproduction, and motivation.[31] The *direct view* is that rather than athletes "remembering" the demonstration, they visually perceive key aspects of the demonstration and can replicate them without accessing memory or conscious thought (see transfer theory 4). The perspective is that athletes can "automatically" perceive and replicate the overall coordination or movement pattern, or the relative timing and coordination of the movement pattern. This direct perception allows the athlete to replicate movement patterns without accessing their memory.[32] We use these views to employ demonstration methods that are more likely to transfer.

What and When to Demonstrate

Demonstrate the coordination initially. When athletes are learning a *new pattern of coordination* (e.g., tennis serve, the cradle of a lacrosse ball), coaches should provide *fundamentally correct* demonstrations of the skill in *real time* (not slow motion), as a *whole* (not part), and *without talking*. The *cognitive* view says athletes need to "get the idea" of a new and complex movement, with less complexity and reduced demands on memory and attention. The *direct* view says athletes need to receive this full-speed whole visual image to replicate and scale the coordination of the movement elements (without storing them in memory). When learning complex new movements, "correct" and silent demonstrations that are whole and full speed are most valuable for athletes to transfer forward.

Demonstrate the specific movement parameters later. Once athletes conceptualize the new skill and can coordinate the basic movement pattern, demonstrations need to become more targeted, specific, and "cognitive" in nature. For the tennis serve, the racket angle might be visually demonstrated, or the wrist action at contact for the lacrosse cradle. These demonstrations should be memory enhancing. For example, they need to be short and simple demonstrations, verbally directing the athletes' attention to the element they are to watch, and coaches should check for understanding by questioning what the athletes saw and retained. Coaches should avoid demonstrating speed or forcing parameters such as "moving faster" or "more forcefully." They are no more effective than using verbal instructions and can waste practice time.

Consider "discovery" before demonstrating. In contrast to starting practice with a demonstration to serve as the template, there is increasing support for the "discovery" practice of new skills prior to demonstrations.[33] For example, rather than start by demonstrating the tennis serve, athletes might be given a task (e.g., to hit the ball over the net into a target zone) or a challenge to complete (e.g., three different ways to serve the ball farther). After a period of exploration, demonstrations of the serve are then provided. The idea is not to *replace* demonstrations with discovery practice, but to let athletes try to solve the movement problem first. Learning from the demonstration becomes more relevant and athletes pay more attention to it. There is also support for discovery methods when learning complex variations of existing skills. For example, the baseball coach might have players explore different ways to touch second base and throw to first base, before providing demonstrations of turning a double play.

Demonstrate with frequency, then fade to self-control. Traditionally, instructors provide an initial demonstration, with few additional demonstrations, while athletes practice the skill(s). However, research shows increased learning by using more frequent demonstrations interspersed with physical practice. This is especially true for new skills or for less-skilled athletes, and providing frequent and *brief* demonstrations interspersed with physical practice is highly recommended. As athletes advance in skill level, demonstrations become less helpful and are needed less.[34]

Interesting research compares practice conditions where athletes are provided demonstrations by request (*self-controlled*) to traditional conditions providing demonstrations on a set schedule. The self-controlled practice conditions often show greater retention and transfer of learning despite receiving less frequent demonstrations.[35] We recommend practice settings where athletes are increasingly given the opportunity to control their own demonstration frequency (and timing) for a few reasons. First, it's a way to manage optimal challenge for individual athletes. Evidence shows that athletes generally request demonstrations that match their individual needs. Less-skilled athletes or those trying new techniques request demonstrations more frequently. Second, self-control over demonstration frequency helps shift the practice environment from coach centered to more athlete centered. Such an approach facilitates a sense of athletes' independence and ownership in skill development (see chapter 3). Third, it can be applied easily in practice. For example, some coaches provide a video station of demonstrations, allowing athletes to self-select different demonstrations "on demand." Finally, self-controlled demonstrations align with a growing body of evidence supporting self-controlled learning in a variety of practice conditions (e.g., feedback, practice schedule).[36] Rather than coaches directly controlling and prescribing all practice conditions to athletes, more transfer of learning occurs in conditions of self-control and choice.

Consider "Learning" Models

While "correct" demonstrations using a skilled model are often recommended (as we did above), there is also value in using less-skilled models to demonstrate. An interesting area of research compares the traditional, correct demonstration using an *expert* model to an alternative demonstration that uses a less-skilled or *learning* model. We distinguish between the two models below. Both involve receiving feedback from the coach during the demonstrations.

Expert Model	*Learning Model*
Skilled, demonstrates skill correctly	Less skilled, demonstrates skill with errors
Includes verbal cues of key points for success	Receives verbal instructions to fix errors
Continues performing correctly with feedback	Continues to correct errors with feedback

It's important to note that a *learning model* is *not* the same as an unskilled model. A learning model is attempting to learn a skill while receiving instructional feedback. Findings from these studies suggest that learning models can better engage athletes and improve the retention and transfer of learning.[37] They can encourage athletes to explore personal movement solutions rather than one ideal movement (recall transfer theory 4, ecological dynamics). While it may be important to see an effective (skilled) movement solution initially to get the idea of the movement, using learning models can help athletes discover their "best" movement solutions while increasing their level of cognitive effort and engagement. We summarize below the potential benefits for athletes observing *learning* models compared to *expert* models.[38]

Expert Models

Encourage imitation of a movement

Generate less self-efficacy: "Can I really replicate that movement?"

Provide less instruction—cues only

Learning Models

Encourage exploration, problem-solving, and discovery of a movement

Generate more self-efficacy and motivation: "I think I can do better than that."

Provide more instruction—cues, error detection feedback, and attempts to correct errors

Implementing Learning Models

Coaches can implement learning models in a variety of ways. Some specific strategies are highlighted below:

1. Use peers as models (teammates) instead of the coach. This can increase the belief (self-efficacy) they can execute the demonstrated skill.
2. Pair athletes to watch each other execute skills. Watch a peer learning model prior to practice. Add a third teammate to watch two peers practice a skill (small group). Watching a variety (more than one) of error correction and learning strategies can further increase learning.
3. Ask athletes to identify and correct key skill elements (provided by the coach) of a peer learning model. Provide athletes with quick checklists where one athlete looks for key aspects and provides corrective feedback to their partner.
4. Mix both expert and learning models. Alternate using models showing the correct technique with unskilled models showing a less-effective technique (with corrective feedback!). This is analogous to the coach instructing by using video replay for side-by-side comparisons (self or other) of a skilled and unskilled performance.

TRANSFER THIS

Recall the purpose of coaches' instructions: *to create the independent, adaptable, and problem-solving athlete.* It appears Coach Beeston is effectively using the method of questioning to facilitate independent thinking and problem-solving in his athletes. He sets the stage for athlete engagement and uses questioning techniques such as hand raising and wait times. Using this method, his players are more likely to remember the instruction and transfer it forward. It captures athlete attention, increases the relevance of instruction, and reduces the quantity of the information. As he teaches through questions, we encourage Coach Beeston to attend to the different question types that facilitate learning and to incorporate short verbal cues and analogies that focus athlete attention externally. He also might consider incorporating some player demonstrations, positioning players to see key elements of performance, using both expert and learning models. It seems Coach Beeston is facilitating an essential element of instruction to engage athletes in the learning process. Instead of providing high amounts of information, his instructions are more athlete centered, and his players share in the process of skill development. They are likely to remember what they practice, and his instructions are likely to transfer well!

Coaches, Transfer This
1. Instructions should help create *the independent, adaptable, and problem-solving athlete.* To facilitate, balance direct and explicit methods with methods that are indirect and implicit.
2. Manage athlete attention to instructions by increasing the relevance and reducing the amount of information. Direct athlete attention by shifting to the most relevant information and to an external focus.
3. Increase the use of verbal cues and analogies. Develop and provide rich and short verbal cues that focus athlete attention externally to key elements of performance. Create and use effective analogies or metaphors instead of lengthy explicit instructions.
4. Use high amounts of questioning to deliver instructions. Be thoughtful about the purpose of the questions (types) and the methods that stimulate thinking and problem-solving in athletes.
5. Use demonstrations strategically. Use them both before practice and after skill exploration (discovery). Intersperse frequent demonstrations in early practice, and move to self-controlled demonstrations in later practice. Use a blend of both expert and learning models and pre-cue athletes to attend to the key skill elements.

Coach Educators and Developers, Transfer This

1. Facilitate reflection and discussion about the role of instruction. Have they ever done or seen too much instruction (over-coaching)? Do they tend to provide more explicit and direct or implicit and indirect instruction? Does their instruction help develop athlete independence, problem-solving, or adaptability for competition? Can they provide examples?
2. How do coaches capture and focus athletes' attention during instruction? When they focus athlete attention, do they use more internal or external cues? Have coaches practice designing external-focused instruction.
3. Have coaches identify five verbal cues or analogies they use in practice or instruction. Evaluate them on the elements of good cues (e.g., content, 3D). If they need to be improved, how can they modify them?
4. Try instructing with questions. Have coaches identify a common drill they use. Instead of delivering their usual explicit instruction by "telling" athletes what to do, have coaches develop at least three different questions (different types) they could ask athletes before, during, or after the drill.
5. Use video-recorded segments of coaches (others or themselves) conducting a practice activity or session. Analyze and reflect on one or more instructional behaviors. Did the coach: Capture the attention of athletes? Use more internally or externally focused instruction? Provide good verbal cues? Use questioning effectively (e.g., different types and techniques)? Use demonstrations effectively? Can the coach improve their instructional methods? If so, how?

7

Repetitions That Transfer

Coach Martel gave a talk to fellow coaches at a high school softball coaches' workshop. She shared her approach to practicing the skill of bunting: "For the first two weeks of spring practice, we are in the gym. Each day, players get 25 repetitions practicing 'bad' bunts. Players have to bunt the ball foul down the two baselines, pop up the bunt, bunt it straight back to the pitcher, and bunt it right in front of the catcher (5 reps of each). We don't instruct much; we just tell them to work on controlling their bat and the ball. We find it's a lot easier to work on bunting when we move to the field later. They seem to have better bat control." Following Coach Martel's talk, a couple of coaches raised their hands to disagree with her approach. They said it made no sense to practice a skill incorrectly, and players only learn by doing things the right way.

I don't understand why I struggled in the game, I did so well in practice! This frustration is all too common. If only successful practice repetitions translated to successful game performance. Consider the basketball player who hits 18 out of 20 three-point shots in practice drills but is 1 out of 5 the next day in the game, or the golfer on the driving range who hits 8 out of 10 mid-iron shots on the flag, only to hit 3 out of 9 in the golf match. The most-offered explanation for this lack of transfer is that they didn't do enough repetitions in practice. Maybe they didn't make it "automatic" and need more practice. The second most-offered explanation is that they didn't practice their reps in game-like conditions (lack of specificity). Both explanations have merit, but both need clarification. Based on the science of transfer, we know a couple of truths:

1. Repetitions are necessary. Repetitiveness is not. The number of repetitions is important, but for transfer, the quality of them, or *how* they are done, is equally (if not more) important. As Kobe Bryant put it, "It's not about the number of hours you practice, it's about the number of hours your mind is present during practice."[1]
2. Specificity of practice repetitions is important, but the *variability* (nonspecific) of them is also important for transfer of learning.

This chapter explores the nature of practice repetitions so that coaches and athletes ultimately transfer more of their "reps" to the competition.

VARY THE PRACTICE REPETITIONS

The traditional view of practice repetitions is that they are necessary to master the ideal or "perfect" movement or technique. They help athletes develop repeatable techniques that become "automatic." Tradition holds that repeating the same, perfect form as much as possible is good, and varying from the perfect technique is bad. However, the idea of perfect practice ignores much of the research on effective practice. In short, more variability in practice repetitions is a good thing! We like the Arnold Palmer quote:

> Swing your swing. Not some idea of a swing. Not a swing you saw on TV. Not that swing you wish you had. No, swing your swing. Capable of greatness. Prized only by you. Perfect in its imperfection. Swing your swing. I know, I did.[2]

Since we rarely, if ever, execute the same movement the exact same way twice in a competition, our practice repetitions should simulate this competitive variability. Successful performance in the sport environment requires a variety of different movement solutions (not just one ideal). The intentional variation of practice repetitions is widely seen as a means of enhancing positive transfer from the practice to the competitive context. Those who study skill expertise make the case that practice should be less about *acquisition* of the skill and more about *adaptability* of the skill. Repetitions high in variability help athletes learn to adapt their skill to dynamic competitive conditions.[3]

Practicing with intentional movement variability has strong support from our theories. Recall transfer theory 2 (motor programs and schemas), that varied practice enhances the development of a stronger schema, enhancing learning of movement relationships that increases adaptability and guides future attempts. Practice should emphasize updating and strengthening schemas, specifically changing the parameters (e.g., force, distance) of a movement pattern (GMP) during repetitions. The intentional variation of movement parameters leads to higher transfer of the skill to a variety of performance conditions, and these movement *errors* (variations) are a necessary part of learning.

Transfer theory 4 (ecological dynamics) also supports movement variation rather than rote, repetitive practice. It endorses the manipulation of constraints that allow athletes to explore and discover optimal movement solutions and techniques that work best for them. Research shows that gaining skill does not result in a decrease in all movement variability, but a restructuring of "good" and "bad" variability. Though skilled performers become highly consistent in their outcome, they do so by keeping some elements of their movement inconsistent and variable. An outcome that is highly consistent (e.g., bat contacting the ball 5 times in a row) does not mean that the movements were executed identically each time. Skilled performers who achieve this consistency do so by showing high levels of movement "adaptability."[4]

Below we highlight a "typical" controlled research study comparing more *repetitive* practice (constant) to more *varied* practice[5]:

- *The Study:* Conduct 400 practice repetitions to learn to reproduce a target amount of force on a grip strength task (60% of max); subjects were divided into two practice groups.
- *Constant Practice:* Subjects performed 400 repetitions at the *target* force (60%). They received feedback of their results after each trial.
- *Varied Practice:* Subjects performed 400 repetitions at four *different* force amounts (40, 50, 70, and 90% of max force). They received feedback of their results after each trial.

- *The Results*: During practice, *constant* practice subjects outperformed *varied* practice subjects (accuracy of producing force amounts). On a retention/transfer test two days later, *varied* practice subjects outperformed the *constant* subjects on reproducing the target force (60%).

Note the fact that despite conducting no practice repetitions at the *specific* or *perfect* target force amount (60%), the *varied* group performed better on the test of the target force (60%). The test was conducted later and without receiving feedback (similar to a game). While varied group was outperformed in practice, they were able to generalize their repetitions and adapt to a new target force, and do it independently, on the test (without feedback). So, "perfect" practice did not transfer well to performance in game-like conditions; varied practice produced more transfer of learning.

Varied practice repetitions should be intentional and planned. Repetitions can be planned to be somewhere between *highly varied* to *highly constant* (or specific). Next, we provide coaches with some strategies to implement practice variability.

Strategy 1: Vary the Movement Parameters
Constant practice is the practice of the identified "best technique" of a skill. The intent of the repetitions is to produce the correct movement and reduce movement variability. *Varied practice* is the intentional variation of the parameters that make up a movement, such as speed of movement (faster vs. slower), size of movement (larger vs. smaller), force of movement (higher vs. lower), and length of movement (shorter vs. longer). Exploring these early and often in the learning process is recommended for athletes to discover movement solutions, and ones that are more adaptable to a variety of performance conditions. Below are examples of *movement parameters* intentionally varied during repetitions:

1. Use three different grip widths (safely) when practicing weightlifting, for example, dead-lifts.
2. Hit tennis backhand strokes using three different racket weights.
3. Serve volleyball using three different forces, for example, very hard, very soft, medium.

4. Strike shots on goal just below the top crossbar, just inside the side bar, and just inside the top corner of the goal.
5. Advance the hockey puck down the ice, skating three different patterns, for example, zigzag, curved, and straight.

Strategy 2: Vary the Environmental or Task Parameters
A second way to implement movement variability is through the intentional variation of the environment or the task. Recall the manipulation of task constraints from earlier (chapter 4). Think of the aspects of the environment or task that, if changed, will elicit a different movement solution from the athlete. Though the intent here is to vary aspects of the environment or task, the outcome is that athletes must apply different movement parameters to be successful. Below are examples of *environmental* or *task parameters* that can be varied during repetitions:

1. Placing a defender positioned at different locations during basketball shooting drills.
2. Using different net heights during practice of down-the-line forehands in tennis.
3. Using different surfaces during field hockey ball-control drills, for example, turf, grass, combinations.
4. Running the soccer dribble keep-away drill in different-sized or -shaped zones.
5. High jumper taking off from different spots (angle or distance) marked on the ground.

Figure 7.1 is an example of implementing *movement* and *environmental* practice variability for athletes practicing *20 repetitions of the soccer chest trap*.

Important Considerations
There are a few important points for coaches to consider when implementing variability. First, when and how often coaches should intentionally vary repetitions has been debated in the practice literature. The consensus is that practice variability is most useful when practicing newer skills or when introducing variations or advanced versions of existing skills. This aligns with

Movement Variability

| Chest trapping—stationary (20) | Chest trapping—stationary (5)
Chest trapping—jumping (5)
Chest trapping—running (5)
Chest trapping—to knees (5) |

CONSTANT PRACTICE   VARIED PRACTICE
◄──►

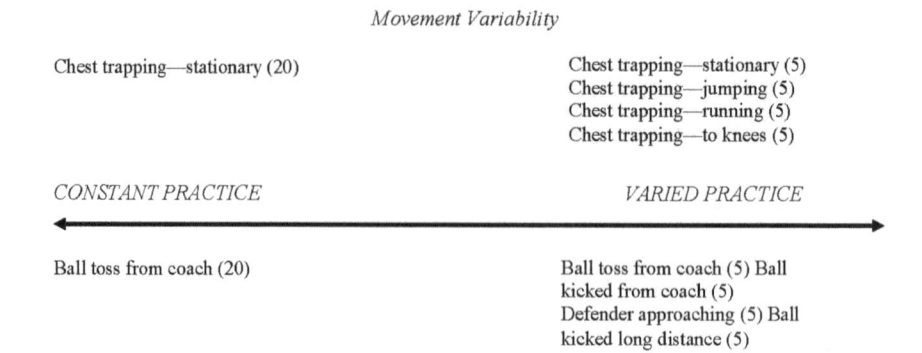

| Ball toss from coach (20) | Ball toss from coach (5) Ball kicked from coach (5)
Defender approaching (5) Ball kicked long distance (5) |

Environmental Variability

FIGURE 7.1
An example of implementing both *movement* and *environmental* practice variability for athletes practicing *20 repetitions of the soccer chest trap*. The coach can manipulate the repetitions along the continuum of low variability (constant) to high variability (varied).

"discovery" learning methods that have proven effective. Shifting the emphasis away from the "one-size-fits-all" approach to one of exploration and adaptation is widely supported in the literature and aligns with the notion of varied practice. Practice variability is also useful when coaches want to guide athletes toward new movement patterns or techniques. For example, repetitions hitting a baseball over a variety of wall heights and distances are more likely to elicit new swing patterns, such as the desirable "upper cut" swing plane with higher exit trajectories.

Second, though variability is generally recommended more for beginning-level athletes, it can be useful for athletes of all levels. The assumption is that high-level athletes, with their long and rich history of movement experiences, will have already learned robust schemas and movement relationships and are able to generalize their skill across a variety of situations. However, coaches and athletes report success using practice variability at all stages of expertise. For example, high-level soccer players practice chest trapping from a variety of kicks, speeds, ball trajectories, locations, and body positions. Professional golfers intentionally practice shot variety on the driving range (e.g., long, short, draw, fade). Accounting for the elements that can vary in the performance context, and intentionally varying those elements, can improve transfer.

Third, practice variability aligns with both practice-to-transfer (PTT) and practice-to-learn (PTL) goals. As such, coaches and athletes should expect lower levels of practice success when repetitions are high in variability. Repetitions that force learners to problem-solve and adapt their movement increase practice difficulty. Remember, the aim of varied practice is *not* "perfect" practice or the continued rehearsal of a specific or ideal technique. The trade-off is deeper learning and better transfer to the dynamic competitive environment.

INTERLEAVE THE PRACTICE REPETITIONS

in·ter·leave: to *combine* different things so that *parts* of one thing are put between *parts* of another thing (verb)

—*Cambridge Dictionary*

Recall transfer theory 3 (cognitive effort) that emphasized the role of memory in producing positive transfer of learning. Practice should improve the functioning of the memory systems and reduce the effects of "forgetting" what was practiced. Interleaved practice should strengthen memory-enhancing processes such as encoding, rehearsal, and retrieval.

Interleaved vs. Repetitive Practice

Coaches can help make repetitions "stick" in the memory of their athletes by manipulating the *order* or the *schedule* of the practice repetitions. In the literature, the varied order of repetitions has been called *random* or *interleaved practice*.[6] Compared to the relative ease of performing consecutive repetitions (*repetitive practice*) of the same skill (e.g., 10 corner kicks in a row), the nonconsecutive order of practicing different skills (e.g., 1 corner kick, 1 pass, 1 chest trap) is more effortful.

Repetitive practice is often the preferred and more traditional way for athletes to "get their reps in." It's enticing; athletes (and coaches) feel satisfied when they get in a groove and repeat several successful repetitions in a row. For example, there is a sense of achievement gained from placing five consecutive bunts down the first-base line in softball practice. "Muscle memory" is often cited as a reason to rehearse a skill until you get it right and then repeat it some more. Athletes like to keep practicing successful repetitions to demonstrate their competence. It's somewhat addictive. If you are a recreational golfer and spend time on the driving range, you know the desire to keep hitting the same shot, using the same club that you can put on the flag. And when you do switch clubs or shots, recall the tendency to want to keep hitting that club until you can put it on the flag consistently. Repetitive (blocked) practice is attractive, indeed.

The problem with repetitive practice is that research shows it to be less effective for long-term learning. Interleaved practice, where repetitions are woven or alternated within the practice of different skills, has consistently shown superior performance in retention and transfer tests (learning).[7] An interleaved practice order can create *cognitive challenge*. This is the *desirable difficulty* necessary for deep and sustainable learning.[8] Put another way, interleaved repetitions can create higher levels of *contextual interference* or the "good" interference that strengthens the memory processes.[9] It's a form of memory enhancement for athletes to better retain their practice repetitions. Compared to repetitive practice, interleaved practice can be challenging for athletes and reduce their practice success.

The difference between interleaved (high interference) and repetitive (low interference) practice is illustrated in figure 7.2. The practice of three different volleyball skills can be scheduled on a continuum of highly repetitive (all repetitions of one skill completed before moving to the next skill) to highly interleaved (completely random and unpredictable order of practicing different skills). In the middle of the continuum is an example of a "hybrid" practice order, which is a mix of both repetitive and interleaved repetitions.

Why Interleaved Practice Promotes Transfer of Learning

Interleaving practice repetitions is a way to manipulate the level of cognitive challenge and transfer of learning. It's worth elaborating on *why* interleaved practice repetitions hold significant transfer of learning advantages over repetitive practice. We provide the most compelling reasons below.

Test Matching

Interleaved practice is more *representative* of the test (game). Does the game encourage variation between different shots at random moments? Recall the practice design tool (chapter 5) to assess the potential for the practice environment to transfer to the competition environment (see table 5.3).

Order of Practice Repetitions

Repetitive	*Hybrid*	*Interleaved*
Forearm Pass (20)	Forearm Pass (5)	Overhead Set (1)
Overhead Set (20)	Overhead Set (5)	Forearm Pass (1)
Spike (20)	Spike (5)	Overhead Set (1)
(60 reps)	*(continue to 60 reps)*	Spike (1)
		Forearm Pass (1)
		(continue to 60 reps in randomized order)

◄──►

Low interference	Medium interference	High interference
Rehearsal		Effortful retrieval
Memorization		Elaboration

Low	*Moderate*	*High*

Amount of Cognitive Challenge (Memory)

FIGURE 7.2
The practice of three different volleyball skills can be scheduled on a continuum of highly repetitive to highly interleaved. In the middle of the continuum is an example of a hybrid practice order (a mix of both repetitive and interleaved).

Many performance conditions require different skills to be performed randomly (e.g., tennis, basketball, volleyball), so interleaving practice repetitions better match the test (game). When the test is interleaved (this is common), the learning advantage of interleaved practice is very large. Even when test order or sequence is different from what was practiced, interleaved practice shows learning advantages. Individuals that train with interleaved sequences are less impacted by changing test conditions (repetitive or interleaved), compared to those who train with repetitive practice. For example, a student who interleaves the study of different concepts rather than rehearsing one concept at a time shows better performance on a test, regardless of test format.[10] Musicians perform better on their test when they practice a piece of music by restarting at different sections of the piece (avoiding getting into a repetitive groove).[11] A cross-country runner might apply the concept by interleaving the order of different course starting and ending points (different running strategies) even though the test is repetitive.

Retrieval and Reconstruction in Memory

Interleaved repetitions are a form of retrieval practice. When you switch from performing a forearm pass to performing a set, you forget the forearm pass solution and retrieve (reconstruct) the memory of the overhead set. The more frequently you forget and reconstruct the movement solution, the stronger memory becomes. Repetitive practice is rehearsal without the retrieval. You are repeating a similar solution, like memorizing a list. It feels good while you practice, but it's easy to forget later.

Elaboration in Memory

When an athlete switches back and forth between the forearm pass and overhead set, there is a "compare and contrast" process that goes on in their memory. They practice recognizing and executing the differences (e.g., elbows together in one, elbows apart in the other) and similarities (e.g., low staggered stance for both) between the two skills. The repeated application of past concepts with new concepts encodes deeper and stronger memory representations and mental models that transfer well to competition.

Psychological Skills

Repetitive practice offers us little in the way of psychological and mental similarity to game conditions. Most sporting competitions give the athlete one chance to solve a specific movement problem and generate a successful performance (exceptions are do-overs in tennis serves, free throws, and high jumps). Interleaved practice simulates the one-chance-for-success mind-set. For example, a golfer has one shot at the green from the fairway. In the moment, they need to forget the last shot, survey the environment, problem-solve the best approach, and create a *new* movement solution. A volleyball player serving in a game has one chance to survey the court, strategize the best serve, and execute successfully. If they practiced this problem-solving process (i.e., interleaved repetitions), then positive transfer is more likely. Managing the pressure of the competitive situation is a skill to be practiced. Success largely depends on athletes' ability to manage their anxiety and direct their attention to the important environmental cues (e.g., opponent positions) during performance. Interleaved repetitions provide athletes with practice managing their arousal, anxiety, and attention.

Implementing Interleaved Practice

Implementing an interleaved practice schedule starts with practice planning. While interleaved practice can depend on logistical aspects, such as transition times and facility issues, we think working through those aspects is well worth the effort. We offer some planning strategies (with examples) below.

Interleave the Order of Different Skills

Different skills require fundamentally different movement solutions and problem-solving. Coaches can interleave repetitions based on amount of time, number of repetitions, or drill design.

Practice time. Below is a sample schedule of practice time (1 hour) for baseball middle infielders on three different fielding skills:

Skill Practice: Middle Infielders (baseball)

Repetitive Schedule (traditional)	*Interleaved Schedule (moderate)*
3:00–3:20 Backhands	3:00–3:10 Slow rollers
3:20–3:40 Slow rollers	3:10–3:20 Backhands
3:40–4:00 Double plays	3:20–3:30 Slow rollers
	3:30–3:40 Double plays
	3:40–3:50 Backhands
	3:50–4:00 Double plays

Repetitions. Below is a sample practice schedule of repetitions (100) for basketball players on four different basketball skills:

Skill Practice: Basketball

Repetitive Schedule	*Interleaved Schedule*
Layup finishes (25 reps)	Layup finishes (5 reps)
Dribble control (25 reps)	Pull-up jumpers (5 reps)
Pull-up jumpers (25 reps)	Dribble control (5 reps)
Entry passes (25 reps)	Entry passes (5 reps)
	(continue in random order to 100)

Drill design. The practice of different skills can be interleaved easily in drill design. Here is a volleyball example:

> Design a rotation in which a player executes a *spike*, then moves to the setting position to perform a *set* to the hitter, then moves to the other side of the net to execute a *block*, then moves to a position to provide *block coverage* behind the next block. In this drill, practice interleaves the repetitions of four different skills.

Interleave the Order of the Same Skill (Parameters)

The practice variability section encouraged coaches to vary the parameters of the same skill (variable practice). Coaches can add more cognitive challenge by interleaving the practice order of varied practice repetitions. Below is an example of scheduling 20 repetitions for four variations (parameters) of the volleyball serve. The interleaved schedule provides the most cognitive challenge (random and unpredictable), but the coach could reduce the amount by using a hybrid schedule, such as changing the order predictably every two or three repetitions.

Skill Practice: Volleyball Serving

Repetitive Schedule of Varied Practice	*Interleaved Schedule of Varied Practice*
5 Long serves	1 Down-the-line serve
5 Short serves	1 Long serve
5 Down-the-line serves	1 Floater serve
5 Floater serves	1 Short serve
	(continue in random order to 20)

Table 7.1 provides some examples of implementing interleaved practice. They also happen to be examples used in actual research studies![12]

Managing Difficulty and Perceptions in Interleaved Practice

In the above examples, interleaved repetitions increased learning in both beginning and advanced athletes. It's a robust and powerful practice effect. However, research is conclusive that high amounts of interference or cognitive challenge may not *always* increase learning.[13] Repetitive or blocked repetitions can be more beneficial when (a) the skill is complex or difficult or

Table 7.1. Research and practical examples of interleaved vs. repetitive practice.

Study	Repetitive	Interleaved	Results
College baseball players: Extra reps of batting practice	15 reps fastball 15 reps curveball 15 reps changeup	Alternate random order of pitch type for 45 reps	Interleaved performed better in game-like test of random pitches, and also performed better in a repetitive test format
Novice gymnasts: 9 weeks of practice on different apparatuses	Complete all trials for one apparatus before beginning practice on another apparatus	Hybrid practice rotating practice trials between the different apparatuses	Interleaved showed higher technical and artistry scores on retention test
Novice badminton players: 3 weeks of practice of long, short, and drive serve types	Practice one serve type each practice session	Practice all 3 serve types each practice session	Interleaved performed more accurately on both retention test and a transfer test serving to a "new" spot on the court

(b) the athlete is a beginner on the skill. As well, repetitions that create moderate levels of interference (hybrid schedule) may sometimes be better. The best use of interleaved practice is when it is matched with athlete readiness. Coaches are encouraged to determine if players can "handle" the interference of interleaved repetitions. When first introducing new skills or variations, repetitive practice may be the desirable difficulty.

We encourage coaches to begin to create interference and cognitive challenge soon after athletes "get the idea" of the skill. Coaches should progressively interleave practice repetitions (e.g., hybrid schedules) and move toward the end of the continuum (unpredictable and random) as athletes gain skill. Repetitions get closest to game conditions when they are varied and interleaved. For example, high-level golfers often have coaches call out shots (e.g., fade, draw, and hook) or distances (e.g., 20, 40, 60, 80 yards) randomly and unpredictably as they practice their reps on the driving range.

In addition to managing the difficulty of repetitions, it's also important to manage the athletes' *perceptions* of the learning process. Athletes should be aware of the trade-off of interleaved practice—the potential sacrifice of successful practice performance for the return of better learning. Interesting research shows that repetitive interleaved practice can mislead athletes' judgments about how much they are learning from practice. When athletes are asked to predict how well they think they will perform on a retention or transfer test later, those using repetitive practice *overestimate* their level of learning and predict significantly higher test performance than actually occurs. To the contrary, those using interleaved practice *accurately predict* test performance.[14]

This "illusion" of higher levels of learning through repetitive practice is potentially harmful to the athlete. Not transferring their predicted success to the game can be a source of frustration and can ultimately lead to a loss of athlete confidence, enjoyment, and motivation to practice. We recommend coaches openly discuss the role of cognitive challenge during repetitions, so athletes recognize the value of the "struggle." Hopefully, when athletes practice independently, away from the watchful eye of a coach, they can better manage their levels of difficulty. Evidence shows that learners privy to a history of interleaved practice can change the way they approach learning situations. In a sense, they can "learn to learn." Learning itself is a transferrable and invaluable skill, and it certainly aligns with the culture of learning and the "growth mind-set" foundations discussed in chapter 3.

SPACE THE PRACTICE REPETITIONS

Another important area for transfer is how coaches distribute or space their practice repetitions over time. For example, is it better to complete your repetitions in fewer but longer sessions or more but shorter sessions? This variable has been researched using the terms *massed practice* and *distributed practice*. Both practice types involve a period of active practice or work and a period of rest. The typical distinction is that a massed practice schedule involves longer practice or work times with shorter rest periods, compared to a distributed schedule, which has shorter work times and longer rest periods.

Research indicates a clear learning advantage for shorter, more frequent practice sessions. Spacing practice of a skill across sessions, compared to practicing a skill for longer periods of time within one session, has been shown to enhance learning. Learning environments should favor conditions that space practice repetitions across shorter, more frequent practice sessions.[15] The learning advantage of distributed practice is well documented in classroom

Table 7.2. Research and practical examples of massed vs. distributed practice schedules.

Study	Massed	Distributed	Results
Target shooting practice	One session of training	Two training sessions separated by one day of no practice	On a retention test, distributed had more hits and less error
Dynamic balance practice	All practice sessions and repetitions conducted in one day	Repetitions and practice sessions distributed across two days	Distributed had less balancing error both during practice and on a retention test
Golf putting practice	240 reps on one day with short breaks between blocks of 10 reps	60 reps per day for four consecutive days	Distributed performed better at end of practice, on a one-day retention test, and on a seven-day retention test

environments where more frequent sessions of less time (e.g., 1-hour classes, 3 times per week) increase learning compared to longer, less frequent class sessions (e.g., 3-hour class, 1 night per week). Recall the transfer theory 3 (cognitive effort) highlight, where surgeons receiving instruction in a distributed format outperformed those who learned in a massed schedule. Table 7.2 provides research examples of massed and distributed practice schedules.[16]

Why Spacing Practice Promotes Transfer of Learning

Concentration

The formula for success is simple: Practice and concentration then more practice and more concentration.

—*Babe Didrikson Zaharias*[17]

Like repetitive practice (vs. interleaved), massed practice repetitions run the risk of becoming monotonous for the athlete. As such, the amount of concentration and attention to practice is reduced during the repetitions. When coupled with an increase in physical and mental fatigue of massed practice, the likely result is less learning from the practice session. Research supports that the benefit of distributed practice shows up later in practice sessions, rather than at the beginning of practice. Learners grow more tired and disinterested as massed practice continues.

Memory Consolidation

Learning is somewhat dependent on the memory and cognitive processes that occur *outside* of practice, not just what goes on *during* practice. Memory consolidation is the result of neural and chemical activities in the brain that occur during periods of rest or time away from the skill practice. It has been described as a process critical for the strengthening of long-term memories and is assumed to be responsible for the gains seen in performance in the period between the end of practice and the subsequent test (the game). Research is consistent that intervals of time away from additional practice increases memory strength. And consolidation has been shown to begin immediately after the completion of practice. Time spent practicing a different skill is also a form of "outside" time that can help memory consolidation (interleaved practice!).

Implementing Spaced Repetitions

We recommend coaches intentionally move toward spacing repetitions, and as much as possible, adopt a distributed schedule, practicing skills in shorter but more frequent time periods. Coaches can consider spacing repetitions along a continuum of low distribution (massed), to moderate, to high distribution (distributed). Table 7.3 provides an example of a weekly basketball plan for four different skills. The spacing is different, but the total amount of practice time is the same (240 minutes, 60 minutes per skill). More distributed practice schedules should help athletes remember more and forget less on game day.

Implementing distributed practice schedules may take some time and patience. Research shows that learners often prefer a more massed learning schedule. This may be due to the desire to complete all repetitions at once and the perception that they are learning better with massed practice (similar to repetitive practice). Sometimes massed practice can be preferable and advisable (e.g., early in the practice of new skills, safety considerations, logistics). For example, coaches may like to spend more time presenting new information and instructions, at least until athletes show they understand it. However, we encourage coaches to begin spacing practice as soon and as much as possible. Even in the early practice of new skills, spacing practice

Table 7.3. Example of a weekly practice plan of four basketball skills, each practiced for 60 minutes. Total practice time (240 minutes) is spaced in low, moderate, or high distribution schedules.

Practice Plan: Week 3, Team Movement Skills			
Target Skills: (1) Defensive Pressure, (2) Offensive Movement, (3) Team Rebounding, (4) Team Defense			
	Low Distribution (Massed)	*Moderate Distribution*	*High Distribution (Distributed)*
Monday	Defensive Pressure (60) Other Practice Activities	Defensive Pressure (30) Offensive Movement (30) Other Practice Activities	Defensive Pressure (15) Offensive Movement (15) Team Rebounding (15) Team Defense (15)
Tuesday	Offensive Movement (60) Other Practice Activities	Team Rebounding (30) Team Defense (30) Other Practice Activities	Defensive Pressure (15) Offensive Movement (15) Team Rebounding (15) Team Defense (15)
Wednesday	Team Rebounding (60) Other Practice Activities	Defensive Pressure (30) Offensive Movement (30) Other Practice Activities	Other Practice Activities
Thursday	Team Defense (60) Other Practice Activities	Team Rebounding (30) Team Defense (30) Other Practice Activities	Defensive Pressure (15) Offensive Movement (15) Team Rebounding (15) Team Defense (15)
Friday	Other Practice Activities	Other Practice Activities	Defensive Pressure (15) Offensive Movement (15) Team Rebounding (15) Team Defense (15)

can be beneficial, and it aligns with earlier recommendations on instructions (chapter 6). Recall the tendency of beginning coaches to present too much information (e.g., over-coaching) rather than instructions that are short and to the point. Rather than trying to communicate and practice lots of new information at one time (massed), consider delivering only a portion of it and saving some for later, or the next session.

"WHOLE" REPETITIONS TRANSFER BETTER

Good teaching sometimes involves breaking skills down into manageable parts and progressively adding complexity as athletes gain skill. For example, teaching an offensive play to a team early in the season often requires practicing one option before adding more complex options or elements. When teaching the freestyle swimming stroke, instructors often practice the foot action first, or separately from the arm action. Many sport instruction books break down a skill into parts and recommend separate practice of them. For example, some tennis instruction books break down the serve into the grip, stance, backswing, ball toss, forward swing, ball contact, and follow-through. Part practice recognizes the attention and memory limitations of beginners trying to learn new skills. From a transfer of learning perspective, the examples above highlight situations of near and high positive transfer. As discussed earlier, a coach isolates or simplifies an element of the skill with the assumption that the part (transfer task) will transfer forward to the whole (target context).

While part practice may be recommended in some cases, we suggest that more often, skills are best practiced whole. We offer an example of a local basketball coach who practiced the mechanics of basketball shooting in parts. He organized a rotation of three shooting stations, each practicing a different part of shooting:

Station 1: Chair shooting; players practiced the upper body mechanics of shooting while seated on a chair (5 minutes).

Station 2: Lie-down shooting; players practiced the wrist release and elbow position while lying flat on the ground (5 minutes).

Station 3: Step-form shots; players practiced stationary set shots at the goal, coordinating the front-foot stepping movement with the shooting arm (5 minutes).

After all players had completed the three stations, players performed several repetitions of the "whole" jump shot.

The parts practiced in the stations above are all important skill elements, but there will be lower-than-expected transfer of learning from the part practice repetitions to the whole skill (jump shot). Why? First, the jump shot in basketball is a highly *organized* skill. Each part depends on the part that preceded it. The coordination, timing, force production, and rhythm of a jump shot depends on the connectedness of its parts. For example, the timing of elbow and wrist extension depends on, and is timed with, the lower body's extension. And when practiced separately, the arms and wrist use a different amount (higher) of relative force than when performed together. Second, the drills are *decomposed* from environmental information of the game-like whole jump shot. The chair and lie-down drills change the visual information and location of the goal. The step drill is missing defenders and speeds that the performer relies on to execute the best step (speed and distance) in the game. We elaborate a bit more below on the two main factors that impact the transfer of part practice repetitions.

Skill Organization

Skill organization refers to the degree in which the parts or components of the skill are connected or related to one another.[18] A *high organization* skill has parts that are interdependent; that is, performance of each part depends on the part performed just before it. The skill is made up of a chain of events (component parts) that are connected in timing, rhythm, or spatial elements. Examples of highly organized skills include a cartwheel in gymnastics, the breaststroke in swimming, and running the hurdles in track. The execution of a hurdle motion, for example, is connected to the performance of the previous hurdle (e.g., adjusting step pattern if cleared last hurdle too high). In general, part practice of high organization skills produces low, zero, or potentially negative transfer. It may create interference in the timing and rhythm of the skill. Isolating the backswing or downswing of a hockey slap shot, for example, is connected to interacting spring-like muscle properties (e.g., stretch reflex), so both parts should work together more as athletes gain skill. The same may apply to backswings in sport skills such as golf and baseball swings or tennis or volleyball smashes.

A *low organization* skill has parts that are independent and not connected. While fewer in number, examples might include the previously mentioned freestyle stroke (leg kick and arm action) or weightlifting movements such as a bench press or bicep curl. Low organization skills are easier to break down given their relatively isolated parts. For these skills, there is little disruption to the timing, coordination, and rhythm of the whole skill, so we might expect positive transfer of learning when practicing parts of the skill.

High organization skills (most sport skills) are difficult to break apart given their connected parts. As such, part practice of these skills produces lower-than-expected transfer of learning.

Skill Decomposition

Decomposition refers to the degree the movement is practiced separately from the environment.[19] Decomposed practice is when a movement is isolated from the competitive environment and practiced in a different (simpler) environment. The movement may stay whole, but it's a form of part practice because the movement is isolated from the environment. For example, in tennis, a coach lobbing the ball softly for the player to hit into an empty court removes the environmental part of an approaching ball off an opponent's racket. In baseball, hitting off a tee, a soft toss, or a pitching machine simplifies the skill but removes the part of a pitcher's release point and ball trajectory. As well, tee and soft-toss drills often encourage a different movement than the one used in the game. Take a look at the side-by-side comparisons offered in the video at https://baseballeducationcenter.com/hitting bundle/stop/?utm_source=email&utm_medium=aweb1.

While these examples are typical "part" practice activities, the movement is "de-coupled" from the perception, and the movement solution is different from the one needed for competition. Another popular part practice method is doing repetitions of the ball toss separately from the serving motion (e.g., volleyball and tennis). But does it transfer? Interesting research shows that experts in these sports don't achieve consistency in the vertical, forward–backward, and side-to-side toss of the ball when serving, and when they practiced only the toss part of the skill, their toss height was much higher than when they performed the whole skill. The only consistent factor that experts developed was the stability between the time of peak height of the ball toss and the initiation of the forward swing of the racquet (or arm).[20] Their toss height (environment) is connected to their swing initiation (movement)! So, while there may be merit in learning parts of an effective toss, transfer improves when most repetitions are kept whole.

For reasons related to skill organization and decomposition, we suggest coaches use part practice on a limited basis. While it has value to manage limitations in athlete attention and memory and serves to progressively add difficulty and challenge, part practice methods may limit positive transfer. We recommend that as soon and as much as possible, practice repetitions should emphasize practice of the "whole" skill. Whole practice better simulates the underlying movement coordination and the perception-action link, which increases the transfer of repetitions to the competition. There may be better ways to simplify skills and progressively add challenge to our practice repetitions, and we point to a few of them next.

Simplify, Don't Separate

When we need to reduce difficulty of skill practice, we recommend a *simplification* approach rather than using a part practice. Three simplification methods are discussed below. Recall that some of these may connect back with the foundation of manipulating constraints from chapter 4.

Simplify the Equipment

Keep the movement structure and environmental information the same but simplify the skill by modifying the equipment. Consider oversized rackets or gloves (easier to make contact/catch), shorter or lighter implements (easier to manipulate), or anti-slip grip surfaces (easier to swing/control). Scaling equipment to match the athlete is preferred over practicing in parts (e.g., young tennis players practicing with modified racket weights and lengths produce more skillful movements compared to using standard/adult equipment). It's a proven way simplify a skill without breaking it apart.[21]

Simplify the Task

Change the design of the drill instead of breaking the skill apart. Instead of decomposing with cone dribbling, using tag games and keep-away can provide similar game-like perceptions of the environment, such as keeping eyes up, scanning the field, searching for teammates, and looking for openings. Instead of hitting balls off tees (decomposed), get closer to the game environment by using balls tossed from shorter distances, slower speeds, or larger balls. Changing the size of zones, number of players, or time requirements in a drill can simplify a skill while keeping the whole intact.

Cue the Attention
Provide attention-directing cues essential to parts of the skill while practicing the whole skill. Internally focused examples during practice of a whole skill might include a focus on the hip rotation part of a volleyball jump serve or the part of a high elbow recovery while swimming the freestyle stroke. Recall too the importance on cueing an external focus of attention for athletes. Examples might include a focus on the ball's height during the ball toss portion of the whole serving skill or the jump portion of the whole serve with an external cue such as "explode off the ground." As mentioned earlier, part-focusing attention cues should be short and simple, consisting of one or two cues at a time.

Clarify the Purpose of Part Practice
There are situations when part practice of a highly organized skill is useful. Athletes learning a new skill or a new modification of an existing skill can benefit from part repetitions, as well as situations where safety is paramount (e.g., football tackle). For example, despite the breaststroke in swimming being highly organized, athletes might better allocate attention to the new part by practicing the arm movement and leg kick independently for a few repetitions before practicing the whole. Beginners can practice the leg kick first, followed by the arm action, then together as a whole unit, when attention is better allocated to the coordination and timing of the whole movement. This *progressive-part practice* limits part practice repetitions and quickly moves to practicing the skill whole. Additionally, a coach might isolate part of a skill for strength and conditioning goals. The swimmer might use a kickboard to remove the arm action and strengthen the kicking motion. The volleyball server might practice the jump portion of the serve to work on conditioning and explosive movements. A coach might also use part practice to isolate strategic concepts, such as conducting an isolated "walk-through" of team strategies before practice or a game to focus athlete attention on tactical elements without distracting movements. In all these situations, we recommend part practices have a specific purpose and be used sparingly and progressively on the way toward repetitions that are performed whole, in game-like environments.

FULL-SPEED REPETITIONS TRANSFER BETTER

A pitcher throws 95 mph pitches, for strikes.

A tennis player drives a forehand shot 1 inch inside the line at 90 mph.

A football quarterback completes a 50-yard pass to the receiver in stride.

A hockey player blasts the puck into the top corner of the net.

An MMA fighter lands the roundhouse kick perfectly to the opponent's head.

How do they do that? High-level athletes perform skills with an incredible blend of speed and accuracy. How did they practice the complex blend of speed-accuracy? What did they practice first, speed or accuracy? What should the coach focus on in practice?

The Golden Rule and Its Exceptions

The *speed-accuracy trade-off* is a well-researched premise that a predictable relationship exists between speed and accuracy when executing a skill—an emphasis on speed will negatively impact accuracy, and vice versa. This golden rule (termed Fitts's Law) was established primarily using simple, manual aiming movements in controlled laboratory environments.[22] As a law, the findings are consistent: when you speed up movement, you lose accuracy. At some point, we likely have all experienced the negative impact of moving too fast. The golden rule is well ingrained in our view of motor control. However, some interesting research shows that there are exceptions to the rule, including[23]:

1. When *timing accuracy* is a factor in the performance (e.g., baseball swing), increasing movement speed improves timing. In other words, timing accuracy improves when athletes swing faster and/or move a shorter distance (this is opposite the golden rule).
2. When making *complex forceful movements*, accuracy is important (e.g., field goal kick); there is an inverted-U relationship. Accuracy is the worst when athletes generate movements at approximately 50 percent of their maximum force, but accuracy improves as they approach near-maximal (80–90%) forces (this modifies the golden rule).

These exceptions suggest that moving harder and faster may not sacrifice accuracy like we think. And these two exceptions (movement timing and force) would apply to many sport skills, such as the examples at the beginning of this section.

Movement Coordination and the Need for Speed

A second important principle informing coaches about balancing speed and accuracy is the importance of developing effective patterns of coordination as a foundation for expertise. An effective coordination pattern is a prerequisite for producing high amounts of speed. As such, it should be emphasized over control elements (such as accuracy). Learning the coordination of a movement skill should come before learning how to control the skill (e.g., being accurate). For example, the pitcher would first develop the coordination of the throw and control the accuracy of pitches later. An effective coordination for throwing positively transfers (far) to more specific learning situations later (e.g., the pitcher learning how to throw a curveball). The importance of developing effective coordination patterns as a foundation was reinforced when we practiced the "fundamental movement patterns" in elementary school (e.g., throwing, kicking, striking). If the fundamental movement coordination is inefficient, then mastering speed and accuracy later is unlikely.

Evidence shows that high-speed movements facilitate more effective coordination patterns. An emphasis on speed in the early stages of learning facilitates the development of efficient movement patterns, while an emphasis on accuracy often impedes the development of efficient movement patterns, especially those of complex forceful movements (like those in our examples). When learners sacrifice velocity to increase accuracy, a "constrained" movement pattern emerges.[24] They don't release their joints, limbs, and muscles to move freely and smoothly. Their body doesn't discover movement solutions that generate higher levels of speed. And with continued repetitions emphasizing accuracy, this constrained and inefficient pattern gets ingrained as a GMP or as a "preferred pattern." (See transfer theories, chapter 2.) It's easy to transfer and hard to change.

The collective evidence suggests that repetitions encouraging speed (over accuracy) in the learning process are key to developing ability in speed-accuracy skills. There are several ways to emphasize speed in practice, and we offer a few suggestions next.

Coach Moving Fast
Emphasizing speed over accuracy requires a long-term development perspective, as it can reduce success in the short term. Allow tennis balls or volleyballs to be hit out long, and full-speed baseball swings to miss during practice. Downplay speed errors; instead encourage other ways to achieve accuracy rather than slowing the movement down. For example, encourage a shorter swing rather than slowing it down to get more accuracy. Instructions and cues that encourage speed, for example, throwing to "bust the beanbag" or "knock the wall down," have proven helpful in developing better movement patterns. Reinforcing speed in the learning process embraces the value of developing foundational movement patterns for far transfer later.

Manipulate the Accuracy Constraints
Traditional drills are often designed to emphasize accuracy. For example, many partner drills requiring players to throw or kick the ball to each other in small spaces are accuracy focused. Players may be encouraged to adopt a less-efficient kicking pattern to get the ball to their partners successfully. Tennis drills are often organized in ways that measure success using accuracy goals, for example, counting how many serves they get in the service box out of 10 repetitions. These drills may not facilitate discovering full-speed movement solutions and developing efficient coordination patterns. Practice tasks can be modified so they naturally encourage faster movements. For example, coaches can eliminate targets or make them larger during skill repetitions, such as soccer kicks, baseball pitching, volleyball or tennis serves, and hockey strikes. The lacrosse coach could use a soccer goal instead of the smaller lacrosse goal. Tennis players can serve into the whole court or against a backstop rather than the smaller service court. Baseball coaches modify pitching practice throwing to a wall rather than a small glove. Consider manipulating the size of balls or equipment during repetitions. Tennis players can use larger rackets and baseball players could use wider bats and/or larger balls to reduce accuracy constraints.

Coaches should remember that the speed emphasis is most effective early in the learning process as athletes are exploring movement solutions at their individual levels. They should allow movement patterns to look different among individual athletes and allow athletes the freedom to adopt their own movement patterns. The pressure to conform to one ideal movement pattern can constrain the development of an effective coordination pattern. Remember, even elite performers show uniquely different coordination patterns. But they all discovered a way to generate high-speed movements first. As athletes consistently produce efficient and high-speed movement patterns, coaches can increase accuracy constraints (e.g., smaller targets) that help them control their skill for competition requirements. Even then, we encourage coaches to continue to monitor their athletes' coordination patterns. For young athletes, the attraction toward accuracy is strong, and they tend to gravitate back toward accuracy-constrained movement patterns.

TRANSFER THIS

Let's return to Coach Martel from our introductory scenario. She effectively used a research-supported *varied practice* strategy for bunting repetitions. Players were practicing different movement parameters of the bunt (e.g., bat angles, forces). While the variations yielded "bad bunts" and reduced practice success, Coach Martel was more concerned about the problem-solving and bat control her players were going to transfer (far) later in practice and games. We recommend she also consider making the practice repetitions progressively more difficult by interleaving them so the athletes are not doing five consecutive reps of the same bunt (e.g., 2 pop-up bunts followed by 2 back-to-pitcher bunts). She could also add difficulty by spacing the bunt repetitions at different times during the practice session (e.g., 10 bunts at the beginning of practice and 10 in the middle of practice). Finally, it appears these repetitions were conducted full speed with the whole movement intact (not part practice). This should also facilitate positive transfer of the repetitions. We recommend Coach Martel stick to her ways and support her methods with the science of transfer (and the purpose of practice). Hopefully, the other coaches will come around!

Coaches, Transfer This
1. Rather than doing all repetitions the "correct" way, design some repetitions that intentionally vary parameters of the movement (e.g., speed, force, size of movement) or the task/environment (e.g., distances, zones, heights). This helps athletes transfer their skill across different performance conditions.
2. Interleave repetitions between different skills (e.g., dribbling and passing) or between different skill variations (e.g., long serves and short serves) of a skill. Progressively increase the amount of cognitive challenge by making repetitions more random, unpredictable, and cognitively challenging.

3. Rather than doing all practice repetitions of a skill in one session (massed), schedule shorter but more frequent practice sessions. While athletes might feel they are not "getting it," their increased concentration and memory consolidation (during more rest periods) will increase transfer of learning.
4. Transfer is enhanced when most practice repetitions are full speed and whole. While both part practice and slow-speed movements can be useful on a limited basis to simplify skills and create optimal challenge, look for alternative methods that keep whole movements intact, at game-like speeds.

Coach Educators and Developers, Transfer This

1. Reflect on the quantity vs. quality of practice repetitions. What is the role of both? What are some popular examples of athletes or coaches emphasizing quantity, quality, or both? What are ways to make repetitions have more quality? Provide real-life examples.
2. Reflect on the opening scenario of practicing with intentional errors to facilitate bat control. Do they support such a method? Have they ever conducted practice in a similar way (intentional errors)? How have they intentionally varied movement or environment parameters (see examples in this chapter)? Ask coaches to apply the variability continuum (see table 7.1) to a familiar skill. How can they modify practice to increase variability?
3. Explore examples of coaches who have used more interleaved or spaced practice schedules (compared to repetitive and massed). Using tables 7.2 and 7.3, have coaches try making repetitions more challenging by developing interleaved (or hybrid) and spaced schedules for familiar skills. Share and discuss examples.
4. How do coaches *simplify* practice repetitions for their athletes? Do they use methods of part practice or slow down movements? If so, provide examples. How did they impact skill development? Do coaches teach for accuracy first or speed first? How do they practice maximizing both? Do coaches like to break skills into parts, practicing them separately? What are ways coaches can simplify skills but keep them whole and full speed?
5. Have coaches reflect on the outdated and discredited adage, "You throw like a girl." What does that really mean? How do you think such a throwing motion was developed? How might their teacher, coach, or parents have emphasized accuracy too much in practice? Connect to other types of speed-accuracy skills and their development.

8

Feedback That Transfers

A travel baseball club (ages 12–15) invited two different private hitting instructors to visit with parents. The instructors were seeking to recruit players for hitting lessons during the fall season ($50 per session). Their "sales pitch" to the parents was captured below.

Hitting Instructor 1: "I will need to meet with your player three times per week over the next 3 months. Your player needs consistent feedback and corrections to create the correct muscle memory needed for good hitting." (36 sessions = $1,800)

Hitting Instructor 2: "I will need to meet with your player three times per week for the first month. After that, I provide workouts for him to do on his own, and he meets with me for feedback on an as-needed basis. Your player needs to learn to make his own adjustments as a hitter." (12 sessions = $600)

Feedback is an important part of the learning process. To continue developing, athletes often need additional skill information from an outside source. The coach is positioned as a primary source of skill information (feedback) for athletes. This chapter focuses on increasing the transfer potential of coach feedback.

THE NATURE OF FEEDBACK
Intrinsic vs. Augmented Feedback
Athletes receive feedback from two primary sources. First, they receive a plethora of *intrinsic feedback* from their internal sensory sources (i.e., visual, auditory, tactile, proprioception). Every sport or task has inherent, or built-in, sensory information that athletes learn how to manage and interpret. Some sports are rich with visual feedback about speed and accuracy outcomes (e.g., soccer), while others are rich with proprioceptive feedback about body position and control (e.g., wrestling). With practice, athletes improve in their ability to perceive and interpret intrinsic information specific to their sport.

To maximize their skill development, athletes need additional or supplemental feedback that guides them to solve problems and achieve higher levels of performance. This *augmented feedback* comes from an external source. External sources that augment athletes' intrinsic feedback can come in a variety of ways, such as a video replay of a movement technique, devices that give information about correct mechanics (e.g., golf putting guide), biofeedback about heart rate or muscle contractions (e.g., EMG, heart rate monitor), or devices giving time-based information (e.g., stopwatch, radar gun). Most often, the coach is the primary source of augmented feedback to the athlete. For example:

"Pull your hips back more before you start your swing."

"How else can you generate more force on your swing?"

"I really liked the way you set your feet and were balanced before your swing."

"You almost have it, remember to finish the follow-through. That's looking much better."

Quality coaching involves providing the augmented information to increase athlete learning (and transfer).

Direct vs. Indirect Feedback
Direct Feedback
This is the explicit type of augmented information designed to "stick" with the athlete as part of their memory of the learned skill (see transfer theory 3,

cognitive effort). Athletes must be able to attend to it, store it in memory, and retrieve it later in practice and competition.[1] As such, direct feedback from the coach should be:

1. Brief (lasting only a few seconds)
2. Specific (e.g., one or two things at a time)
3. Focused (attention directed to the key elements)
4. Explicit (athletes are *aware* of the purpose of the feedback, e.g., to correct an error)

An example of a verbal feedback statement that is brief, specific, focused (external), and explicit might be: "Snap your racquet face toward the ground at contact."

Indirect Feedback
This type of augmented information is designed to "constrain" skills and help athletes discover more effective movement solutions (see transfer theory 4, ecological dynamics), often without athlete awareness. It's often considered a *hands-off* way to provide feedback.[2] An example of a coach providing indirect feedback is manipulating practice constraints (chapter 4) that can correct an error (in absence of direct feedback). The coach might see the need for the athlete to "pull the hips back farther before contact." Instead of delivering direct feedback, the coach increases the distance to hit a ball, so the athlete discovers a different solution, such as pulling the hips back farther. To correct a poor entry in diving, the coach might place a foam noodle at shin height and ask the learner to dive over without touching it. The swimmer naturally pushes harder off the side of the pool, correcting the error. To correct tense running posture, the runner can be asked hold potato chips in each hand without crushing them, and to encourage more arm extension, players could hit playground balls off a tee rather than baseballs. The sports world is full of equipment and ideas that can fix errors using the indirect method, and we encourage coaches to use them.

A second way to provide indirect feedback is to blend it with direct methods by using guided discovery questions that encourage players to discover their own corrections rather than directly telling them what to fix. For example, "How else can you generate enough force to hit it deep?"

encourages self-discovery of a solution that further enhances athlete memory of the correction or solution. Coaches should use both direct and indirect methods when providing feedback.

SHAPE BEHAVIOR WITH FEEDBACK

What is "good" feedback? We suggest feedback is good when it:

1. is a valued part of the learning culture,
2. shapes athletes' future behavior(s), and
3. facilitates athlete independence and adaptability.

Recall in chapter 4 that a foundation for transfer is a culture of learning. Quality practice conditions embrace the role of errors and mistakes. They are viewed by players and coaches as essential to the process of skill development. A learning culture has athletes more receptive to coach feedback, and they are less defensive when errors are pointed out. This culture can be communicated through the coaches' feedback to athletes.[3] For example:

> "I'm glad I saw that mistake. It tells us something we need to fix before the next game."

> "This is a tough skill, even college players struggle with it. Let's fix this part first."

It is important athletes don't try to hide their mistakes from the coach. Doing so creates a gap in teaching and learning and results in a lack of transfer. Coaches and athletes should be able to openly discuss mistakes so they are viewed as a positive, not a negative. A culture of feedback encourages athletes to take more risks during practice, and they will welcome information that helps them improve.

Some coaches endorse the term "feedforward" rather than "feedback."[4] Rather than providing information about the past error (which can be seen as criticism), coaches and athletes should provide information that helps them better control their next attempt, in a feedforward way. Feedback, to be most effective, should shape how athletes behave not only in their next attempt, but ultimately in game conditions. In this sense, feedback should always be information that athletes can positively transfer forward (near and far).

Effective feedback helps athletes be more independent and adaptable. That is, they can detect and correct their own errors in a variety of competitive situations. Since coach feedback is limited during competition, athletes should be able to make their own performance adjustments, absorb input during the game, independently solve problems, and seek guidance when they need it. This level of independence is developed in practice and can be facilitated with augmented feedback. It's more than just fixing errors in practice. We suggest coaches view feedback as a form of "behavior modification." It should shape the way athletes think and behave in the future. To begin the process of behavior modification, coaches should recognize the three primary *functions* of feedback.[5]

Function 1: Error Correction
The most obvious role of feedback is to provide information that corrects errors. This information might point out incorrect aspects of the performance, explain why an error occurred, or correct a specific error(s):

"You're shifting your weight too much and too early; stay back and centered."

The information would be used by athletes to modify their future attempts with the goal to improve learning and transfer. We discuss important elements of error correction later in this section.

Function 2: Motivation
Feedback can be used to increase athlete effort, persistence, and enjoyment during practice, and should be targeted to achieve this function:

"Your dribbling is looking much better. Keep up the effort; it's paying off!"

Evidence suggests that motivational feedback is not just a temporary effect to increase effort, but one that impacts long-term retention and transfer. Providing motivational feedback to athletes about their successful performances, compared to errors-only feedback, has been shown to increase learning.[6] As well, when athletes receive feedback after repetitions they perceive as more successful, they show higher levels of self-efficacy and request feedback more often. Positive feedback increases an athlete's expectancies for success and perceptions of competence. This has positive effects on learning and athletes' desire to improve. We strongly recommend coaches provide a healthy dose of motivational feedback that is specific and sincere.

Function 3: Reinforcement
Feedback can function to strengthen desirable behaviors or skills. The role of feedback here is to increase the likelihood of a similar (positive) response occurring in the future, whether it be on the next attempt, the next practice, or in the game:

> "I really liked the way you set your feet and were balanced before your swing."

Reinforcing feedback can be the reward associated with an improvement or a successful effort. Humans (including athletes) generally crave reinforcement. Praise behaviors you want athletes to replicate, or "catch them doing good" by reinforcing successful efforts and performances during practice. For reinforcement to work, the feedback should be targeted toward *specific* behaviors. For example, "Yes, Luke, love the first contact!" is more effective than "Great job, Luke!" especially if other players can hear the praise (they are likely to learn from it). Reinforcement works when coaches are sincere and selective. Overuse of the same words such as "awesome" eventually reduces the impact of the reinforcement.

Find the Balance
Given their importance in shaping behavior, coaches should seek to provide information that achieves *all* the functions of feedback. And coaches should be deliberate with their feedback relative to the three functions. Feedback should have a clear purpose (one or more functions). Sometimes the purpose is to modify a technique or strategy for the next performance (error correction), while other times the goal is to confirm progress in a technique (reinforcement), or to encourage effort or persistence (motivation). Rather than delivering only one type of feedback, we encourage coaches to combine the types to harness their cumulative effect in shaping behavior. The often-cited method of "sandwich" feedback is an approach that puts the error correction

feedback (the meat) between the reinforcement and motivation feedback (the bread).[7] The coach first provides information that reinforces a skill or effort, then provides information that corrects the skill, and finally offers information that motivates future efforts. For example:

Reinforcement: "I really liked the way you set your feet and were balanced before your swing." (bread)

Error Correction: "Next time, try and pull your hips back more before you start your swing." (meat)

Motivation: "You almost have it. Keep up the effort! That's looking much better." (bread)

Research is clear: information that combines the feedback functions maximizes athletes' learning and transfer.[8] Coaches are encouraged to exploit the functions of feedback and find the right balance between highlighting mistakes and successes. For coaches, it will take some practice, but it's worth the effort!

BEFORE THE FEEDBACK: LEARN TO WATCH

Good feedback starts with good observation skills. The ability to watch might be the most overlooked part of effective feedback. Sometimes "observing" doesn't feel like coaching, so we don't recognize its importance or spend much time planning for it. It's a critical skill to be developed. Like the expert athlete seeing the whole field and anticipating the next best move, good coaches seem to be able to see and anticipate errors during practice. Though it comes with experience, good observation skills can be developed. Some guidance is offered below.

Make a Checklist of the Key Elements

Prior to observing the athletes' performance, coaches should clearly identify the purpose of the skill and its key elements. Key elements are the critical features essential to successful performance of the skill. While these elements leave room for individual exploration and solutions, they identify the things that make the skill successful. Coaches are encouraged to develop and use a checklist to organize what they are looking for in a skill. This narrative or list is a reminder of what successful performance looks like (and what to look for). Numerous sport-specific books, web pages, and journals offer a variety of checklists, some of which are very specific. Key elements to checklist for the volleyball set might include, for example:

1. Eyes under fingers and ball
2. Hips open to direction pass was received
3. Elbows out at ball contact
4. Extend follow-through in direction of pass

Once the key elements of the skill have been identified, we encourage coaches to write down what a *great* performance looks like. How is it different than a good or average performance? Including this information in a practice plan will focus coaches on what to watch for, and as a result, their feedback (direct or indirect) will be more focused and effective.

Collect Data First
One way to improve the skill of watching is to collect data before providing feedback. Rather than locking in on the first mistake you see from an individual player, take the time to observe and track the most common or important error(s) players are struggling with (use your checklist). As well, collect data on as many players as possible prior to giving feedback. Most coaches understand the challenge of getting feedback to all players equally in a short amount of time. Observing all players and tracking the most common and important error(s) allows coaches to provide "data-driven" feedback on corrections that impact the most players. We recommend that coaches take notes and tallies during skill observations. This keeps the coach on task and helps them be more selective in providing feedback with the most impact. The act of taking notes enables coaches to be more intentional about *how* they are looking and *what* they are looking for. It's also a way to prevent the natural bias of giving feedback to a select few players at the expense of neglecting others.

Anticipate Errors[9]
An important element of effective observation is identifying errors or mistakes coaches are most likely to see in a practice activity. What are the

things the players are most likely to get wrong as they perform this? What are they likely to misunderstand? Writing this down makes it more likely that coaches will see these mistakes when they happen. Coaches get better at this with practice. The impact of anticipating errors is that coaches can better plan their responses to the errors they expect to see. What will you do, say, or show when you see these errors? This makes feedback more effective and increases the chances athletes will learn from it. One of the ways to anticipate errors is to identify the possible reasons or underlying causes of an observed error. After observing an error, ask *why* questions such as: Why did I see this mistake? Why was the pass not accurate? Why was the athlete out of position? The cause of the error might not always be related to a technique error. An inaccurate pass could be due to incorrect anticipation or decision-making or errors in comprehension or attention. Effective feedback depends on identifying the true cause of the error or mistake. Being aware of and looking for the potential sources of error helps coaches provide more effective feedback. Building off Cheryl Coker's model[10] of diagnosing errors, figure 8.1 highlights the five major categories of error, and we briefly discuss them below.

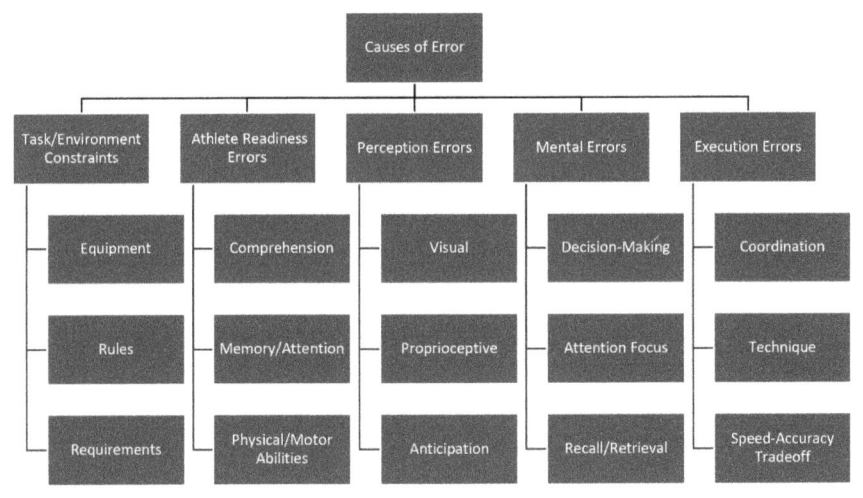

FIGURE 8.1
Categories for diagnosing errors. Coaches should identify the type(s) or cause(s) of error before providing feedback. (Adapted from Coker, *Motor Learning and Control for Practitioners*)

Errors Due to Task or Environmental Constraints
Sometimes an ineffective bat swinging motion is the result of the ball being too small or the bat being too heavy. Changing the ball or bat size may "fix" the swing as the hitter extends their arms and rotates their hips (indirect feedback). An immature throwing motion might be the result of a short distance, the target, or the ball not fitting the thrower's hand. Changing these constraints might produce a longer step with the lead foot. Lowering the basketball goal might encourage the use of an elbow-in, wrist-snap technique. Addressing task or environmental constraints and fixing the environment or task first is a good principle to follow before providing direct feedback to fix the error.

Errors Due to Athlete Readiness
Sometimes athletes may not understand the instructions, the practice activity, or the skill requirements. In other cases, it may exceed their capacity in attention and memory. We highlighted individual constraints in chapter 3, many of them related to developmental factors, such as physical, cognitive, and psychological issues. Is the error due to lack of physical strength? Motivation? Attentional capacity? Comprehension? Short-term memory? Sometimes athletes may not possess the underlying motor abilities necessary to perform the skill at a high level (e.g., dynamic balance, explosive strength, range of motion). In these cases, feedback may not bring about the desired effect, and athletes need to develop other skill solutions or strategies to compensate (e.g., relying on strengths or an alternative strategy). The volleyball player may not execute the block at the net correctly because of immature visual abilities (e.g., depth perception), an overload of information (attention), or a fear of a fast-moving ball coming toward them. In this case, the coach might adjust the difficulty of the task rather than provide direct feedback.

Errors Due to Perception
Sometimes the error is due to the inability to distinguish what is relevant vs. irrelevant information. Athletes may be looking at cues that don't contribute to good performance, such as watching the ball in soccer or basketball rather than the hips of the dribbler. Errors often result when an athlete doesn't know what cues to look for in the environment. In some cases, athletes might understand what cues are relevant but fail to look at the information-rich areas where those relevant cues occur. In these cases, coaches'

feedback might be about where to look and when. Perceptual errors might also include athletes not being attuned to proprioceptive feedback from their body. The inability to sense or feel weight shift, joint angles, or speed of movement might be a cause of an error. It's worth noting that nonoptimal levels of arousal and anxiety can lead to perceptual errors. Arousal levels that are too low or too high often result in athletes "missing" the most important cues in the environment. To address these errors, coaches can modify anxiety conditions during practice as they direct attention to the important environmental information.

Errors Due to Mental Factors
Sometimes errors are due to athletes making incorrect decisions. They may be due to an ineffective focus of attention (e.g., too narrow or internal) or an inability to visualize a movement pattern. Errors may be the result of too many movement choices for athletes to make, so they missed one or selected the wrong response. For example, the volleyball setter is faced with multiple attack options, so errors are likely in decision-making. Errors might also occur because athletes have difficulty remembering or recalling solutions or concepts. They might forget to use a certain technique due to excitement or anxiety. To address these errors, coaches might use feedback that "prompts" the recall of skills previously practiced (see questioning in chapter 7), or they might adjust the decision-making difficulty (e.g., reduce the number of possible options) of the practice activity.

Errors Due to Execution
The most "obvious" type of error coaches observe are errors in technique or movement execution. Execution errors may occur because athletes haven't yet had enough practice time to establish the coordination or technique(s). Execution errors may be caused by an ineffective coordination of the movement pattern or errors in parameters or techniques (e.g., too fast or too long of a step). In general, coaches should look to address errors in the coordination first, then look to correct errors in control. For example, a pitcher who can't locate her pitch consistently (control) may need feedback related to the timing of her arm and leg movements (coordination). As well, the error might be due to an imbalance of speed and accuracy. As mentioned in chapter 6, feedback should, when possible, maintain a "full speed" emphasis.

After observation and determining the likely cause(s) of errors or mistakes, the coach is now in a better position to deliver targeted feedback. Still, providing feedback might not always be the best strategy. Should the error or mistake be corrected? We encourage coaches to ask the following questions first[11]:

1. Is the athlete capable of making the correction?
2. How much time is needed to make the correction?
3. Is the athlete motivated to make the correction?

The lack of transfer from a coach's feedback may be due to one or more of these reasons. Corrections that seek to refine or rebuild skills require a mix of time, effort, and motivation. For example, an athlete may not be motivated to make a change in their coordination the week before playoffs, as it takes too much time and may produce negative transfer to the next game.

GIVING THE FEEDBACK: THE CONTENT MATTERS

The content of the coach's feedback is of the more heavily researched areas of motor-skill learning. Below are some findings that can make feedback more transfer appropriate.

Outcome or Process Feedback?

There are two primary types of augmented feedback. One type is *outcome* feedback (called knowledge of results, or KR, in the literature). The other type is *process* feedback (called knowledge of performance, or KP, in the literature).[12] Outcome feedback is information about the results or outcome of a performance attempt (e.g., how far a person long jumped), whereas process is information about the movement characteristics that led to a particular outcome (e.g., the projection angle at takeoff in the long jump). Continuing with the long jumper, the coach might tell the athlete his foot landed 2 inches past the takeoff board (outcome), and/or the coach might tell the jumper he needs to coordinate his arm action better at takeoff (process). Which information is better to give? The short answer is, it depends. But coaches should be aware that each impacts learning differently.

Outcome feedback can be useful but is often redundant. Telling an athlete that she has missed her shot long when the outcome is clearly visible, for example, would be unnecessary. It is important for coaches to recognize and resist the temptation to verbalize the obvious, as it results in a loss of credibility and reduces athlete attention to more useful feedback when delivered. Still, outcome feedback can play an important role in skill acquisition for a few reasons. First, it can be useful to reinforce performance and motivate athletes to continue practicing. Keeping track of score improvements, for example, can be both reinforcing and motivating. Second, some research suggests that using outcome-only feedback can encourage problem-solving of movement solutions. Learners are not told how to fix the movement, so they instead explore and discover techniques for themselves. And third, outcome-only feedback is one way to encourage athletes to adopt an external focus of attention (discussed in chapter 6). Though outcome-only feedback is useful, it should be balanced it with process feedback.

Process feedback is useful when there are clear and identified movement elements, characteristics, or techniques that are necessary for success. For example, we know that a coordinated arm action is important for propelling the long jumper to longer distances, so feedback about that element is useful. Most sport skills have critical movement elements, so it's used naturally by experienced coaches (who know a lot about the skill). Process feedback from coaches can either be *descriptive* or *prescriptive*. Feedback that is *descriptive* simply detects or describes errors that were committed, while *prescriptive* feedback provides a solution, or how to correct the error on the next attempt. A coach might tell a gymnast that her back was overly arched during her last handstand (descriptive) and to further tuck the hips and hold the stomach tight during the next attempt (prescriptive). A tennis coach might provide feedback such as:

"You need more topspin when you hit the ball." (descriptive)

"Start your racket low and roll over the top of the ball when you hit." (prescriptive)

In general, prescriptive feedback is more useful for less-skilled athletes, who need the information to improve. Descriptive feedback can be useful for more-skilled athletes who understand the skill and can use the description to make their own corrections.[13] Coaches may want to encourage problem-solving in their athletes by providing descriptive feedback only and see if their athletes can fix the error(s) on their own.

Like outcome-only feedback, process feedback can be less useful in certain situations. First, providing too much of it can often overload athletes' memory and attention limits. Second, process feedback often induces an internal focus during performance, which can hurt learning and performance (see chapter 6). Third, an imbalanced amount of process feedback may not match athlete readiness. For example, a lack of prescriptive feedback can hinder learning for less-skilled athletes, and providing too much prescriptive feedback can hinder the development of error correction for more-skilled athletes. When coaches are intentional in balancing outcome and process feedback (including descriptive and prescriptive), they better facilitate the tennis player (in the example above) who can independently detect the error of topspin and make their own correction during a match.

Show and Tell the Feedback
Feedback transfers well when provided visually. The importance of a demonstration was discussed earlier (chapter 6), but it's also an effective method of providing feedback. Demonstration feedback can help with athlete memory and attention since it adds a visual element to the verbal correction. After observing the error, the coach may quickly show the athletes:

"Now, try the drop step more like this." (Coach demonstrates.)

We also encourage coaches to use *peer models* for demonstration feedback:

"Take a look at Katie and what she does with her drop step." (Katie demonstrates.) "Let's try it more like that next time, go!"

A third variation of demonstration feedback is using *comparative models*, which harnesses the power of learning models (see chapter 6):

"What do you notice about my drop step on this move?" (Coach demonstrates the error.)

"What do you notice about how this one is different?" (Coach demonstrates correctly.)

"Right! Let's go try that!"

When using demonstration feedback, we encourage coaches to plan for it and to use the same demonstration principles discussed in chapter 6. Make sure athletes can see it and focus their attention on the key elements, and be sure to keep it short and simple with one or two corrections at a time.

Actions and Aspirations[14]
An important principle to increase the motivational function of feedback is that it should be based on athletes' actions, not character flaws. Remember the adage, "Judge the action (or behavior) not the person." Compare the two feedback statements below:

"Mike, you don't hustle back on defense after a turnover."

"Mike, you didn't hustle back on defense after the turnover."

The word "don't" judges the person. It comes off as a global, enduring character flaw. The word "didn't" judges the action. It's temporary, and it can be fixed with a change in behavior. Athletes need to know that the purpose of feedback is not to judge, but to correct and make them better: "Here is what you did wrong; here is what you need to do better." It feels more respectful and is intrinsically motivating. The reinforcement of efforts and actions (not genetic abilities) also aligns with developing the all-important growth mindset and culture of learning (chapter 3).

A second method to increase the motivational function of feedback is to use challenging and aspirational content. Athletes are naturally competitive; they want to prove they can achieve things. Consider the two feedback statements below:

"Now, Thomas, can you do that quicker?"

"Your racket control is good enough now; you can try to spin the ball down the line."

The first one is a *challenge* statement. The second one is an *aspiration* statement. Both reinforce past achievement and challenge athletes to keep going with their corrections.

First, Estimate

A research-supported method to increase athlete independence in error detection and correction is to ask them to evaluate or estimate their own performance errors before receiving augmented feedback.[15] Coaches should encourage athletes to develop error-detection skills by using questioning methods that provoke reflection about their last practice attempt. After athletes provide their estimate, the coach then follows up with feedback. For example:

> "How was your knee bend that time?" (Athlete estimates.) "Yes, I agree, get lower next time."
>
> "Why do you think your throw went left?" (Athlete estimates.) "Perhaps, and it could also be your release point."

Estimating first also creates a delay between the repetition and the feedback. Compared to feedback that is provided immediately after the athlete's attempt, delaying feedback (a few seconds after the repetition) has been shown to increase learning. When feedback from an outside source is provided too soon after a repetition, athletes are prevented from interpreting and evaluating their own intrinsic feedback (e.g., vision, proprioception) relative to the outcome. They instead defer to the coach's error detection and correction.[16]

Initially, athletes might have difficulty reflecting on their errors. Coaches who use questioning in their instruction (see chapter 6) and facilitate two-way communication (see chapter 2) will find it easier to use this feedback method. If athletes have difficulty estimating errors to begin with, coaches can start with either/or questions such as, "Do you think your ball went left because of body position or arm angle?" Ultimately, the goal is for athletes to independently assess and adjust their own performances. The estimations-first method facilitates the type of cognitive effort important for transfer—independent error detection and correction.

GIVING THE FEEDBACK: NOT TOO MUCH

A misconception about feedback is that more is better; it should be provided as often as possible. To the contrary, research shows that athletes learn better when the frequency or amount of feedback is strategically reduced. Too-frequent feedback reduces the amount of athlete thinking and problem-solving, and creates passive learning conditions. While high amounts of feedback can guide athletes to correct performance in practice, performance can suffer when feedback is no longer available (e.g., during the game).[17] Guiding a learner toward successful performance (with feedback) while at the same time creating a dependency on it has clear implications for the transfer of learning. Coaches should provide an optimal amount of feedback that facilitates athletes' learning of independent error detection and correction.

So, how much feedback should the coach give? As usual, it depends! The general rule of thumb is that feedback frequency should be adjusted to the athletes' level of readiness. Younger or less-skilled athletes need higher amounts of process feedback, and that amount should be reduced, or faded, as expertise increases. When coaches introduce new skills or variations to existing skills, feedback should be more frequent and faded to lower amounts as practice continues. Fading the frequency of feedback as athletes develop skill is a way to manage practice difficulty and create optimal challenge. There are a few research-supported methods to systematically reduce the amount of feedback to maximize transfer.[18]

Summarize the Feedback

One strategy is to provide feedback in a *summary* form. In this approach, the coach saves their feedback and provides it to the athlete after a certain number of trials. For example, the coach provides feedback to the less-skilled athlete after watching three repetitions. For the more-skilled athlete, coaches may summarize their feedback after watching 10 trials. The coach predetermines the summary length based on skill difficulty and/or athlete readiness. The reduced frequency (also delayed) is designed to facilitate athletes' interpretation of their own feedback and problem-solving before getting the coach's feedback. The summary feedback can be provided to the athlete as an average or general representation of performance—for example, "Overall you were stepping too far"—or about performance on each repetition—for example, "You stepped too far on your first three repetitions, and too short on your last two."

Bandwidth the Feedback

We recommend a second strategy, called *bandwidth* feedback. In this approach, the coach predetermines a range of "correctness" for performing a skill. Athletes are informed of this bandwidth and are told they will get feedback when their performance is outside the bandwidth (incorrect, outside the range of correctness). If the athlete gets no feedback or hears nothing after a repetition, then it was "correct" (or within the range).

Let's provide an example. We recently watched a high school baseball coach conduct a practice session on controlling the speed of the "changeup" pitch compared to the fast ball. The changeup is a pitch that looks like a fastball to the hitter but is thrown 5–10 mph slower than a fastball. Common mistakes are throwing the changeup at speeds too fast (too close to fastball speed) or too slow (too far from fastball speed). The coach gave feedback to pitchers using a radar gun measuring the speed of the changeup (outcome feedback) relative to their fastball speed. Below is an example of bandwidth feedback provided to "Gus," a pitcher who performed 10 changeup pitches (between fastball pitches). The coach established a bandwidth of 66–70 mph based on Gus's fastball average of 75 mph. He alerted Gus to the bandwidth and that he would receive feedback if his pitch speed was outside the range. Hearing no feedback meant Gus was within range of a good pitch speed. An "X" on the chart shows he performed outside the bandwidth and received feedback (pitch speed, or mph) on that trial.

Drill: Control changeup speeds (using circle change technique)

Pitcher: Gus

Fastball Average: 75 mph

Pitch speeds *(changeups, 10 reps)*	*Bandwidth: 66–70 mph* *(target range)*
1. 74 mph	X
2. 72 mph	X
3. 69 mph	
4. 64 mph	X
5. 65 mph	X
6. 69 mph	
7. 68 mph	
8. 64 mph	X
9. 69 mph	
10. 67 mph	

Notice the reduced frequency of the feedback provided (trials with X). Gus received feedback a total of five times, or 50 percent of the time (10 reps). As well, notice the fading of the feedback. As he improved his speed control (in the range), he received less feedback. The important point is the coach resisted providing explicit or direct feedback after every trial. In doing so, he likely facilitated more independence and problem-solving in Gus. As well, he provided implicit feedback that *reinforced* Gus's successful attempts—he knew that if he received no feedback, he was performing correctly. This can increase confidence and motivation—important for shaping behavior.

The bandwidth method is particularly effective for other reasons. First, it can be individualized to match with athlete readiness. The boundaries of the bandwidth could be adjusted to athlete skill level to increase (less skilled) or decrease (more skilled) the frequency of feedback. Second, it has more potential to shape behavior with its "hidden" reinforcement function. When the athlete does not receive feedback (performance within the bandwidth), it serves as reinforcement that they are performing successfully. Ironically, the no-feedback trials are providing feedback to shape the desired behavior!

Advance toward Independence

As athletes gain skill, coaches should begin to shift the control of feedback frequency to the athletes. Evidence supports increased learning when athletes self-control their feedback frequency. In these practice conditions, rather than the coach determining when to provide feedback, athletes choose when they receive it, getting it only by request. They request feedback to reinforce their successes and/or correct their errors. Interestingly, research shows that athletes who self-control when they receive feedback often seek *increased* amounts of feedback compared to athletes who practice with traditional coach-controlled feedback. Benefits of self-controlled feedback include: athletes being more actively involved in the learning process; increased attention to the feedback; increased memory; and increased autonomy, perceived competence, and intrinsic motivation.[19]

While it may take awhile for athletes and coaches to adopt self-controlled feedback, some coaches have found success with specific methods. Some use *small-group sessions* where players are working on the same skill(s) and feedback is shared among players and coaches. In these situations, discovering solutions is a shared endeavor and a form of self-controlled feedback.[20] For example, the coach can ask one of the players who is observing, "What did you see there?" One player might share with another player, "Here's what I am trying, and it seems to work." By sharing feedback, athletes are building knowledge together, and it's an effective way to individualize and personalize practice that can increase learning. A second method uses video-feedback stations for athletes to access during practice. Stations can be set up with the coach present to provide guidance, in small groups or individually, with skill checklists. Video-feedback stations can show a variety of models, including an individual athlete, a peer model, an expert model, or learning models. A particularly effective technique is to provide a comparative model by request, for example, a split screen showing learning and skilled models. Self-controlled feedback often requires patience from the coach and experience from the athlete (e.g., knowing what to ask). The learning advantages may not show up immediately during practice but become more visible as athletes gain skill and when they perform the skill in new situations (transfer).[21]

CLOSE THE FEEDBACK LOOP
Good feedback has the athlete using the information to change future behavior. To increase the likelihood of the feedback being used in the future, the coach needs to close the feedback loop.[22] The feedback loop checks to see if the athlete "got it" and if the coach's feedback was "any good." The loop consists of:

> Coach Gives Feedback—Athlete Tries It—Athlete Reflects—Coach Reinforces or Redirects

Let's highlight the importance of the feedback loop with an example. Recently, we observed a softball coach give solid feedback to a player about footwork for fielding a ground ball from the shortstop position:

> Coach: "Tia, make sure to field the ball off your front foot as you move toward first."
>
> Tia: "I got it coach." (Nodding her head positively)

The coach moved on to watch other players, continuing to provide useful feedback to several players. But we stuck around to watch. In Tia's next five repetitions, she fielded the ball off the front foot only one time; the other four times she went back to fielding it off her back foot. In the observation above, the feedback was provided but the player did not learn from it. Closing the feedback loop may be the most overlooked elements of feedback. Well-intentioned coaches are often thinking of their next move. In this case, the coach was looking to give helpful feedback to more players (admirable) and failed to check if the first player learned from the original feedback. Let's pick it back up and help our coach close the loop:

Tia: "I got it coach." (Nodding her head positively)

Coach: "Ok, now show me. . . . Not quite, show me again. . . . That's it. Did you feel the difference?"

Tia: "Yes, but it feels a lot slower now."

Coach: "That makes sense; staying down low might help the speed."

In the feedback loop, athletes should try out the correction immediately and then reflect on the new action. Trying it immediately allows the athlete to use it while fresh in memory and reduces the chances the feedback will be ignored, forgotten, or misunderstood. Reflecting on the correction provides a delay that increases active learning and problem-solving. Following the reflection, the coach can either confirm or redirect the athlete's correction. Closing the feedback loop helps athletes transfer more of the coach's feedback. It may help prevent the frustration that occurs when coaches know they have corrected something but athletes don't use it later. As a deliberate effort to observe and check for understanding, it holds both players and coaches accountable for making feedback more effective.

TRANSFER THIS

Let's return to our two hitting instructors soliciting parents to work with their young baseball players. Which one would you hire? Assuming everything else was equivalent between the two instructors, we endorse the approach offered by instructor 2. He seems to embrace the role of feedback for transfer—to develop independent, problem-solving athletes who can detect and correct their own errors. He doesn't want athletes to be dependent on him to make their own hitting adjustments. This instructor likely has developed good observation skills. We bet he has developed skill checklists and can anticipate errors in hitting. He probably is good at individualizing and targeting his feedback by identifying why errors are occurring in each hitter (using the five categories of error). It's likely this instructor uses a blend of indirect and direct feedback to shape behavior and balances process and outcome feedback that corrects errors, motivates, and reinforces his hitters. To facilitate the independence he speaks of, he probably reduces the amount of direct feedback and instead uses methods such as summary or bandwidth feedback. As well, he might delay his feedback, encouraging hitters to engage in their own error detection by using methods like athlete estimation and questioning. It appears the coach holds both himself and his hitter accountable for learning from feedback (feedback loop). Finally, it appears that this instructor's feedback is advancing athletes toward independence (important for transfer). And since research shows athletes who choose their feedback schedule often request *more* feedback, we think he will do just fine financially, as players might return for lessons on their own accord for more feedback. For the parents, it looks to be money well spent.

Coaches, Transfer This
1. View feedback from a perspective of shaping behavior. Provide a blend of direct, brief, and targeted feedback with indirect task and environment modifications that can shape behavior. Blend feedback that functions to correct, motivate, and reinforce behaviors, and be deliberate and balanced with feedback around these functions. Practice delivering feedback using the "feedback sandwich."
2. Hone the skills of watching before providing feedback. Develop skill checklists, observe, and anticipate errors. See if you can differentiate between what a good and a great performance looks like, and identify *why* you see the error (using the five categories of error) before delivering feedback.
3. Provide a mix of outcome and process feedback, as well as prescriptive and descriptive. Avoid redundant outcome feedback and offering too much process/prescriptive feedback that can overload athletes and overly direct athlete attention internally (vs. externally).
4. Have athletes estimate their performance errors prior to giving feedback. Use demonstrations to deliver feedback, and challenge athletes to fix specific actions (not genetic traits).

5. Use methods that decrease athlete dependence on coach feedback and increase independent problem-solving. These include reducing feedback frequency with strategies such as summary and bandwidth feedback, closing the feedback loop, and incorporating more athlete self-control of feedback.

Coach Educators and Developers, Transfer This
1. If possible, have coaches choose a skill, make a checklist with cues, and then videotape a practice activity. View the practice activity and take notes (digital or paper/pen) on players' skill performance using the checklist. Ask coaches to classify their feedback as process, outcome, descriptive or prescriptive.
2. Review figure 8.1 and the possible causes of motor-skill errors. Have coaches choose one or two important skills in their sport. Reflect (anticipate) on the causes of error in that skill(s) by addressing the question, "Why am I seeing this mistake?" Use the five causes of error categories (see figure 8.1) and fill in according to the skill(s) you chose.
3. Have coaches practice writing four different feedback statements—outcome, process, prescriptive, and descriptive feedback statements. Check to see if your outcome statement is redundant with what athletes already get from their intrinsic feedback. Show examples of a "Coach Obvious" who provides ineffective feedback (e.g., www.classicseagles.com/news_article/show/1174715). Facilitate a discussion on types of feedback statements and when to best use them.
4. Have coaches practice designing bandwidth feedback and sandwich feedback. Refer to the earlier sandwich and bandwidth examples (e.g., Gus; see figure 8.1). If possible, have coaches demonstrate and share their sandwich and bandwidth feedback methods.
5. Have coaches role-play situations of providing effective feedback. This might include, among others: (a) using demonstration feedback, (b) using athlete estimations before feedback, or (c) closing the feedback loop. Did they role-play effectively, and what can be improved?

9

The Games That Transfer

Coach Jones, a middle school basketball coach, designed a practice session to work on the skills of boxing out and rebounding. He demonstrated and explained the key elements of the boxing out and securing the rebound. He designed several structured and isolated block-out drills (e.g., no-ball contact drill, 3-second keep-out drill) where players took turns executing the key techniques. He delivered quality feedback during the drills, and the players showed significant improvement. During the drills, Coach Jones felt really good about their rebounding skills, and he told his players to apply them in the scrimmage at the end of practice. During the scrimmage, Coach Jones was dismayed to see that very few of the players executed their practiced rebounding techniques during the scrimmage. Too, those who looked the best in the drills were the ones who executed most poorly in the scrimmage!

We close the book by saving the best for last. We argue that nothing offers more potential for transfer than a good game! We remember (and you might too) our favorite tag, wiffleball, or kickball games as children. We chose our equipment, modified the rules, and set the field dimensions. We chose even teams and changed things up so that the competition was fair. We made trades, shortened the bases, and changed the scoring. Most of the time, we played for a long, long time, and it was fun! Of course, things are different now—we are the coaches, and our job is to design high-quality purposeful practice. How can we design practice so that our athletes experience the joy of those childhood games, yet are equipped to compete successfully in the competitive sport environment? If we could only find the balance between intrinsically fun play and high-level learning (and transfer).

This chapter explores the transfer of learning benefits of a games-based approach (GBA) to practice. It is contrasted with the traditional drills approach (TDA). First, we ask coaches to review table 9.1, which shows elements of two different practice plans for soccer dribbling and passing (A and B). After reviewing, take the pretest, answering the questions below.

Pretest Questions
1. Which practice looks more enjoyable (A or B)? Why?
2. Which practice better develops athletes' technical, tactical, and mental skills (A or B)? Why?
3. Which practice better engages athletes mentally and with more touches/repetitions (A or B)? Why?

Practice A is an example of a traditional drills approach. Practice B is an example of a games-based approach. Let's compare the key differences between the two practice approaches.[1]

COMPARING THE TDA AND THE GBA PRACTICE SESSION

The TDA is a coach-centered "skills first, game second" approach which seeks to isolate the development of technical skills through a combination of coach-led instructions, demonstrations, feedback, isolated skill drills, and scrimmages. In a typical TDA practice session:

1. The coach conveys skill information to the athlete via verbal instructions and demonstrations of the best technique(s).
2. Athletes take turns practicing the skill in isolated and controlled drill(s).
3. The coach provides corrective feedback about the technique(s) and athletes make corrections.
4. Players participate in more complex or advanced drill(s), again receiving corrective feedback from the coach.
5. Athletes apply their practiced techniques to a scrimmage at the end of practice.

Table 9.1. Comparison of traditional drills approach (practice A) to games-based approach (practice B). After reviewing, answer the pretest questions.

	Practice A: Soccer Dribbling and Passing		Practice B: Soccer Dribbling and Passing	
	Practice Activity	*Coaching Points*	*Practice Activity*	*Coaching Points*
3:00–3:15	Warm-up laps and team stretch Light jog two laps Static stretching	Review and demonstrate effective dribbling and passing during static stretching	Half-speed zone run and dynamic stretching Dribble tag (2 dribblers) Keep-away (pass and dribble in circle, keep ball from getting stolen by 2 players in the middle)	Cues: • Quick movements • Look up • Keep ball close • Crisp passes Question: What strategies worked or didn't work for you?
3:15–3:30	*Slalom dribble drill* Four lines of four take turns Cones 10 feet apart Change cone distances Practice different turn angles (e.g., 180 degrees) Move faster through the cones	Instep control Touch and speed Use both feet Keep ball close Head up Inside-outside touches Stop and demonstrate best techniques	*Heads-up activity* Players dribble randomly in penalty area and call out number of fingers coach holds up Change zone size to manage challenge Rotate players in and out at 30-second intervals Other players watch with questions	Cues: • Keep moving • Seek open areas • Keep the ball close • Change speeds when seeking space Players watching: • What do you notice about ball control when other players get close? • Are they changing speeds when moving to open spaces?

(continued)

Table 9.1. *Continued*

	Practice A: Soccer Dribbling and Passing		Practice B: Soccer Dribbling and Passing	
	Practice Activity	*Coaching Points*	*Practice Activity*	*Coaching Points*
3:30–3:45	Partner pass and move drill Two lines with partner in other line Take turns advancing ball down field by passing ball back and forth with partner to end of field No more than two touches before passing Change speeds; start moving faster	Pass with good pace Use instep Lead partner with passes Keep close to body, within 2 feet, before pass Stop to show good partner-passing techniques	2 on 2 game Multiple 15 × 20 yard grids All players play at same time in separate areas Advance ball past end line, then opposing team takes possession and attacks Scoring past end line earns 2 points, three consecutive passes earn 1 point Play 2-minute games, rotating grids to play different teams; 1-minute rest between games	Pause and question: • Are you keeping ball close and changing speeds? • What are you looking at when ball is being passed? • How did you anticipate the defender? • What were the passing options? • How do you know when to pass or dribble? What are you reading?

The GBA, in its simplest terms, designs games and activities to look and feel more like the real game or competition. It is an athlete-centered "learn skills through competitive games" approach that balances technical skill development with tactical and mental skills development. In a typical GBA practice session:

1. The coach identifies the target skills and behaviors to be learned, or the practice session's intent, and how they can be practiced in the context of a game environment.

2. The coach designs a game or activity that facilitates athletes' discovering solutions to the targeted skills or behaviors. Game constraints are manipulated so that skills are practiced with perceptual and tactical aspects of the game intact.
3. The coach focuses the players during game play through a series of pauses and questions to highlight important areas of performance (technical, tactical, mental skills).
4. The coach carefully observes and continues to modify game elements that match athlete readiness and facilitate achievement of target skills and behaviors.
5. The coach enhances game play by creating additional challenges that simulate skills needed in game-like competitive situations.

When implemented effectively, the GBA holds more potential for the transfer of practice conditions to the game. But why?

WHY THE GBA BETTER FACILITATES TRANSFER OF LEARNING[2]

We highlight the "Top 10" reasons for coaches to implement the GBA. They might look familiar; they reinforce theories and concepts emphasized throughout this book (e.g., the purpose of practice, chapter 1).

1. *Coach Centered vs. Athlete Centered.* The TDA is coach controlled. The coach makes all decisions about the drills, the techniques, and the corrections for the skill(s). It typically uses the command style of coaching. The GBA is more athlete centered—the coach uses more cooperative coaching, balancing directing athletes with allowing athletes to direct themselves. Athletes are encouraged to discover movement solutions at their own level of readiness.
2. *Reproduction vs. Adaptability.* The TDA focuses on reproducing an ideal movement model or the "perfect" technique. An emphasis on reproduction often occurs at the expense of learning to adapt the skill to the dynamic and competitive environment. The GBA emphasizes skill acquisition through developing adaptable movement solutions to fit the dynamic competitive environment (e.g., opponents' action, speed of play, fatigue).

3. *Complete Skill Development.* The TDA emphasizes development of the technical skills and techniques. It often neglects the tactical and mental aspects of skill development, which limits the transfer of practice. The GBA emphasizes learning tactical and mental skills while practicing and applying the technical skills. Technical skills are often practiced while simulating targeted perceptual (e.g., anticipation) and mental (e.g., anxiety) elements required for game performance.
4. *Engagement, Discovery, and Learning.* A Ben Franklin quote applies: "Tell me and I forget, teach me and I may remember, involve me and I learn." The TDA tells and teaches athletes skills and restricts athlete engagement in the learning process. The GBA, through game play, discovery, and questioning, increases athlete participation and engagement during practice, which is fundamental for transfer of learning.
5. *Isolation vs. Integration.* The TDA often isolates skills to be practiced separately from other skills. However, successful game performance often depends on how skills are executed in combination with other skills. Effective passing in soccer depends on whether you are passing off a dribble, off a stop, or with advancing defenders. The GBA encourages learning of skills in an integrated fashion; athletes practice connected skills similar to those required in the game.
6. *Perception-Action Link.* The TDA often "de-couples" the execution of the skill from the game-like environmental information available (e.g., cones, lines, one at a time). As such, skills and movement solutions are often learned out of context, and are less likely to be transferred. The GBA facilitates athletes' perceptual skills and the solution of movement problems in environments more "representative" of the competitive environment.
7. *Dependence vs. Independence.* In the TDA, athletes depend on the coach for their skill development. They are told the techniques to use, what they are doing wrong, and how to correct their errors. The GBA, through game shaping and focusing, encourages athletes to discover mistakes and explore better solutions. This transfers well to the competition, where they must problem-solve and perform independently.
8. *Communication.* The TDA relies on one-way communication of the coach delivering explicit and direct instruction, so it may not enhance coach–athlete communication. The GBA uses play stoppages and questioning

in ways that facilitate two-way communication. The GBA also facilitates intra-athlete communication, as they talk and work together to achieve the game's objectives; this transfers well to the competition.

9. *Sense of the Game.* Since the TDA encourages athletes to reproduce skills in closed or controlled environments, athletes engage in less game-like thinking and decision-making. The GBA requires athletes to make skill adjustments and change strategy or tactics based on changing dynamics and within the "chaos" of the game. The GBA is viewed as a method to create "thinking" players with a sense of the game; they can sense where to go and when. This "game sense" can be improved through a compilation of game-based learning experiences.[3]

10. *Challenge, Motivation, and Enjoyment.* Since it is drill based, the TDA often uses repetitive or boring practice activities that are less interesting and motivating for athletes. In GBA, players are challenged to refine and apply skills in a variety of competition-like situations. When coaches shape games to match athlete readiness, they are likely to find the optimal *challenge point* for athletes, or the *sweet spot* where motivation and enjoyment is maximized.

Barriers to the GBA

Despite the clear benefits of the GBA for transfer of learning, the TDA remains a popular approach for many coaches and practice environments. It's helpful here to understand why more coaches stick with the TDA rather than moving toward the GBA.

First, the traditional emphasis on the technical aspects of sport performance is strong. Search the Internet and you will most readily find a plethora of drills and skill breakdowns to help coaches and athletes learn the ideal technique(s). As well, coaching clinics and teaching aids sold on the market emphasize technical solutions to coaching skills. The popular clichés "fundamentals first," "muscle memory," "perfect practice makes perfect" reinforce the TDA. We are encouraged to design drills and purchase products that perfect the ideal technique(s). The related assumption is that the fundamentals must first be acquired (through repetitive drilling) before playing games.

Second, the lure of immediate gratification is more prevalent in the TDA. Observable and more immediate improvement is likely since coaches are controlling the drills and offering instruction and feedback to master the skill(s). It can look like great teaching and coaching, as athletes are coached to get the drill right. On the other hand, the GBA has more "chaos," with starts and stops, a lot of questioning, players moving unpredictably, and frequent errors or mistakes. There is significant trial and error, and improvement is more gradual. The GBA can require patience and a long-term development perspective. Practical aspects, such as limited practice time or parental pressures, can also play a role in a coach's desire to see immediate improvements. Regardless, it's difficult for many coaches to see the GBA's return on investment since it takes time and patience; athletes coached via the GBA may acquire the technical skills a little slower, but when they do, their higher level of "game sense" facilitates more transfer to the game.[4]

Third, there is a prevalent image and perception of what a great coach "looks like." They move about practice providing high amounts of verbal instructions and feedback to fix athlete mistakes as they see them. They are often loud and direct and are clearly in control of practice conditions. On the other hand, the GBA coach may look less engaged, as they shape and manipulate game elements indirectly or behind the scenes. Rather than provide answers, they ask athletes questions. They may know the answer(s) to performance problems, but they want athletes to discover and experience them. The GBA often requires a higher level of knowledge, planning, and understanding of skill development and transfer of learning—it just may not "look" that way—and an entry-level coach often feels the pressure to look and act like a coach in control.

Finally, the "linear" and controlled method of skill development is easier for entry-level coaches to conceptualize. Planning and preparation of the TDA is straightforward. Practices or drills are planned around a single focus. Isolating skills and simplifying environments make it easier to control and give skill corrections and feedback. The TDA offers a "tight" and predictable structure: a controlled warm-up drill, followed by isolated technique drills, stopping frequently to give feedback, followed by more complex drills, and culminating in a scrimmage. There is a simplicity to the teaching and organization, and it is relatively easy to plan and replicate.[5] We provide an example of why less-experienced coaches tend to gravitate toward the TDA:

Long ago as a graduate student, one of the authors of this book was asked to teach a new sport for which she had no background—fencing. She prepared by studying the fundamental techniques and movements, watching skilled performers, identifying the essential teaching cues, and planning the fundamental drills. She developed a great lesson plan of skill drills that culminated in a modified fencing activity. However, her lesson lost momentum when the students started asking questions during the drills such as, "How do I know when to lunge?" "What should I be looking at, their foil or their arm?" "What happens if my opponent comes in from a different direction?" Along with being unprepared to answer the questions, she began to wonder about the isolated nature of her drills, and if there might be a better approach to practice and learning.

Our author was drawn to the linear nature of skill development, and she adopted the traditional approach, likely because her knowledge base was fairly limited to the technical skills of the sport and her focus was on improving those skills. The author/instructor would have been much more likely to teach field hockey or softball using the GBA approach, given her extensive knowledge of game principles and strategic concepts in those sports. While it's natural for less-confident coaches to gravitate toward the TDA, we recommend the GBA be implemented as early as possible. It can be implemented progressively, as coaches grow more comfortable with their knowledge and shaping the "chaos" of the practice games. And less-experienced coaches can successfully implement the GBA, and we provide this guidance next.

IMPLEMENTING THE GBA

As much as possible, practice activities should provide players with opportunities to learn how the real game works. While repetitions are important for technical skill development (see chapter 7), the GBA emphasizes repetitions of technical skills in perceptually rich environments that help develop game-like tactical and mental skills. Transfer is increased because the skills practiced are more like the competition (see chapter 5). From our earlier discussion of practice representativeness and perception-action coupling, the key principle for implementing the GBA is that the information available to the athlete in the practice environment should resemble the information available in the game environment. A well-accepted process for implementing the GBA is to *shape, focus,* and *enhance* the games.[6]

Shape the Game

We highlight some important elements for coaches to consider in *shaping* the game to be more "competition like."

Identify the Game-Like Behaviors, Skills, or Actions

Remember, coaches are teaching through the game. What does the coach want to reinforce or see more frequently? These are a blend of technical, tactical, and mental skills. For example, in basketball, the coach might identify the following skills to be developed through the game:

> *Technical:* Crisp passing and receiving techniques (bounce passes and entry passes)
>
> *Tactical:* Floor balance and moving without the ball (with a specific purpose)
>
> *Mental:* Handle pressure and anxiety of time constraints (shot clock); see the whole floor

Distort or Manipulate Aspects of the Game (Constraints)

Once the practice intentions are clear (see above), the coach works on manipulating the practice activity. As discussed in chapter 4, the STEPS approach to manipulating constraints can also apply to shaping the game. These include *Space, Task, People, Equipment,* and *Speed*. The coach strategically distorts key aspects of the game (constraints) so that certain behaviors are practiced more often. Examples of common distortions, or constraint manipulations, to increase game-like behaviors include:

1. Using fewer players, such as two-on-two or four-on-four lacrosse games, to increase touches and use of tactics and gain confidence.
2. Imbalanced numbers of players in a three-on-two fast-break basketball activity to facilitate increased spacing and seeing the whole floor.
3. Larger grid or zone for three-on-two field hockey game to practice the concept of passing and receiving in passing lanes and to manage anxiety.
4. Modify scoring in a game to reward 2 points for successful box outs to facilitate a mental focus on rebounds and the visual search of players to box out.

5. Restriction that defenders must remain within certain parts of the grid, but attackers can move freely in soccer, to encourage more offensive movements and team communication.

In short, constraints are shaped to make the practice environment more representative of the real game. We point to an interesting video that shows how modifying the equipment (low ball compression and larger racquet sizes) and space (court size and zones) in youth tennis can make the practice look and feel like the real game: https://www.youtube.com/watch?v=3IbzcttoDuY.

Redesign Drills

Many traditional drills encourage movements that are not very game-like, and they do little to practice tactical and mental skills. Coaches can shape practice by considering how drills might be modified to be more game-like. Table 9.2 provides three examples of how coaches can redesign drills to align with the GBA.

Small-Sided Games

One of the more common ways to shape the game is by using small-sided games (SSGs).[7] Sometimes called small-area games (SAGs) or conditioned games, they have become increasingly popular and are used by a variety of sports-governing bodies in hockey (e.g., USA Hockey), soccer, basketball, tennis, etc. We encourage coaches to search the Internet for small-sided game ideas. Even if not in your sport, you can adapt some of the ideas to fit your sport. Note the key elements of any SSG:

1. Decreasing the number of players participating and the space in which the game is played. This generally results in more touches or repetitions and a greater focus on the target behavior(s).
2. Maintaining the fundamental mental and tactical elements of the game. Keeping the competitive aspects of the game (e.g., against other players) to encourage game-like mental skills (e.g., pressure). Retaining also the foundational, tactical aspects of the game (e.g., attacking, defending, spacing) to encourage game-like decision-making and problem-solving.

Table 9.2. Examples of redesigning traditional drills into games-based activities.

Traditional Drills	Redesigned Games
Baseball batting practice	*Baseball batting activity*
Each player rotates to do 3 bunts then 15 full swings. Other players are positioned around the infield and outfield, returning balls to bucket and ball collector behind the pitcher's mound.	Each player gets six pitches to hit, one must be a bunt. Other players are at their fielding positions. Additional players are baserunners to create game-like situations. Fielders make the play on each hit, executing both the appropriate technical (make the play), tactical (to the right base), and mental (focus) responses. Coach creates game-like situations players must solve (e.g., puts runner on second with one out).
	Questions: Strategies and tactics (e.g., Why should the cutoff man be at this location and not the other one?)
Soccer agility drill	*Soccer agility game*
Each player takes turns doing zigzag through cones at a fast pace. Repeat five times. Feedback: Work on changing directions quickly, getting low, and accelerating.	Tag game: Players move in a 20 x 30 zone without getting tagged. Tagger scores 1 point for tags made in 30 seconds. Add variations to increase fast and agile movements: two taggers, dribble ball, freeze and release tag, etc. Repeat game five times.
	Questions: How can you best keep space around you? How do you best avoid getting tagged? How can tagger make more tags? How can you trick or mislead your opponent?
Basketball box-out drill	*Basketball box-out game*
3-second box-out drill	Rack up rebounding drill
https://www.youtube.com/watch?v=qBPgi9hdeVw	https://www.basketballforcoaches.com/box-out-drills/
Place ball on a cone in the lane. Four players partner up and position themselves 10 feet from the ball/cone. On the whistle, one player turns to box out the other player, who tries to get to the ball. The goal is for the player boxing out to keep the player from getting to the ball for 5 seconds. Feedback: Pivot to make contact; elbows out to feel player; keep contact; body position	One player will continuously shoot from the top of the key while four players (2 on 2) battle to secure rebounds. When a player rebounds the basketball, they receive 1 point for their team and then must immediately pass the ball out to the shooter who will shoot again. The team who accumulates 10 points first is the winner. Variations: shoot from different spots on the court; change number of players, e.g., three on three or four on four; modify scoring, e.g., 2 points for defensive rebound and 1 point for offensive rebound.
	Questions: Where are you looking to predict where the ball will come off the rim? What techniques best help you keep contact with your player?

Designed effectively, the specific benefits of the SSG become clear. Smaller fields and fewer players afford more repetitions with technical skills like protecting the ball, passing, moving, defending dribblers, and shooting. But the increased repetitions are not just technical. With SSGs, players get more practice:

1. Making decisions and problem-solving in the chaos of the game.
2. Working with teammates to communicate, cooperate, and discover team-oriented solutions (e.g., adapting to teammate strengths and weaknesses).
3. Reading the game and anticipating (e.g., the game sense of being in the right place at the right time).
4. Being creative with techniques and strategies that can help game performance.

Table 9.3 provides examples of two SSGs. In each game, the space and number of players are distorted, and the rules/scoring facilitate the targeted skills while retaining fundamental game-like elements of competition and tactics.

Closer analysis reveals the two games in table 9.3 may differ in their transfer value. The SSG "counterattack" (field hockey) is highly representative of the game environment and is likely to yield high transfer of learning.[8] The perceptual information available to the athletes is very similar to that of a game. "Slick shot" (basketball) is less representative of the real game.[9] It distorts game elements to a larger degree. For example, it removes dribbling for the offense and stealing for the defense, both of which are valuable sources of information available to players in the real game. Offensive players need practice making decisions about whether to shoot or dribble, and defensive players need to practice deciding when to intercept or go for a steal. As much as possible, the game should include game-like decision-making. So, while we like the slick shot game for manipulating key constraints to develop target skills, all games are not created equally, and coaches should find ways to make this game more representative of the game environment as players become more proficient (e.g., allow steals by the defense).

Avoid "Over-Shaping" Games
In chapter 4 (designing practice), we advised coaches to avoid manipulating or "over-constraining" practice activities in ways that decrease game-like

Table 9.3. Examples of small-sided games (SSGs).

Field Hockey SSG: "Counterattack" (4 on 4) Target Behaviors: Skill in tackling and interceptions Manage attack after transitions in possession Manage counterattacks after transitions in possessions	Rules: Pitch boundaries narrowed/funneled toward the goal to reduce space and increase numbers of tackles, interceptions, and transitions in possession. Other side of field pitch boundaries opened to facilitate a larger space to attack after transition of possession. Points awarded for dissolving a counterattack opportunity and for goals. 4- to 5-minute game blocks.
Basketball SSG: "Slick Shot" 3 (offensive) vs. 2 (defensive) players Target Behaviors: Defensive pressure and rotations Offensive passing and ball movement	Rules: Playing area is inside the 3-point line bounded by the baseline. Offensive players may not dribble, and they may only receive the ball in the designated area (inside 3-point line). Defensive players may only intercept the pass; they cannot steal the ball from the offensive players. Offense scores 1 point for each unguarded (3-ft. distance away) shot, 2 points for making the shot. Defense scores points for intercepting the ball or forcing offensive team to make more than three passes. Keep score, playing each game to 10.

similarity. Remember, changing game constraints forces players to behave a certain way. Some constraints may force behaviors that are not similar to the game. The slick shot game is somewhat guilty of over-shaping, as discussed above. Two other examples are the "minimum of five passes" rule in basketball, soccer, or field hockey. The intent is to encourage players to develop passing skills such as looking up to find open players and moving into position to pass and receive. As well, the "two-touch only" rule is to encourage players to move the ball forward quickly and not over-dribble. Both conditions remove the decision-making about when to pass early or when to hold on to the ball. Players are not actively searching the environment for information that best informs these decisions. Their perception of the environment is constrained in ways that are dissimilar to the game. In addition, the *defenders* are also deprived of game-like perception and decision-making. In the two-touch rule, once the attacker has touched the ball the first time, the defender knows a pass is coming next and stops actively solving the problem of "what's the attacker going to do next?" So, while the shaping (rule constraints) of the game develops target behaviors, it can inadvertently facilitate decision-making and problem-solving that is *not* game-like.[10]

Recall from chapter 4 (designing practice) the value of the common soccer *platform* activity called "rondos." We come back to it here as a great example of an SSG. The game involves a group of players (e.g., 4 to 5) with a numerical advantage playing keep-away from opponents (e.g., 2 to 3) in the middle. The objective is for the players with the ball to keep it within their team without the players in the middle intercepting it. While the number of players involved varies, you will often see three vs. one, five vs. two, or seven vs. three rondos, and sometimes a whole team can be involved. The drill offers endless variations that can be shaped to improve both skill (e.g., passing and receiving) and perception (e.g., head up and eyes ahead, determine/anticipate space, judge speed of pass). Coaches can easily extend the drill to small-sided games to add more game-like variations, which can be distorted to focus on whatever game element(s) the coach identifies. For example, some coaches use it to improve receiving a pass under pressure, protecting and retaining possession, or reading the defense. As stated on the *Soccer Coaching Pro* website:

> In general, rondos help with your decision-making, creativity, passing abilities, and overall teamwork although there are a plethora of other skills you'll also develop through playing this fun game.[11]

The website offers multiple variations (9) of the rondo so that coaches can progressively make it more difficult and/or game-like or use it to distort specific game aspects. With a little creativity, coaches can use a similar design for other sports to teach technical, tactical, and mental skills. Finally, rondos align well with the importance of designing optimal challenges, as athletes can progress from lower-difficulty individual games (1 on 1) to more complex team play (e.g., 4 on 4) to overloaded challenge situations (e.g., 3 on 4).

Focus the Game

The game is the best teacher.

We agree with the above quote, but it needs some clarification. Coaches using the GBA have a more cooperative (vs. command) style of coaching; they guide players to discover solutions and make better decisions. The GBA repositions the coach as a skilled facilitator of athlete learning and performance. By itself, the game won't teach athletes all the techniques, tactics, and decision-making skills they will need to transfer. The best learning occurs when the coach is actively involved as a teacher. The effectiveness of the GBA depends largely on how coaches *focus* the game after they have shaped it. In shaping the game, coaches manipulate constraints in ways that "do much of the talking" for the coach. This does not mean coaches stop teaching or remain silent during the game(s). Within game play, coaches can help focus it in ways that maximize learning, and we provide some key elements of focusing the game below.

Focus Players' Attention on What You Want to See
Direct your athletes to the behaviors, game elements, and skills you want them to learn. They may not always understand what the game is trying to distort or teach. What are the key elements of the game you will be looking for during the game? Providing brief explanations about the purpose of the game and labeling the key elements of game concepts or skills can be helpful. Clear labels (e.g., "push forward") of the desired elements help athletes' working memory and retrieval when you pause play later to question them.

Create "Pause Moments"
The GBA is all about the coach stopping or pausing to help facilitate more effective solutions, perceptions, and tactical decisions.[12] Good coaches seize the "teachable moments" that can enhance transfer of learning, for example, "Freeze . . . take a look at your teammates' location at the end of this play. How is Amanda's position?" Here is further guidance for creating *effective pause moments* in the GBA:

Focus on the tactical. Remember, the strength of the GBA is focusing athletes' perception so they develop tactical skills. Pauses for technical skills, or pauses done too quickly or too frequently, may prevent tactical problem-solving and decision-making. Wait a few minutes to see if players can figure it out before pausing play. Rather than stopping play, consider using quick cues to focus athletes' attention on the technical skills (e.g., "stay low" or "head up") or remind athletes of previously learned concepts, for example, "Remember to sag below the ball." Some coaches use their assistant coaches to look for and deliver cues or reminders of important technical skills while athletes play on. This frees the head coach to observe and stop play to question athletes about larger tactical concepts.

One at a time, quickly. Keep pause moments to 30 seconds or less, and focus on one key idea during the pause. Get back to play as soon as possible. This helps maximize both attention and memory and increases chances feedback will be applied when play is resumed.

Use clear and memorable language. During the pause, use concise language that is easy to remember. Ideally, use the common or shared language developed earlier (chapter 4). Combine verbal language with an image, analogy, or demonstration, if possible (e.g., "Make a ball-me-you triangle"). Use consistent language to pause and resume play such as "Freeze" or "And stop," and "Play on" or "And go."

Extend playing time and check. After the pause, increase the amount of playing time so you can clearly check to see players are applying the concept. Move to the next pause only after the previous one has been applied.

Check for understanding. Replicate a pause moment later in practice to see if players can generate the same solution. This retrieval practice spaced between other concepts increases retention and transfer of the concept and provides the coach with good feedback.

It's All in the Questions

Coaches in the GBA guide players to tactical skill solutions using a heavy dose of questioning. Questioning is the recommended method to focus athletes during practice games. Recall the importance of using questions in instruction (chapter 6), and the five types of questions from chapter 6: knowledge building, discovery, environment, check for understanding, and decision-making. Coaches are encouraged to get in the habit of using questions during pause moments.

Pause moments filled with effective questioning are where game-like perception can be shaped and developed.[13] As such, we suggest questions should emphasize the *perceptual* elements of the game. These are environment questions, such as:

"Where were you looking?"

"Where is the most important information to anticipate that play?"

"What do you see?"

"What will tell you where the dribbler is going?"

Better perception leads to better *decision-making*. Poor decisions are often failures in perception. Players will be better prepared to answer decision-making questions such as:

"What should you do here?"

"Why did we go wide on that play?"

"What's our best option next?"

A related technique advocated by experienced coaches and teachers is that of the "freeze replay."[14] The coach pauses play with a "freeze" command and rewinds the play back to the critical point, and through questioning, the coach helps players "replay" the situation for a better solution. The coach draws out the more desirable perceptions, decisions, and behaviors of game play through targeted questioning.

Since SSGs are best used to develop perception and tactical skills, most questions during play stoppage should be environment and decision-making types of questions. Questioning related to technical aspects of the skill should be limited. If the coach observes during game play that athletes need improvement on technical skills, they can try our earlier suggestion to use assistant coaches to deliver cues and remind athletes about better techniques. We also recommend the practice method of rotating in brief TDA practice of technical skills (drills and repetitions) within and between small-sided games, as needed. Such a method takes advantage of the learning benefits of *interleaving* and *spacing*, discussed in chapter 7.

Enhance the Game

The third element of implementing the GBA is to further *enhance* the game. This is sometimes called "conditioning" the game, in which the game is further distorted to enhance learning. Typically, these enhancements are progressive in nature and add further challenge to players as they gain expertise. Enhancements can both increase the fun and enjoyment of game play and simulate game elements, such as the mental skills required in competition (e.g., anxiety). Below are some of the more effective examples of enhancing game play.

Further Constrain Game Rules or Conditions
The game can be enhanced by changing the rules or scoring conditions. For example, basketball coaches practicing team defense can modify game scoring to match specific game situations, such as rewarding 3 points for a forced turnover, 2 points for forcing a "bad shot," and 1 point for a successful stop at the end of a time period. Or they can modify constraints such as requiring the defense to force the ball into certain zones or areas on the court during a play. Or they could require three "callouts" to be heard from the defensive team before giving up a shot. In soccer, a dribbling/protection game could extend the time or space to dribble or add a "floater," who always plays on the attacking team, or establish a maximum number of passes per possession.

Challenge the Sideline Players
Game play often has players rotating out to rest or watch from the sidelines. Rather than watch passively, sideline players can be challenged with questions about what they see.[15] For example, "I'm going to ask you guys where the ball should have gone in this next sequence." Coaches can get more specific with observation tasks or checklists that grade teams or individual players on how many successful actions they saw during game play. For example, they could record how well a team communicated on defense (basketball): "Let's grade the blue team on the number of callouts they made on the screens."

Use Data to Enhance the Competition
A powerful method of enhancing game play is the use of objective data tracking to inform and question players of their game performance. We provide the example of Kika Toulouse, a coach and coach educator with the New York Red Bulls (soccer).[16] Watch her method in the video at https://www.youtube.com/watch?v=zjIBJiDnVRM. She tells the team she will be tracking certain behaviors and actions during their next competitive game segment. She later pauses and delivers the data, for example, as excerpted from the video:

> Who do you think won? ... I counted six opportunities and you got points on 5 out of 6. ... Orange, you had 7 opportunities; you created more chances but only capitalized on three of them. ... Why do you think you weren't able to capitalize more?

Such an enhancement not only makes the game more interesting but makes the questioning more relevant and memorable to the players.

Tournaments, Leagues, or Competitions
Coaches can create fun and competitive tournaments for small-sided games or drills.[17] For example, the slick shot game could have a tournament with divisions, team names, and keeping track of team records and standings. Games could be tracked all season, recording individual and/or team improvements with awards and recognitions. Some soccer coaches have created tournaments and competitions using the rondo game discussed earlier. There are also examples of coaches creating high-stakes competitions (not so fun) in game activities to increase the transfer of mental skills to the game. We use the example of high school basketball coach and skills trainer Colin Stevens, who designed practice games to simulate game-like mental elements:

> At the beginning of a practice week, players are randomly assigned to teams of three for a set of modified practice games such as rebounding, defensive stops, and 3 v. 3. For each game, assistant coaches keep score, and winning teams are determined. To win each game, the team has to find ways to be successful. While it requires using their learned skills (e.g., blocking out), it also requires using effective team strategies that help them win such as recognizing teammate strength and weakness, cooperating, and communicating with teammates. It also helps them learn to compete. They have to fight to win, control their emotions and anxiety, and maintain their focus under pressure. To simulate the pressure, we make it high stakes. At the end of the practice week, the players with the highest cumulative number of wins are named starters for next game(s). Players have to fight to earn their starting spot in practice drills. We talk to the players about the process. Independent of skills, they have to learn to compete, elevate their teammates, and control their emotions. They are accountable for helping their team win (or lose). Sometimes parents struggle with the outcome, especially if their star player is not starting. But players understand. And yes, the more skilled players who can help us win still get the most minutes, even if they don't start.[18]

Like Coach Stevens, coaches can enhance games to prevent athletes from "going through the motions" that can often occur with TDA practice conditions. The inability to control mental skills like emotions, anxiety, and attention often undermine the positive transfer of skills to the game. Below are two more examples of enhancing game play by manipulating mental skills.

Interleave Consequences with Game Play
As an example, a basketball player may miss the free throw in the game not because he hasn't learned the skill, but because he hasn't learned to manage high levels of fatigue, shift attention from the previous play, or control the anxiety of the situation. The GBA coach might periodically stop the game activity and quickly line up players on the foul lane for a player to shoot free throws with team-based consequences. If it's made, the player's team gets an extra point, but if missed, the team loses a point. Game play activities might also be interleaved with game-like stoppages for servers in volleyball or tennis, or hitters in baseball or softball. In a similar way, gymnasts or track or field athletes (i.e., throwers and jumpers) might lengthen the time between performance attempts to simulate the typical wait time (and pressure and focus) they face in a meet. The interleaved rotation of game play with high-stakes individual performances is one way players can further practice the mental skills that transfer to the game.

Authentic Repetitions
Games, drills, and repetitions can be enhanced by making them representative of the pressure and emotions of the competition. For example, golf coaches might provide "scenarios with consequences" at the driving range, where a golfer is challenged to "hit this shot on the last hole with a one-stroke lead." A basketball coach might design a simulation for basketball players to run a play with 5 seconds on the clock and down by 1 point. There are coaches who intentionally create distractions (e.g., noise) and environmental conditions (e.g., wind, heat) to simulate performance under game-like conditions. The possibilities of enhancing SSGs along these lines are endless, limited only by practice logistics and the creativity of the coach.

As coaches look to implement the GBA, we recommend accessing several sources provided in the notes. An excellent resource for creating games-based practice plans and activities is provided by Koekoek and colleagues and Launder and Piltz.[19]

TRANSFER THIS

Let's return to Coach Jones, the middle school basketball coach who was frustrated when his players didn't apply their rebounding skills to the scrimmage at the end of practice. This lack of positive transfer can be partially explained by his coach-centered use of traditional drills (TDA). He employed a "skills first, game second approach" that focused on isolated technical skill development. He might have fallen into the trap of coaching to get the drill right rather than transferring the skills to the competition. We encourage him to employ a games-based approach (GBA) in which his players learn rebounding skills through the design of competitive games. Along with other benefits, the GBA helps develop athletes' tactical and mental skills important for transfer.

He should explore methods to implement the GBA, including shaping, focusing, and enhancing games. Table 9.2 provides a specific example of how he can redesign a traditional rebounding drill to be more game-like. He might find benefits in designing small-sided games (SSGs) that increase the number of repetitions with game-like decision-making. Successful rebounding requires a great deal of perception and problem-solving (e.g., perceiving shot angle, reading opponent), and SSGs are a great way to practice this. We also encourage Coach Jones to focus his players during games by using "pause moments" and a variety of questioning methods to guide his players' perception and decision-making. As he gets better at shaping and focusing his games, he can further enhance them by adding creative elements that challenge his players and improve mental skills, such as handling the pressure and anxiety of competition.

Coaches, Transfer This

1. Ponder this question: If your sport changes its format and the game requires telling the athletes where to start and where to finish, and then has them go through a bunch of cones, would your team win the championship? (Hint: we hope not.)
2. Compared to traditional practice methods, the games-based approach is an excellent way to increase transfer of learning. It offers benefits that align with most concepts and theories discussed in this book.
3. Shape your games systematically. Identify the target behaviors and skills you want to see and manipulate the game constraints to facilitate those skills.

4. Consider redesigning some traditional drills into games (table 9.2), and design SSGs that increase repetitions under game-like conditions (see table 9.3).
5. Teach through focusing the game, using the methods such as "pause moments" and questioning. This helps shape athletes' perception of the environment and facilitates better decision-making.
6. Further condition games in ways that enhance athlete enjoyment/engagement (e.g., tournaments or leagues) and/or the mental skills specific to competition (e.g., simulate pressure situations).

Coach Educators and Developers, Transfer This
1. Facilitate discussions about the benefits of the GBA. Which of the Top 10 reasons for the GBA do they think is most important? What elements of the GBA and TDA are they currently using? Provide examples if possible. If coaches rely heavily on the TDA, discuss possible reasons why.
2. Provide resources that highlight examples of SSGs and other games-based drills or practice activities (e.g., rondos). Show videos, if possible, of the GBA in action, and evaluate how they might impact transfer of learning.
3. The GBA is implemented through shaping, focusing, and enhancing games. Have coaches discuss examples of drills or activities that align with one or more of those methods. How have they shaped, focused, or enhanced play? For example, have they collected and shared data during game play (enhanced) or purposefully imbalanced the number of players in a game (shaped)?
4. If possible, have coaches videotape one or two drills for critique (or provide one). Share how coaches might:

  - Redesign the drill to align with the benefits of the GBA (see examples).
  - Shape the constraints of the game to facilitate target behaviors.

5. Ask coaches to share how they focus games by using methods such as pause moments and questioning. How have they tried to shape athletes' perception of the environment and better decision-making? If possible, provide an example of a practice activity and have coaches develop pause moments and questions.

Notes

INTRODUCTION

1. Anders Ericsson and Robert Pool, *Peak: Secrets from the New Science of Expertise* (New York: Houghton Mifflin Harcourt, 2016).

2. Pete Van Mullem and Lori Gano-Overway, *To Be a Better Coach: A Guide for the Youth Sport Coach and Coach Developer* (Lanham, MD: Rowman & Littlefield, 2021), 4.

3. Van Mullem and Gano-Overway, *To Be a Better Coach*, 4.

CHAPTER 1

1. Lori Gano-Overway, Melissa Thompson, and Pete Van Mullem, *National Standards for Sport Coaches: Quality Coaches, Quality Sports* (Burlington, MA: Jones and Bartlett, 2020), 22–27.

2. Swen Nater and Ronald Gallimore, *You Haven't Taught Until They Have Learned: John Wooden's Teaching Principles and Practices* (Morgantown, WV: Fitness Information Technology, 2010).

3. Richard A. Magill and David I. Anderson, *Motor Control and Learning*, 12th ed. (New York: McGraw Hill, 2021), 265–75.

4. Magill and Anderson, *Motor Control*, 265–75.

5. Richard A. Schmidt and Timothy D. Lee, *Motor Learning and Performance*, 6th ed. (Champaign, IL: Human Kinetics, 2020), 182–89.

6. Anders Ericsson and Robert Pool, *Peak: Secrets from the New Science of Expertise* (New York: Houghton Mifflin Harcourt, 2016).

7. Ericsson and Pool, *Peak*, 97–100.

8. Ericsson and Pool, 22.

9. Jean Côté and Karl Erickson, "Diversification and Deliberate Play During the Sampling Years," in *The Handbook of Sport Expertise*, ed. Joe Baker and Damian Farrow, pp. 305–16 (London: Routledge, 2015).

10. Paul R. Ford and Edward K. Coughlan, "Operationalizing Deliberate Practice for Performance Improvement in Sport," in *Skill Acquisition in Sport: Research, Theory and Practice*, 3rd ed., ed. Mark A. Williams and Nicola J. Hodges, pp. 189–90 (New York: Routledge, 2020).

11. Craig A. Wrisberg, *Sport Skill Instruction for Coaches* (Champaign, IL: Human Kinetics, 2007), 33–72.

12. Gano-Overway et al., *National Standards for Sport Coaches*.

13. Daniel Coyle, *Little Book of Talent: 52 Tips for Improving Skills* (New York: Random House, 2012), 17–28.

14. Stephen R. Covey, *The 7 Habits of Highly Effective People: Powerful Lessons in Personal Change* (New York: Free Press, 2004), 344.

15. Nater and Gallimore, 48.

16. Nater and Gallimore.

CHAPTER 2

1. Richard A. Magill and David I. Anderson, *Motor Control and Learning*, 12th ed. (New York: McGraw Hill, 2021), 307.

2. Magill and Anderson, *Motor Control and Learning*, 308–10.

3. Rob Gray, "Sports Training Technologies: Achieving and Assessing Transfer," in *Skill Acquisition in Sport: Research, Theory and Practice*, 3rd ed., ed. Nicola J. Hodges and Mark Williams, pp. 202–18 (Routledge, 2020).

4. Chris Button, Ludovic Seifert, Jia Yi Chow, Duarte Araújo, and Keith Davids, *Dynamics of Skill Acquisition: An Ecological Dynamics Approach*, 2nd ed. (Champaign, IL: Human Kinetics, 2021), 182–86.

NOTES

5. Gray, "Sports Training Technologies," 204.

6. "A Women's Softball Pitcher vs. The Top Baseball Hitters . . . Who Wins?" accessed March 11, 2022, https://jugssports.com/blog/a-womens-softball-pitcher-vs-the-top-baseball-hitterswho-wins/.

7. Magill and Anderson, *Motor Control and Learning*, 312.

8. Richard A. Schmidt and Timothy D. Lee, *Motor Learning and Performance*, 6th ed. (Champaign, IL: Human Kinetics, 2020).

9. Timothy Lee, "Transfer-Appropriate Processing: A Framework for Conceptualizing Practice Effects in Motor Learning," in *Complex Movement Behaviour: The Motor-Action Controversy*, pp. 201–15 (Amsterdam: Elsevier Science Publishers, 1988).

10. Simon M. Rosalie and Sean Muller, "A Model for the Transfer of Perceptual-Motor Skill Learning in Human Behaviors," *Research Quarterly for Exercise and Sport* 83, no. 3 (September 2012): 413–21.

11. Laurette Hay and Pierre Schoebel, "Spatio-Temporal Invariants in Hurdle Racing Patterns," *Human Movement Science* 9, no. 1 (February 1990): 37–54.

12. Richard A. Schmidt, "A Schema Theory of Discrete Motor Skill Learning," *Psychological Review* 82 (1975): 225–60.

13. Cheryl A. Coker, *Motor Learning and Control for Practitioners*, 5th ed. (New York: Taylor & Francis, 2021), 75–79.

14. Schmidt and Lee, *Motor Learning and Performance*, 117.

15. Robert Kerr, "Getting into the Scheme of Things," *Coaching Science Update* (Coaching Association of Canada, 1979): 48–51.

16. Timothy D. Lee, Stephan P. Swinnen, and Deborah J. Serrien, "Cognitive Effort and Motor Learning," *Quest* 46 (1994): 328–44.

17. A. E. Moulton, A. Dubrowski, H. MacRae, B. Graham, E. Grober, and R. Reznick, "Teaching Surgical Skills: What Kind of Practice Makes Perfect?" *Annals of Surgery* 244 (2006): 400–409.

18. Alan Baddeley, "Working Memory: Looking Back and Looking Forward," *Nature Reviews: Neuroscience* 4 (2003): 829–39.

19. Nicholas C. Soderstrom and Robert Bjork, "Learning versus Performance: An Integrative Review," *Perspectives on Psychological Science* 10, no. 2 (2015): 176–99.

20. Soderstrom and Bjork, "Learning versus Performance," 192.

21. Soderstrom and Bjork, 193.

22. Trevor Ragan, "How to Get More Out of Practice," Train Ugly, accessed May 11, 2022, https://thelearnerlab.com/train-ugly/.

23. Rob Gray, *How We Learn to Move* (Perception Action Consulting and Education LLC, 2021).

24. Button et al., *Dynamics of Skill Acquisition*.

25. Ian Renshaw, Keith Davids, Daniel Newcombe, and Will Roberts, *The Constraints-Led Approach: Principles for Sports Coaching and Practice Design* (New York: Routledge, 2019).

26. Gray, *How We Learn to Move*.

27. Jia Yi Chow, Keith Davids, Chris Button, and Ian Renshaw, *Nonlinear Pedagogy in Skill Acquisition*, 2nd ed. (New York: Taylor & Francis, 2021).

28. Renshaw et al., *The Constraints-Led Approach*.

29. Tim Buszard, Machar Reid, Rich Masters, and Damian Farrow, "Scaling the Equipment and Play Area in Children's Sport to Improve Motor Skill Acquisition: A Systematic Review," *Sports Medicine* 46, no. 6 (2016): 829–43.

30. Linda Griffin and Joy Butler, *Teaching Games for Understanding: Theory, Research, and Practice* (Champaign, IL: Human Kinetics, 2005).

31. Ross Pinder, Keith Davids, Ian Renshaw, and Duarte Araújo, "Representative Learning Design and Functionality of Research and Practice in Sport," *Journal of Sport and Exercise Psychology* 33, no.1 (February 2011): 146–55.

32. Button et al., *Dynamics of Skill Acquisition*.

33. Pinder et al., "Representative Learning Design."

34. Ross Pinder, Ian Renshaw, Keith Davids, and Hugo Kerherve, "Principles for the Use of Ball Projection Machines in Elite and Developmental Programmes," *Sports Medicine* 41, no. 10 (2011): 793–800.

35. Rob Gray, *The Perception & Action Podcast*, https://perceptionaction.com/.

NOTES 217

CHAPTER 3

1. Wade Gilbert, *Coaching Better Every Season: A Year-Round System for Athlete Development and Program Success* (Champaign, IL: Human Kinetics, 2017), 32–33.

2. Gilbert, *Coaching Better Every Season*, 34.

3. Rainer Martens, *Successful Coaching*, 2nd ed. (Champaign, IL: Human Kinetics, 2012), 28–32.

4. Martens, *Successful Coaching*.

5. Lori Gano-Overway, Melissa Thompson, and Pete Van Mullem, *National Standards for Sport Coaches: Quality Coaches, Quality Sports* (Burlington, MA: Jones and Bartlett, 2020), 7.

6. Gilbert, *Coaching Better Every Season*, 112–16.

7. Gilbert, 114.

8. Red Auerbach, "Sports Quotes," accessed May 25, 2022, https://sportsquotes.us/basketball/author/red-auerbach.

9. Martens, *Successful Coaching*, 90–101; Robert Weinberg and Daniel Gould, *Foundations of Sport and Exercise Psychology*, 7th ed. (Champaign, IL: Human Kinetics, 2019), 241–42.

10. Weinberg and Gould, *Foundations of Sport*, 243.

11. Damon Burton and Thomas Raedeke, *Sport Psychology for Coaches* (Champaign, IL: Human Kinetics, 2019), 18–21.

12. Doug Lemov, *The Coach's Guide to Teaching* (Clearwater, FL: John Catt, 2020).

13. Lemov, *The Coach's Guide to Teaching*, 52–54.

14. Doug Lemov, Erica Woolway, and Katie Yezzi, *Practice Perfect: 42 Rules for Getting Better at Getting Better* (San Francisco: Jossey-Bass, 2012), 66–68.

15. Lemov, *The Coach's Guide to Teaching*, 193.

16. Lemov, 52–54.

17. Martens, *Successful Coaching*, 62–80.

18. Nick Winkelman, *The Language of Coaching: The Art and Science of Teaching Movement* (Champaign, IL: Human Kinetics, 2021).

19. Gilbert, *Coaching Better Every Season*, 127–30.

20. Ashley Gill, *Foundations of Sports Coaching*, 3rd ed. (New York: Routledge, 2021), 68–73.

21. Peter C. Brown, Henry L. Roediger III, and Mark A. McDaniel, *Make It Stick: The Science of Successful Learning* (Cambridge, MA: Harvard University Press, 2014).

22. Brown et al., *Make It Stick*, 153–58.

23. Brown et al., 156–61.

24. Brown et al., 146–50.

25. Martens, *Successful Coaching*.

26. Richard A. Schmidt and Timothy D. Lee, *Motor Learning and Performance: From Principles to Application*, 6th ed. (Champaign, IL: Human Kinetics, 2020).

27. Lemov, *The Coach's Guide to Teaching*.

28. Weinberg and Gould, *Foundations of Sport*, 66–74.

29. Amy Edmondson, *The Fearless Organization: Creating Psychological Safety in the Workplace for Learning, Innovation, and Growth* (Hoboken, NJ: John Wiley & Sons, 2019).

30. Edmondson, *The Fearless Organization*.

31. Malcolm Forbes, AZQuotes.com, Wind and Fly LTD, accessed July 16, 2022, https://www.azquotes.com/quote/519722.

32. Michael Jordan, AZQuotes.com, Wind and Fly LTD, accessed January 15, 2022, https://www.azquotes.com/quote/150618.

33. Mark Anshel, *In Praise of Failure: The Value of Overcoming Mistakes in Sports and Life* (Lanham, MD: Rowman & Littlefield, 2016).

34. Chris Sokoloski, "JV Coach Steps up to Lead Program," *Coastal Observer*, January 27, 2022, p. 16.

35. Trevor Ragan, "Modeling Builds Safety," Train Ugly, accessed January 12, 2022, https://thelearnerlab.com/karchkiralymodeling-can-build-safety/.

36. Carol Dweck, *Mindset: The New Psychology of Success* (New York: Ballantine, 2016).

NOTES

37. Rebecca Chidley, "Utilising a Growth Mindset Within a Young Athlete's Sport Journey," accessed June 5, 2022, https://believeperform.com/utilising-a-growth-mindset-within-a-young-athletes-sport-journey/.

CHAPTER 4

1. Stefan Koehn, Tony Morris, and Anthony Watt, "Flow State in Self-Paced and Externally Paced Performance Contexts: An Examination of the Flow Model," *Psychology of Sport and Exercise* 14, no. 6 (November 2013): 787–95.

2. Mihaly Csikszentmihalyi, *Flow: The Psychology of Optimal Experience* (New York: Harper & Row, 1990), 74.

3. Gabriele Wulf and Rebecca Lewthwaite, "Optimizing Performance Through Intrinsic Motivation and Attention for Learning: The OPTIMAL Theory of Motor Learning," *Psychon Bull Rev* 23, no. 5 (October 2016): 1382–414.

4. Mark A. Guadagnoli and Timothy D. Lee, "Challenge Point: A Framework for Conceptualizing the Effects of Various Practice Conditions in Motor Learning," *Journal of Motor Behavior* 36 (June 2004): 212–24.

5. Nicola Hodges and Keith Lohse, "An Extended Challenge-Based Framework for Practice Design in Sports Coaching," *Journal of Sports Sciences* 40, no. 7 (January 2022): 754–68.

6. Wulf and Lewthwaite, "Optimizing Performance."

7. Doug Lemov, *The Coach's Guide to Teaching* (Clearwater, FL: John Catt, 2020).

8. Cameron Schildt, personal communication.

9. Ian Renshaw, Keith Davids, Daniel Newcombe, and Will Roberts, *The Constraints-Led Approach: Principles for Sports Coaching and Practice Design* (New York: Routledge, 2019).

10. Cheryl A. Coker, *Motor Learning and Control for Practitioners*, 5th ed. (New York: Taylor & Francis, 2021).

11. Renshaw et al., *The Constraints-Led Approach*.

12. Chris Brammall and Jonathan Lowes, "Coaching Pedagogy," in *Foundations of Sports Coaching: Applying Theory to Practice*, 3rd ed., ed. Ashley J. G. Gill, pp. 142–43 (New York: Routledge, 2021).

13. Renshaw et al., *The Constraints-Led Approach*.

14. Chris Button, Ludovic Seifert, Jia Yi Chow, Duarte Araújo, and Keith Davids, *Dynamics of Skill Acquisition: An Ecological Dynamics Approach*, 2nd ed. (Champaign, IL: Human Kinetics, 2021).

15. Renshaw et al., *The Constraints-Led Approach*.

16. Renshaw et al., *The Constraints-Led Approach*, 144.

17. Richard A. Schmidt and Timothy D. Lee, *Motor Learning and Performance*, 6th ed. (Champaign, IL: Human Kinetics, 2020).

18. Doug Lemov, Erica Woolway, and Katie Yezzi, *Practice Perfect: 42 Rules for Getting Better at Getting Better* (San Francisco: Jossey-Bass, 2012), 40–44.

19. Lemov, *The Coach's Guide to Teaching*.

20. "What Is a Rondo in Soccer? (Includes 9 Variations)," *Soccer Coaching Pro*, March 2020, accessed May 6, 2022, https://www.soccercoachingpro.com/rondo-soccer/.

21. Lemov, *The Coach's Guide to Teaching*, 89–92.

22. Coker, *Motor Learning and Control for Practitioners*, 266.

23. Rob Gray, "Sports Training Technologies: Achieving and Assessing Transfer," in *Skill Acquisition in Sport: Research, Theory and Practice*, ed. Nicola J. Hodges and A. Mark Williams, pp. 202–18 (New York: Routledge, 2019).

24. Gray, "Sports Training Technologies."

CHAPTER 5

1. Richard A. Magill and David I. Anderson, *Motor Control and Learning*, 12th ed. (New York: McGraw Hill, 2021); Cheryl A. Coker, *Motor Learning and Control for Practitioners*, 5th ed. (New York: Taylor & Francis, 2021); Richard A. Schmidt and Timothy D. Lee, *Motor Learning and Performance: From Principles to Application*, 6th ed. (Champaign, IL: Human Kinetics, 2020).

2. Rob Gray, *How We Learn to Move* (Perception Action Consulting and Education LLC, 2021).

3. Chris Button, Ludovic Seifert, Jia Yi Chow, Duarte Araújo, and Keith Davids, *Dynamics of Skill Acquisition: An Ecological Dynamics Approach*, 2nd ed. (Champaign, IL: Human Kinetics, 2021).

4. Richard Light, "Making Sense of Chaos: Australian Coaches Talk about Game Sense," in *Teaching Games for Understanding: Theory, Research, and Practice* (Champaign, IL: Human Kinetics, 2005), 111–129; Gray, *How We Learn to Move*.

5. Wikipedia, http://en.wikipedia.org/wiki/Parkour.

6. Wikipedia, http://en.wikipedia.org/wiki/Capture_the_flag.

7. Keith Davids, Duarte Araújo, Luís Vilar, Ian Renshaw, and Ross A. Pinder, "An Ecological Dynamics Approach to Skill Acquisition: Implications for Development of Talent in Sport," *Talent Development & Excellence* 5, no. 1 (2013): 21–34.

8. Ian Renshaw, Keith Davids, Daniel Newcombe, and Will Roberts, *The Constraints-Led Approach: Principles for Sports Coaching and Practice Design* (New York: Routledge, 2019).

9. Sian Barris, Damian Farrow, and Keith Davids, "Increasing Functional Variability in the Preparatory Phase of the Takeoff Improves Elite Springboard Diving Performance," *Research Quarterly for Exercise and Sport* 85, no. 1 (2014): 97–106.

10. Lyndon Krause, Damian Farrow, Machar Reid, Tim Buszard, and Ross Pinder, "Helping Coaches Apply the Principles of Representative Learning Design: Validation of a Tennis Specific Assessment Tool," *Journal of Sport Sciences* 36, no. 11 (2018): 1277–86.

CHAPTER 6

1. Doug Lemov, *The Coach's Guide to Teaching* (Clearwater, FL: John Catt, 2020), 152.

2. Timothy Gallwey, *The Inner Game of Tennis* (New York: Random House, 1974), 36–42.

3. Rich Masters, Tina van Duijn, and Liis Uiga, "Advances in Implicit Motor Learning," in *Skill Acquisition in Sport: Research, Theory and Practice*, 3rd ed., ed. Nicola J. Hodges and A. Mark Williams, pp. 77–95 (New York: Routledge, 2020).

4. Richard A. Magill and David I. Anderson, *Motor Control and Learning*, 12th ed. (New York: McGraw Hill, 2021), 208–14.

5. Richard A. Schmidt and Timothy D. Lee, *Motor Learning and Performance*, 6th ed. (Champaign, IL: Human Kinetics, 2020).

6. Cheryl A. Coker, *Motor Learning and Control for Practitioners*, 5th ed. (New York: Taylor & Francis, 2021).

7. Craig A. Wrisberg, *Sport Skill Instruction for Coaches* (Champaign, IL: Human Kinetics, 2007).

8. Wrisberg, *Sport Skill Instruction for Coaches*, 60–61.

9. Wrisberg, 61.

10. Gabriele Wulf, "Attentional Focus and Motor Learning: A Review of 15 Years," *International Review of Sport and Exercise Psychology* 6, no. 1 (2013): 77–104.

11. Wulf, "Attentional Focus and Motor Learning."

12. Magill and Anderson, *Motor Control and Learning*, 218–19.

13. Nick Winkelman, *The Language of Coaching: The Art and Science of Teaching Movement* (Champaign, IL: Human Kinetics, 2021), 85.

14. Rob Gray, *How We Learn to Move* (Perception Action Consulting and Education LLC, 2021).

15. Magill and Anderson, *Motor Control and Learning*.

16. Magill and Anderson.

17. Winkelman, *The Language of Coaching*, 142–45.

18. Winkelman, 142.

19. Coker, *Motor Learning and Control for Practitioners*, 195.

20. Winkelman, *The Language of Coaching*, 78.

21. Magill and Anderson, *Motor Control and Learning*.

22. Winkelman, *The Language of Coaching*.

23. Hatsuho Zeniya and Hideyuki Tanaka, "Effects of Different Types of Analogy Instruction on the Performance and Inter-Joint Coordination of Novice Darts Learners," *Psychology of Sport and Exercise* 57 (November 2021): 1–11.

24. Masters et al., "Advances in Implicit Motor Learning."

25. Zeniya and Tanaka, "Effects of Different Types of Analogy Instruction."

26. Lemov, *The Coach's Guide to Teaching*.

27. Wrisberg, *Sport Skill Instruction for Coaches*; Lemov, *The Coach's Guide to Teaching*.

28. Marcos Daou, Keith Lohse, and Matthew Miller, "Expecting to Teach Enhances Motor Learning and Information Processing During Practice," *Human Movement Science* 49 (October 2016): 336–45.

29. Greg Neeley, personal communication.

30. Neeley, personal communication.

31. Magill and Anderson, *Motor Control and Learning*.

32. Magill and Anderson, *Motor Control and Learning*.

33. Masters et al., "Advances in Implicit Motor Learning."

34. Coker, *Motor Learning and Control for Practitioners*.

35. Diane Ste-Marie, Michael J. Carter, and Zachary D. Yantha, "Self-Controlled Learning: Current Findings, Theoretical Perspectives, and Future Directions," in *Skill Acquisition in Sport: Research, Theory and Practice*, 3rd ed., ed. Nicola J. Hodges and A. Mark Williams, pp. 119–39 (New York: Routledge, 2020).

36. Ste-Marie et al., "Self-Controlled Learning."

37. Edward Hebert, "The Effects of Observing a Learning Model (or Two) on Motor Skill Acquisition," *Journal of Motor Learning and Development* 6, no. 1 (2018): 4–17.

38. Gibson F. Darden, "Demonstrating Motor Skills—Rethinking That Expert Demonstration," *Journal of Physical Education, Recreation, and Dance* 68, no. 6 (1997): 31–35.

CHAPTER 7

1. Kobe Bryant, AZQuotes.com, Wind and Fly LTD, 2022, last accessed April 30, 2022, https://www.azquotes.com/quote/700736.

2. Arnold Palmer, AZQuotes.com, Wind and Fly LTD, 2022, last accessed October 14, 2022, https://www.azquotes.com/quote/1059958.

3. Rob Gray, *How We Learn to Move* (Perception Action Consulting and Education LLC, 2021); Richard A. Schmidt and Timothy D. Lee, *Motor Learning and Performance*, 6th ed. (Champaign, IL: Human Kinetics, 2020).

4. Gray, *How We Learn to Move*.

5. Charles H. Shea and Robert M. Kohl, "Specificity and Variability of Practice," *Research Quarterly for Exercise and Sport* 61, no. 2 (1990): 169–77.

6. Peter C. Brown, Henry L. Roediger III, and Mark A. McDaniel, *Make It Stick: The Science of Successful Learning* (Cambridge, MA: Harvard University Press, 2014); Schmidt and Lee, *Motor Learning and Performance*.

7. David L. Wright and Taekwon Kim, "Contextual Interference: New Findings, Insights, and Implications for Skill Acquisition," in *Skill Acquisition in Sport: Research, Theory, and Practice*, 3rd ed., ed Nicola J. Hodges and A. Mark Williams, pp. 99–118 (New York: Routledge, 2020).

8. Robert A. Bjork and Elizabeth L. Bjork, "Desirable Difficulties in Theory and Practice," *Journal of Applied Research in Memory and Cognition* 9, no. 4 (2020): 475–79.

9. Wright and Kim, "Contextual Interference."

10. Brown et al., *Make It Stick*.

11. Julia Schorn and Barbara Knowlton, "Interleaved Practice Benefits Implicit Sequence Learning and Transfer," *Memory and Cognition* 49 (April 2021): 1436–52.

12. Richard A. Magill and David I. Anderson, *Motor Control and Learning*, 12th ed. (New York: McGraw Hill, 2021).

13. Magill and Anderson, *Motor Control and Learning*.

14. Dominic A. Simon and Robert A. Bjork, "Metacognition in Motor Learning," *Journal of Experimental Psychology: Learning, Memory, and Cognition* 27, no. 4 (2001): 907–12.

15. F. Martijn Merhoeven and Karl M. Newell, "Unifying Practice Schedules in the Timescales of Motor Learning and Performance," *Human Movement Science* 59 (2018): 153–69.

16. Magill and Anderson, *Motor Control and Learning*.

17. Babe Didrikson Zaharias, AZQuotes.com, Wind and Fly LTD, 2022, last accessed May 15, 2022, https://www.azquotes.com/quote/542326 .

18. Cheryl A. Coker, *Motor Learning and Control for Practitioners*, 5th ed. (New York: Taylor & Francis, 2021).

19. Jia Yi Chow, Keith Davids, Chris Button, and Ian Renshaw, *Nonlinear Pedagogy in Skill Acquisition: An Introduction*, 2nd ed. (New York: Routledge, 2021).

20. Chow et al., *Nonlinear Pedagogy in Skill Acquisition*, 26.

21. Coker, *Motor Learning and Control for Practitioners*.

22. Schmidt and Lee, *Motor Learning and Performance*.

23. Schmidt and Lee.

24. Pamela S. Haibach-Beach, Gregory D. Reid, and Douglas H. Collier, *Motor Learning and Development*, 2nd ed. (Champaign, IL: Human Kinetics, 2017).

CHAPTER 8

1. Richard A. Magill and David I. Anderson, *Motor Control and Learning*, 12th ed. (New York: McGraw Hill, 2021).

2. Cheryl A. Coker, *Motor Learning and Control for Practitioners*, 5th ed. (New York: Taylor & Francis, 2021).

3. Doug Lemov, *The Coach's Guide to Teaching* (Clearwater, FL: John Catt, 2020), 152.

4. John Kessel with Trevor Ragan, "Learning to Learn," last accessed August 6, 2018, https://thelearnerlab.com/trainugly/.

5. Magill and Anderson, *Motor Control and Learning*.

6. Athanasios Mouratidis, Maarten, Vansteenkiste, Willy Lens, and Georgios Sideridis, "The Motivating Role of Positive Feedback in Sport and Physical Education: Evidence for a Motivational Model," *Journal of Sport and Exercise Psychology* 30 (2008): 240–68.

7. Craig A. Wrisberg, *Sport Skill Instruction for Coaches* (Champaign, IL: Human Kinetics, 2007), 119.

8. Magill and Anderson, *Motor Control and Learning*.

9. Lemov, *The Coach's Guide to Teaching*, 169.

10. Coker, *Motor Learning and Control for Practitioners*, 277.

11. Coker, 286.

12. Magill and Anderson, *Motor Control and Learning*, 354–56.

13. Coker, *Motor Learning and Control for Practitioners*, 304.

14. Lemov, *The Coach's Guide to Teaching*, 111–16.

15. John W. Liu and Craig A. Wrisberg, "The Effect of Knowledge of Results Delay and the Subjective Estimation of Movement Form on the Acquisition and Retention of a Motor Skill," *Research Quarterly for Exercise and Sport* 68, no. 2 (June 1997): 145–51.

16. Magill and Anderson, *Motor Control and Learning*.

17. Alan Salmoni, Richard Schmidt, and Charles Walter, "Knowledge of Results and Motor Learning: A Review and Critical Reappraisal," *Psychological Bulletin* 95, no. 3 (1984): 355–86.

18. Magill and Anderson, *Motor Control and Learning*; Richard A. Schmidt and Timothy D. Lee, *Motor Learning and Performance*, 6th ed. (Champaign, IL: Human Kinetics, 2020).

19. Diane Ste-Marie, Michael J. Carter, and Zachary D. Yantha, "Self-Controlled Learning: Current Findings, Theoretical Perspectives, and Future Directions," in *Skill Acquisition in Sport: Research, Theory and Practice*, 3rd ed., ed. Nicola J. Hodges and A. Mark Williams (New York: Routledge, 2020), 119–140.

20. Lemov, *The Coach's Guide to Teaching*, 173–74.

21. Ste-Marie et al., "Self-Controlled Learning."

22. Nick Winkelman, *The Language of Coaching: The Art and Science of Teaching Movement* (Champaign, IL: Human Kinetics, 2021), 78–79.

CHAPTER 9

1. Rainer Martens, *Successful Coaching* (Champaign, IL: Human Kinetics, 2012), 150–60.

2. Martens, *Successful Coaching*; Linda Griffin and Joy Butler, eds., *Teaching Games for Understanding: Theory, Research, and Practice* (Champaign, IL: Human Kinetics, 2005); Brendan SueSee and Shane Pill, "Game-Based Teaching and Coaching as a Toolkit of Teaching Styles," *Strategies* 31, no. 5 (September/October 2018): 21–28.

3. Richard Light, "Making Sense of the Chaos: Australian Coaches Talk about Game Sense," in *Teaching Games for Understanding: Theory, Research, and Practice*, ed. Linda Griffin and Joy Butler, pp. 169–81 (Champaign, IL: Human Kinetics, 2005), 176.

NOTES

4. Jia Yi Chow, Keith Davids, Chris Button, and Ian Renshaw, *Nonlinear Pedagogy in Skill Acquisition*, 2nd ed. (New York: Taylor & Francis, 2021).

5. Chow et al., *Nonlinear Pedagogy in Skill Acquisition*.

6. Martens, *Successful Coaching*; Craig A. Wrisberg, *Sport Skill Instruction for Coaches* (Champaign, IL: Human Kinetics, 2007), 94–97.

7. Doug Lemov, *The Coach's Guide to Teaching* (Clearwater, FL: John Catt, 2020); Ian Renshaw, Keith Davids, Daniel Newcombe, and Will Roberts, *The Constraints-Led Approach: Principles for Sports Coaching and Practice Design* (New York: Routledge, 2019).

8. Renshaw et al., *The Constraints-Led Approach*, 122.

9. Martens, *Successful Coaching*, 158–59.

10. Renshaw et al., *The Constraints-Led Approach*.

11. "What Is a Rondo in Soccer? (Includes 9 Variations)," *Soccer Coaching Pro*, March 2020, last accessed May 6, 2022, https://www.soccercoachingpro.com/rondo-soccer/.

12. SueSee and Pill, "Game-Based Teaching and Coaching"; Shane Pill, "Informing Game Sense Pedagogy with Constraints-Led Theory for Coaching in Australian Football," *Sport Coaching Review* 3 (2014): 46–62.

13. Lemov, *The Coach's Guide to Teaching*.

14. Martens, *Successful Coaching*, 156.

15. Lemov, *The Coach's Guide to Teaching*.

16. Lemov, 170.

17. Martens, *Successful Coaching*, 154–57.

18. Colin Stevens, personal communication.

19. Jeroen Koekoek, Ivo Dokman, and Wytse Walinga, *Game-Based Pedagogy in Physical Education and Sports: Designing Rich Learning Environments* (New York: Routledge, 2023); Alan Launder and Wendy Piltz, *Play Practice: Engaging and Developing Skilled Players from Beginner to Elite*, 2nd ed. (Champaign, IL: Human Kinetics, 2013).

Bibliography

Anshel, Mark. *In Praise of Failure: The Value of Overcoming Mistakes in Sports and Life.* Lanham, MD: Rowman & Littlefield, 2016.

Baddeley, Alan. "Working Memory: Looking Back and Looking Forward," *Nature Reviews: Neuroscience* 4 (2003): 829–39.

Barris, Sian, Damian Farrow, and Keith Davids. "Increasing Functional Variability in the Preparatory Phase of the Takeoff Improves Elite Springboard Diving Performance," *Research Quarterly for Exercise and Sport* 85, no. 1 (2014): 97–106.

Bjork, Robert A., and Elizabeth L. Bjork. "Desirable Difficulties in Theory and Practice," *Journal of Applied Research in Memory and Cognition* 9, no. 4 (2020): 475–79.

Brammall, Chris, and Jonathan Lowes. "Coaching Pedagogy." In *Foundations of Sports Coaching: Applying Theory to Practice*, 3rd ed. Edited by Ashley J. G. Gill, pp. 142–43. New York: Routledge, 2021.

Brown, Peter C., Henry L. Roediger III, and Mark A. McDaniel. *make it stick: The Science of Successful Learning.* Cambridge, MA: Harvard University Press, 2014.

Burton, Damon, and Thomas Raedeke. *Sport Psychology for Coaches.* Champaign, IL: Human Kinetics, 2019.

Buszard, Tim, Machar Reid, Rich Masters, and Damian Farrow. "Scaling the Equipment and Play Area in Children's Sport to Improve Motor Skill Acquisition: A Systematic Review," *Sports Medicine* 46, no. 6 (2016): 829–43.

Button, Chris, Ludovic Seifert, Jia Yi Chow, Duarte Araújo, and Keith Davids. *Dynamics of Skill Acquisition: An Ecological Dynamics Approach*, 2nd ed. Champaign, IL: Human Kinetics, 2021.

Chidley, Rebecca. "Utilising a Growth Mindset within a Young Athlete's Sport Journey," https://believeperform.com/utilising-a-growth-mindset-within-a-young-athletes-sport-journey/, last accessed June 5, 2022.

Chow, Jia Yi, Keith Davids, Chris Button, and Ian Renshaw. *Nonlinear Pedagogy in Skill Acquisition*, 2nd ed. New York: Routledge, 2021.

Coker, Cheryl A. *Motor Learning and Control for Practitioners*, 5th ed. New York: Taylor & Francis, 2021.

Côté, Jean J., and Karl Erickson. "Diversification and Deliberate Play During the Sampling Years." In *The Handbook of Sport Expertise*. Edited by Joe Baker and Damian Farrow, pp. 305–16. London: Routledge, 2015.

Covey, Stephen R. *The 7 Habits of Highly Effective People: Powerful Lessons in Personal Change*. New York: Free Press, 2004.

Coyle, Daniel. *Little Book of Talent: 52 Tips for Improving Skills*. New York: Random House, 2012.

Csikszentmihalyi, Mihaly. *Flow: The Psychology of Optimal Experience*. New York: Harper & Row, 1990.

Daou, Marcos, Keith Lohse, and Matthew Miller. "Expecting to Teach Enhances Motor Learning and Information Processing During Practice," *Human Movement Science* 49 (October 2016): 336–45.

Darden, Gibson F. "Demonstrating Motor Skills—Rethinking That Expert Demonstration," *Journal of Physical Education, Recreation, and Dance* 68, no. 6 (1997): 31–35.

Darden, Gibson F., and David J. Sallee, "From Practice to Game: It's All a Matter of Transfer," *Virginia Journal* (Fall 1997).

Darden, Gibson F., and Jane E. Shimon. "Seven Habits of Developmental Coaches," *Strategies* 17, no. 5 (2004): 25–29.

Davids, Keith, Duarte Araújo, Luís Vilar, Ian Renshaw, and Ross A. Pinder. "An Ecological Dynamics Approach to Skill Acquisition: Implications for Development of Talent in Sport," *Talent Development & Excellence* 5, no. 1 (2013): 21–34.

Dweck, Carol. *Mindset: The New Psychology of Success*. New York: Ballantine, 2016.

Edmondson, Amy. *The Fearless Organization: Creating Psychological Safety in the Workplace for Learning, Innovation, and Growth.* Hoboken, NJ: John Wiley & Sons, 2019.

Ericsson, Anders, and Robert Pool. *Peak: Secrets from the New Science of Expertise.* New York: Houghton Mifflin Harcourt, 2016.

Ford, Paul R., and Edward K. Coughlan. "Operationalizing Deliberate Practice for Performance Improvement in Sport." In *Skill Acquisition in Sport: Research, Theory and Practice*, 3rd ed. Edited by Mark A. Williams and Nicola J. Hodges, pp. 189–90. New York: Routledge, 2020.

Gallwey, Timothy. *The Inner Game of Tennis.* New York: Random House, 1974.

Gano-Overway, Lori, Melissa Thompson, and Pete Van Mullem. *National Standards for Sport Coaches: Quality Coaches, Quality Sports.* Burlington, MA: Jones and Bartlett, 2020.

Gilbert, Wade. *Coaching Better Every Season: A Year-Round System for Athlete Development and Program Success.* Champaign, IL: Human Kinetics, 2017.

Gill, Ashley. *Foundations of Sports Coaching*, 3rd ed. New York: Routledge, 2021.

Gray, Rob. *How We Learn to Move.* Perception Action Consulting and Education LLC, 2021.

———. *The Perception & Action Podcast,* https://perceptionaction.com/, last accessed September 11, 2022.

———. "Sports Training Technologies: Achieving and Assessing Transfer." In *Skill Acquisition in Sport: Research, Theory and Practice*, 3rd ed. Edited by Nicola J. Hodges and Mark Williams, pp. 202–18. New York: Routledge, 2020.

Griffin, Linda, and Joy Butler. *Teaching Games for Understanding: Theory, Research, and Practice.* Champaign, IL: Human Kinetics, 2005.

Guadagnoli, Mark A., and Timothy D. Lee. "Challenge Point: A Framework for Conceptualizing the Effects of Various Practice Conditions in Motor Learning," *Journal of Motor Behavior* 36 (June 2004): 212–24.

Haibach-Beach, Pamela S., Gregory D. Reid, and Douglas H. Collier. *Motor Learning and Development*, 2nd ed. Champaign, IL: Human Kinetics, 2017.

Hay, Laurette, and Pierre Schoebel. "Spatio-Temporal Invariants in Hurdle Racing Patterns," *Human Movement Science* 9, no. 1 (February 1990): 37–54.

Hebert, Edward. "The Effects of Observing a Learning Model (or Two) on Motor Skill Acquisition," *Journal of Motor Learning and Development* 6, no. 1 (2018): 4–17.

Hodges, Nicola, and Keith Lohse. "An Extended Challenge-Based Framework for Practice Design in Sports Coaching," *Journal of Sports Sciences* 40, no. 7 (January 2022): 754–68.

Hoff, David, and Brad Strand. "Youth Coaching: Creating Effective Practice Sessions," Sport Coach America, 2021, https://sportcoachamerica.org/youth-coaching-creating-effective-practice-sessions/, last accessed May 11, 2022.

JUGS Sports Blog. "A Women's Softball Pitcher vs. The Top Baseball Hitters . . . Who Wins?" https://jugssports.com/blog/a-womens-softball-pitcher-vs-the-top-baseball-hitterswho-wins/, last accessed March 11, 2022.

Kerr, Robert. "Getting into the Scheme of Things," *Coaching Science Update* (Coaching Association of Canada, 1979): 48–51.

Kessel, John, with Trevor Ragan. "Learning to Learn," Learner Lab, https://thelearnerlab.com/train ugly/, last accessed August 6, 2018.

Koehn, Stefan, Tony Morris, and Anthony Watt. "Flow State in Self-Paced and Externally Paced Performance Contexts: An Examination of the Flow Model," *Psychology of Sport and Exercise* 14, no. 6 (November 2013): 787–95.

Krause, Lyndon, Damian Farrow, Machar Reid, Tim Buszard, and Ross Pinder. "Helping Coaches Apply the Principles of Representative Learning Design: Validation of a Tennis Specific Assessment Tool," *Journal of Sport Sciences* 36, no. 11 (2018): 1277–86.

Launder, Alan, and Wendy Piltz. *Play Practice: Engaging and Developing Skilled Players from Beginner to Elite*, 2nd ed. Champaign, IL: Human Kinetics, 2013.

Lee, Timothy D., "Transfer-Appropriate Processing: A Framework for Conceptualizing Practice Effects in Motor Learning." In *Complex Movement Behaviour: The Motor-Action Controversy*, pp. 201–15. Amsterdam: North Elsevier Science Publishers, 1988.

Lee, Timothy D., Stephan P. Swinnen, and Deborah J. Serrien. "Cognitive Effort and Motor Learning," *Quest* 46 (1994): 328–44.

Lemov, Doug. *The Coach's Guide to Teaching*. Clearwater, FL: John Catt, 2020.

Lemov, Doug, Erica Woolway, and Katie Yezzi. *Practice Perfect: 42 Rules for Getting Better at Getting Better.* San Francisco: Jossey-Bass, 2012.

Light, Richard. "Making Sense of Chaos: Australian Coaches Talk about Game Sense." In *Teaching Games for Understanding: Theory, Research, and Practice.* Edited by Linda Griffin and Joy Butler, pp. 169–81. Champaign, IL: Human Kinetics, 2005.

Liu, John W., and Craig A. Wrisberg. "The Effect of Knowledge of Results Delay and the Subjective Estimation of Movement Form on the Acquisition and Retention of a Motor Skill," *Research Quarterly for Exercise and Sport* 68, no. 2 (June 1997): 145–51.

Magill, Richard A., and David I. Anderson. *Motor Control and Learning*, 12th ed. New York: McGraw Hill, 2021.

Martens, Rainer. *Successful Coaching*, 2nd ed. Champaign, IL: Human Kinetics, 2012.

Masters, Rich, Tina van Duijn, and Liis Uiga. "Advances in Implicit Motor Learning." In *Skill Acquisition in Sport: Research, Theory and Practice*, 3rd ed. Edited by Nicola J. Hodges and A. Mark Williams, pp. 77–95. New York: Routledge, 2020.

Merhoeven, F. Martijn, and Karl M. Newell. "Unifying Practice Schedules in the Timescales of Motor Learning and Performance," *Human Movement Science* 59 (2018): 153–69.

Moulton, A. E., A. Dubrowski, H. MacRae, B. Graham, E. Grober, and R. Reznick. "Teaching Surgical Skills: What Kind of Practice Makes Perfect?" *Annals of Surgery* 244 (2006): 400–409.

Mouratidis, Athanasios, Maarten Vansteenkiste, Willy Lens, and Georgios Sideridis. "The Motivating Role of Positive Feedback in Sport and Physical Education: Evidence for a Motivational Model," *Journal of Sport and Exercise Psychology* 30 (2008): 240–68.

Pill, Shane. "Informing Game Sense Pedagogy with Constraints-Led Theory for Coaching in Australian Football," *Sport Coaching Review* 3 (2014): 46–62.

Pinder, Ross, Keith Davids, Ian Renshaw, and Duarte Araújo. "Representative Learning Design and Functionality of Research and Practice in Sport," *Journal of Sport and Exercise Psychology* 33, no. 1 (February 2011): 146–55.

Pinder, Ross, Ian Renshaw, Keith Davids, and Hugo Kerherve. "Principles for the Use of Ball Projection Machines in Elite and Developmental Programmes," *Sports Medicine* 41, no. 10 (2011): 793–800.

Ragan, Trevor. "Modeling Builds Safety," Train Ugly, https://thelearnerlab.com/karchkiralymodeling-can-build-safety/, last accessed January 12, 2021).

———. "Train Ugly: How to Get More Out of Practice," Learner Lab, https://thelearnerlab.com/train-ugly/, last accessed August 6, 2022.

Renshaw, Ian, Keith Davids, Daniel Newcombe, and Will Roberts. *The Constraints-Led Approach: Principles for Sports Coaching and Practice Design.* New York: Routledge, 2019.

Rosalie, Simon M., and Sean Muller. "A Model for the Transfer of Perceptual-Motor Skill Learning in Human Behaviors," *Research Quarterly for Exercise and Sport* 83, no. 3 (September 2012): 413–21.

Salmoni, Alan, Richard Schmidt, and Charles Walter. "Knowledge of Results and Motor Learning: A Review and Critical Reappraisal," *Psychological Bulletin* 95, no. 3 (1984): 355–86.

Schmidt, Richard A. "A Schema Theory of Discrete Motor Skill Learning," *Psychological Review* 82 (1975): 225–60.

Schmidt, Richard A., and Timothy D. Lee. *Motor Learning and Performance*, 6th ed. Champaign, IL: Human Kinetics, 2020.

Schorn, Julia, and Barbara Knowlton. "Interleaved Practice Benefits Implicit Sequence Learning and Transfer," *Memory and Cognition* 49 (April 2021): 1436–52.

Shea, Charles H., and Robert M. Kohl. "Specificity and Variability of Practice," *Research Quarterly for Exercise and Sport* 61, no. 2 (1990): 169–77.

Simon, Dominic A., and Robert A. Bjork. "Metacognition in Motor Learning," *Journal of Experimental Psychology: Learning, Memory, and Cognition* 27, no. 4 (2001): 907–12.

Soderstrom, Nicholas C., and Robert Bjork. "Learning versus Performance: An Integrative Review," *Perspectives on Psychological Science* 10, no. 2 (2015): 176–99.

Sokoloski, Chris. "JV Coach Steps up to Lead Program," *Coastal Observer*, January 27, 2022, 16.

Ste-Marie, Diane, Michael J. Carter, and Zachary D. Yantha. "Self-Controlled Learning: Current Findings, Theoretical Perspectives, and Future Directions." In *Skill Acquisition in Sport: Research, Theory and Practice*, 3rd ed. Edited by Nicola J. Hodges and A. Mark Williams, pp. 119–39. New York: Routledge, 2020.

SueSee, Brendan, and Shane Pill. "Game-Based Teaching and Coaching as a Toolkit of Teaching Styles," *Strategies* 31, no. 5 (September/October 2018): 21–28.

Van Mullem, Pete, and Lori Gano-Overway. *To Be a Better Coach: A Guide for the Youth Sport Coach and Coach Developer*. Lanham, MD: Rowman & Littlefield, 2021.

Weinberg, Robert, and Daniel Gould. *Foundations of Sport and Exercise Psychology*, 7th ed. Champaign, IL: Human Kinetics, 2019.

"What Is a Rondo in Soccer? (Includes 9 Variations)," Soccer Coaching Pro, March 2020, https://www.soccercoachingpro.com/rondo-soccer/, last accessed May 6, 2022.

Wikipedia. "Capture the Flag," http://en.wikipedia.org/wiki/Capture_the_flag.

———. "Parkour," http://en.wikipedia.org/wiki/Parkour.

Winkelman, Nick. *The Language of Coaching: The Art and Science of Teaching Movement*. Champaign, IL: Human Kinetics, 2021.

Wright, David L., and Taekwon Kim. "Contextual Interference: New Findings, Insights, and Implications for Skill Acquisition." In *Skill Acquisition in Sport: Research, Theory and Practice*, 3rd ed. Edited by Nicola J. Hodges and A. Mark Williams, pp. 99–118. New York: Routledge, 2020.

Wrisberg, Craig A. *Sport Skill Instruction for Coaches*. Champaign, IL: Human Kinetics, 2007.

Wulf, Gabriele. "Attentional Focus and Motor Learning: A Review of 15 Years," *International Review of Sport and Exercise Psychology* 6, no. 1 (2013): 77–104.

Wulf, Gabriele, and Rebecca Lewthwaite. "Optimizing Performance through Intrinsic Motivation and Attention for Learning: The OPTIMAL Theory of Motor Learning," *Psychon Bull Rev* 23, no. 5 (October 2016): 1382–414.

Zeniya, Hatsuho, and Hideyuki Tanaka. "Effects of Different Types of Analogy Instruction on the Performance and Inter-Joint Coordination of Novice Darts Learners," *Psychology of Sport and Exercise* 57 (November 2021): 1–11.

Index

Note: Page numbers in *italics* refer to tables and figures.

accuracy. *See* speed-accuracy elements
acquisition of skills, 7, 24, 139, 194, 196–97. *See also* instructional elements; learning; practice
adaptability, 16, 18, 139, 193
analysis of practice: about, 93–94; best practices for transfer, 109–10; Coach Shane example, 93, 109–10; elements of similarity, 94–96; environment-based, 104–8, *107*; principles-based, 100–104, *102*; specificity-based, *96*, 96–100
anatomical age differences in athletes, 60–61
Anshel, Mark, 63
anticipation skills, 17
anxiety of athletes, 115–16, 118, 175
athlete-centered coaches, 46–49, 101, 192–93. *See also* games-based approach (GBA)

athletes: anxiety of, 115–16, 118, 175; background self-assessments, 55–56; development of, 47–49, 60–61; independence of, 17, 194; individual differences, 56–61; not accurately predicting performance, 150; questioning by, 180; readiness of, 80–81, 148–50, 174, 178, 181, 183; self-controlled demonstrations, 131–32; self-controlled feedback, 183–84. *See also* attention of athletes; individuals, athletes as
attention of athletes: capturing, 113–15; directing to the external, 116–19; engaging with, 62; importance of, 17; shifting in practice, 115–16
Auerbach, Red, 49
augmented feedback, 166
automaticity, 16, 76–77

background self-assessments, 55–56
badminton, 26, 55, *149*
baseball/softball: analyzing practice, 95, *96*, 97–98, 99–100, 105; designing practice, 89; donor activities, *102*, 104; feedback, 165, 166, 174, 175, 182–83, 184–86; games-based activities, *200*, 209; repetitions, 137, 142, 147, *149*, 155, 156, 160, 161; science of transfer, 23, 28, 29, 30, 32, 33–34, 42, 43; skill instruction, 131
basketball: analyzing practice, 94, 96, *96*, 97, 100, 101, 105, 106–9, *107*; Bryant on, 138; building foundation, 48, 54, 55–56; designing practice, 72, 85, 86, 88; feedback, 174; games-based activities, 198, *200*, 201, *202*, 202–3, 207, 208, 209; Jordan on, 62; repetitions, 141, 147, *153*, 154–55; science of transfer, 25, 27, 31, 35, 40; skill instruction, 119; soccer transferring to, 55
Beeston, Coach, 111, 124–25, 126, 133–34
behavior modification, feedback as, 169
best practices. *See* coach educators' (and developers') best practices for transfer; coaches' best practices for transfer
Brill Bend, 39
Bryant, Kobe, 138

Capture the Flag game, *102*, 103–4
challenge points, 72–73, 195
checklists of skill elements, 171–72
CLA (Constraints-Led Approach), 40–41
coach-controlled approach, 15, 19, 193

coach educators' (and developers') best practices for transfer: analyzing practice, 109–10; building foundation, 67; designing practice, 91; feedback, 187; games-based approach, 210–11; purpose mind-set, 20–21; skill instruction, 134–35; theoretical perspective, 44
coaches: Beeston, 111, 124–25, 126, 133–34; Johnson, 23, 43; Jones, 189, 210; Martel, 137, 162; Rodriguez, 1, 18–19; Stevens, 52–53, 208; Toulouse, 207–8
coaches' best practices for transfer: analyzing practice, 109; building foundation, 66–67; designing practice, 90–91; feedback, 186–87; games-based activities, 210–11; purpose mind-set, 20; skill instruction, 134; theoretical perspective, 43–44
The Coach's Guide to Teaching (Lemov), 124
coach's role, 40–41
cognitive challenges, 144, *145*
cognitive differences in athletes, 58–60
cognitive effort theory, 36–38, *37*, 143, 151
cognitive view of learning, 129–30
Coker, Cheryl, *173*, 173–76
cold calls, 127–28
communication: electronic, 50; explaining the *why*, 114; fundamental skills, 49–54; in GDA *vs.* TDA, 194–95; language usage, 51–54, 205; nonverbal, 50; players giving feedback, 63–64; questions, 123–29, *125*, 180, 205–6. *See also* feedback (for athletes); information

comparative feedback models, 178
competition in practice, 10, 208–9. See also games-based approach (GBA)
conditioned games, 199, 201, *202*, 203
consistency in coaching, 49–50
constant *vs.* varied practice, 140–43
constraints: interaction of, 39–41, 87, 198–99, 201–3, 207; manipulating, 41, 78–83, *81*, 99
Constraints-Led Approach (CLA), 40–41
context variations, 5–6
cooperative coaching style, 47, 112
copycat approach to practice, 16–17
Covey, Stephen, 13
Coyle, Daniel, 12
credibility, 49
cross-country running, 145
Csikszentmihalyi, Mihaly, 70
culture, 53, 61–65, 168, 179

darts, 123
data collection, 172, 207–8
decision-making, 17–18
deliberate play, 9, *10*
deliberate practice, 7–8, *9*
demonstrations, 129–33
descriptive feedback, 177
design of practice: around goals, 73–78, *77*; avoiding gadgets, 69; balancing, 77–78; best practices for transfer, 90–91; building toward transfer, 83–86; manipulating constraints, 78–83, *81*; maximizing time on task, 86–90; for optimal challenges, *70*, 70–71
direct feedback, 166–68
direct messages, 50
direct view of learning, 130

"discovery" practice of new skills, 130–31
dissimilar skills, 32
distance, direction, and description (3D) in cues, 121
distributed *vs.* massed practice, 150–54, *151*, *152*
diversification in sports, 27–28, 32, 47–48, 101
diving events. See swimming and diving events
donor sports, 27–28, 101–4, *102*
downtime, 87
dynamic balance practice, *151*

early success, 60
ecological dynamics theory, 38–42, 43, 78–79, 104, 139
electronic communication, 50
encoded learning, 52
engagement of athletes, 62
environment, 156, 174–75
environmental parameter variations, 141–43, *142*
equipment manipulation, 80, *81*, 157
Ericsson, Anders, 7–9
errors: anticipating, 172–73, *173*; athletes reflecting on, 180; detecting and correcting, 18, 169; diagnosing, *173*, 173–76. See also feedback (for athletes)
example *vs.* rule learning, 58–59
execution, errors due to, 175–76
expert model, 132–33
explicit methods of coaching, 15–16

failure and success, 62–63
far (general) transfer of practice, *26*, 27–28, 100–104, *102*

feedback (for athletes): bandwidth strategy, 181–83; as behavior modification, 169; best practices for transfer, 186–87; closing loop, 184–85; content, 176–80; direct *vs.* indirect, 166–68; estimating first, 180; frequency, 183–84; impact of, 3–7, *4, 5,* 168–71; importance of, 165; intrinsic *vs.* augmented, 166; less is more, 180–81; observing before offering, 171–76; outcome *vs.* process, 176–78; from private hitting instructors, 165, 185–86; show and tell, 178–79; summarizing, 181; video stations, 184. *See also* communication; errors
feedback (for coaches), 63–64
feedforward information, 168
field events. *See* track and field events
field hockey: analyzing practice, 95; designing practice, 79; game-based activities, 201, *202,* 202–3; repetitions, 141
Finch, Jennie, 29
Fitt's Law, 159–60
fixed mind-set, 64–65
flow experiences, 70–71, *71*
football, 95, 96
Forbes, Malcolm, 62
Fosbury, Dick, 38–39
foundation for transfer: athlete-centered coaching, 46–49, 101, 192–93; culture of learning, 61–65, 168, 179. *See also* communication; individuals, athletes as
freeze replay, 206
"full speed" emphasis, 175

functional task difficulty, 72

gadgets and devices, 69, 82, 90
Gallwey, Tim, 112
games-based approach (GBA): barriers to, 195–97; benefits, 193–95, 197, 210; best practices for transfer, 210–11; Coach Jones on, 189; enhancing learning, 206–9; focus of, 204–6; implementing, 198–203; modifying constraints, 41; traditional drills *vs.,* 190–93, *191–92*
"game sense," 195, 196
GBA. *See* games-based approach (GBA)
generalized motor program (GMP), 32–34, *34*
Gilbert, Wade, 46
Giles, Brian, 29
GMP (generalized motor program), 32–34, *34*
goals of practice, 73–78, *77*
golden rule, 159–60
Goldilocks principle, 72–73
golf: analyzing practice, 95; games-based activities, 209; Palmer on, 138; repetitions, 142, 144, 146, 149, *151,* 155; science of transfer, 25–26, 40; skill instruction, 12–13, 122
Gould, Daniel, 50
Gray, Rob, 42
growth mind-set, 17, 64–65, 179
gymnastics: diving and, 101; feedback, 177; games-based activities, 209; repetitions, *149,* 155; skills for, 12

hand raises, 126–27
hard skills, 12–13, *13,* 19

high organization skill, 155–56
hockey, 82, 141, 155, 198
honesty, 49

identical elements theory, 30
immediacy of results, 15, 19
"imperfect" practice, 14
implicit methods of coaching, 15–16
independence of athletes, 17, 194
indirect feedback, 167–68
individuals, athletes as: cognitive differences, 58–60; fairness and, 54; fixed *vs.* growth mind-set, 60; growth and development levels, 60–61; intelligence levels, 59–60; learning modes/preferences, 57–58; motor differences, 56–57; prior knowledge and experiences, 55–56
information: feedforward, 168; learning during practice, 72–73; players providing, 63–64; prior knowledge and experiences, 55–56, 113; quantity of, 114–15. *See also* feedback (for athletes); learning
in-game coaching, 52–53
The Inner Game of Tennis (Gallwey), 112
In Praise of Failure (Anshel), 63
instructional elements: analogies and metaphors, 122–23; best practices for transfer, 134–35; demonstrations, 129–33; goals, 111–12; less *vs.* more, 112; questions as, 123–29, *125,* 180, 205–6; verbal cues, 119–21. *See also* attention of athletes
integration of practice, 194. *See also* games-based approach (GBA)

intelligence of athletes, 59–60
intentional movement variability, 138–39
interleaved repetitions: about, 87, 143–44, 162; in games-based activities, 206, 209; implementing, 147–48, *149*; managing difficulties and perceptions, 148–50; promoting transfer of learning, 143–46, *145*
internal attention, 116–19, 120
inter-task transfer of learning, 100–101
intrinsic feedback, 166
"invasion" sports of soccer and lacrosse, 31–32

Johnson, Coach, 23, 43
Jones, Coach, 189
Jordan, Michael, 62

Karaly, Karch, 63
key elements checklist, 171–72
kickball, 32, *102,* 104
"knock out" game, 101
knowledge of performance (KP), 176, 177–78
knowledge of results (KR), 176–76, 178
Koekoek, Jeroen, 209
KP (knowledge of performance), 176, 177–78
KR (knowledge of results), 176–77, 178

lacrosse: analyzing practice, 95; designing practice, 85; games-based activities, 198; repetitions, 160; science of transfer, 31–32; skill instruction, 130
leagues, 208

learning: athlete engagement and, 194; culture of, 61–65, 168, 179; modes/preferences of athletes, 57–58; new information in, 72–73; overlearning, 76–77; performance vs., 3–7, *4, 5*; rule vs. example, 58–59. *See also* analysis of practice; design of practice; transfer of learning
learning curve, 4–6, *5*
learning model, 132–33
Lemov, Doug, 84, 124
listening skills, 50
The Little Book of Talent (Coyle), 12
long-term memory, 37, *37*
low organization skill, 156

maintenance practice, 9–10
main things, 13–18
Martel, Coach, 137, 162
massed *vs.* distributed practice, 150–54, *151, 152*
memory: consolidation of, 152; direct feedback and, 166–68; elaboration and, 146; importance of, 18; relationships and, 34–35; repetitions and, 144, *145*; retrieval of, 37, *37*, 146. *See also* design of practice; muscle memory
mental elements of practice, 95–99, *96*, 101–4, *102*, 208–9
mental skills, 11, 18, 31, 194, 198
mind-set perspective, 64–65
mistakes. *See* errors; feedback (for athletes)
modeling behavior, 63–64
"moderate distance" transfer of practice, 28

motivation, 169–70, 176, 179
motor programs theory, 32–34, *34*
movement elements of practice, 94, *96*, 97–99, 101, *102*, 103
movement stability and consistency, 18
multisport participation, 27–28, 32, 47–48, 101
muscle memory, 23, 33, 143–44
musician analogy, 145

naïve practice, 10
National Standards for Sports Coaches, 2, 11–12, 47
near transfer of practice, *26*, 26–27
Neeley, Greg, 128–29
negative transfer of learning, *25*, 25–26, 55, 88
new information in learning, 72–73
Nonlinear Pedagogy (NLP), 40
nonverbal messages, 50
notetaking for feedback, 172

objectives of practice, 83–84
observation, 171–76
outcome feedback, 176–77
outcome-oriented practice, 16
over-coaching perils, 112
over-constraining, 82
"overlearned" deep memory, 76–77
over-shaped games, 201–3

Palmer, Arnold, 138
Parkour challenge courses, *102*, 103
parts *vs.* "whole" practice, 154–58
pause moments, 204–6
Peak (Ericsson and Pool), 7–9
peer feedback models, 178

perception-action coupling, 41–42, 81–82, 104–5
Perception and Action Podcast (Gray), 42
perception skills, 206
perceptual elements of games, 205–6
perceptual elements of practice, 95, *96,* 97–99, 101, *102,* 103
perceptual errors, 174–75
perfect practice, 19
performance curve, 4–6, *5*
performance *vs.* learning, 3–7, *4, 5*
personalization of instruction, 113. *See also* individuals, athletes as
Piazza, Mike, 29
platform activities, 84–85, 88
play practice, 9, *10*
Pool, Robert, 7–9
positive failure, 63
positive feedback, 169–70
positive transfer of learning, *25,* 25–26, 28
positivity, 49
PoTSS (Pyramid of Teaching Success in Sport), *46,* 46–47
practice: deliberate *vs.* purposeful, 7–9; focusing on main thing, 13–18; prompting athletes on, 113–14; reasons for, vii; role of, 1–2, 3; transferring to performance, 18–19; types, 7–11, *10. See also* analysis of practice; design of practice; foundation for transfer; repetitions; transfer of learning
practice-to-learn (PTL) goals, 74–75, *77,* 78, 84, 85–86, 99, 143
practice-to-maintain (PTM) goals, 76–77, *77,* 78, 84, 85–86, 99

practice-to-transfer (PTT) goals, 75–76, *77,* 78, 85–86, 99, 143
praise. *See* feedback (for athletes)
prescriptive feedback, 177
"pretty drills," 14
principles-based transfer, 31–32, 100–104, *102*
problem-solving perspective, 62
process feedback, 176–78
process-oriented practice, 16
process-related goals, 65
progressive-part practice, 158
psychological control. *See* mental skills
psychological safety, 61–63
Pujols, Albert, 29
purposeful practice, viii, 8–9, 83–84. *See also* design of practice
Pyramid of Success, 46
Pyramid of Teaching Success in Sport (PoTSS), *46,* 46–47

quantity of information, 114–15
questioning method, 205–6

random practice. *See* interleaved repetitions
reinforcement of skills, 170
relationships between skills, 34–35
relative force, 33
relative timing, 33
relevance of instruction, 113–14
repetitions: best practices for transfer, 162–63; Coach Martel on, 137, 162; constancy *vs.* variability in, 138–43, *142;* as distraction, 14; frustrations with, 137–38; games-based activities, 209; interleaved, 143–50, *145,* 162;

memory and, 35, *35*; spacing of, 38, 150–54, *151, 152,* 162; speed of, 159–62; "whole" *vs.* parts practice, 154–58, 162
representative learning design (RLD), 42, 105–6, *107*
rest, 87
retention tests, 4–5. *See also* memory
RLD (representative learning design), 42, 105–6, *107*
Rodriguez, Coach, 1, 18–19
rondos, 85, 203, 208
rule *vs.* example learning, 58–59

safe environments, 61–63
SAGs (small-area games), 199, 201, *202*, 203
"sandwich" feedback, 170–71
schemas (movement relationships), 34–36, *35*
Schildt, Cameron, 63, 78
science of transfer: direction and amount of transfer, *25,* 25–26; distance of transfer, *26,* 26–28; reasons for coaching for transfer, 24–25; theory of muscle memory, 23. *See also* theories of transfer
self-assessment, 51, 55–56
self-controlled demonstrations, 131–32
self-controlled feedback, 183–84
sensory memory, 37, *37*
sensory sources of feedback, 166
"shell" drill, 85
show-and-tell feedback model, 178–79
sideline players, 207
similarity-based transfer model, 30–31
simplification approach, 157–58

simulation of game-like elements, 75–76
"16 Guidelines for Sending Effective Messages," 51
skill organization, 155–56, 157
skills: acquisition of, 7, 24, 139, 194, 196–97; checklist of key elements, 171–72; decomposition of, 156–57; "discovery" practice, 130–31; dissimilar, 32; types of, 11–13, *13*. *See also* instructional elements; learning; practice
small-area games (SAGs), 199, 201, *202,* 203
small-group sessions, 183–84
small-sided games (SSGs), 199, 201, *202,* 203
soccer: analyzing practice, 95, *96,* 98–99; building foundation, 48; designing practice, 81–82, 85; donor activities, 55, 101–4, *102*; feedback, 174; games-based activities, 199, *200,* 202–3, 207, 208; GBA *vs.* TDA, *191–92*; Parkour challenge courses, *102, 103*; repetitions, 141, 142, *142*; science of transfer, 24, 27, 28, 31–32, 34–35, 36, 41–42; skill instruction, 118
Soccer Coaching Pro website, 203
social media, 50
softball. *See* baseball/softball
soft skills, 12–13, *13,* 19
spaced repetitions, 87, 162
specificity of practice repetitions, 138–43
specificity of transfer theory, 29–32, 94
speed-accuracy elements, 95, *96,* 97–99, *102*
speed of repetitions, 159–62

spontaneous practice, 9, *10*
spot shot drill, 106–8, *107*
SSGs (small-sided games), 199, 201, *202,* 203
STEPS process, 80–83, *81,* 198–99
Stevens, Colin, 52–53, 208
strategic and conceptual elements of practice, 94–95, *96,* 97–100, 101, *102,* 103
stress, 115–16, 118, 175
structure-building (high *vs.* low), 58
success and failure, 62–63
surgeon analogy, 36, 151
sweet spot for motivation, 70–71, *71,* 195
swimming and diving events: analyzing practice, 101, 105; feedback, 166; repetitions, 154, 155, 156, 158; science of transfer, 26, 27; skill instruction, 117

tactical skills, 11, 194, 198, 199, 204–5, 206
"Talk about it!," 51, 52
target behaviors, 79
target shooting, *151*
target tasks, 100
task parameter variations, 141–43, *142*
task simplification, 157–58
teachers, coaches as, *46,* 46–47
Teaching Games for Understanding (TGfU), 41
technical skills, 11, 194, 198, 206
technology, 88–90
tennis: analyzing practice, *102,* 104; designing practice, 85; feedback, 167, 177; games-based activities, 199, 209; multisport experience and, 55; repetitions, 140, 141, 154, 155, 156–57, 160; science of transfer, 26, 33–34, 42; skill instruction, 130, 131
TGfU (Teaching Games for Understanding), 41
theories of transfer: about, 28–29; cognitive effort, 36–38, *37,* 143, 151; ecological dynamics, 38–42, 43, 78–79, 104, 139; motor programs, 32–34, *34;* schemas, 32, 34–36, *35;* specificity of transfer, 29–32, 94. *See also* science of transfer
Thomas, Mrs., 69, 82, 90
Thorndike, Edward Lee, 30
3D (distance, direction, and description) in cues, 121
timing and accuracy, 159–62
Toulouse, Kika, 207–8
tournaments, 208
track and field events: analyzing practice, 94, 95; building foundation, 65; designing practice, 88; feedback, 166, 176, 177; games-based activities, 209; repetitions, 141, 155; science of transfer, 26, 32; skill instruction, 117, 120
traditional drills *vs.* games-based approach, 189, 190–93, *191–92,* 210
transfer-appropriate processing, 30–31
transfer of learning: direction and amount, *25,* 25–26; distance, *26,* 26–28; gardening analogy, 45; negative, *25,* 25–26, 55, 88; from practice to competition, vii–x; reasons to coach for, 24–25. *See also* coach educators' (and developers') best practices for

transfer; coaches' best practices for transfer; foundation for transfer; science of transfer; theories of transfer
transfer tests, 4–6, *5*
"two-touch only" drill, 82
two-way communication, 50

variablity in practice, 138–43, *142*, 162
verbal cues, 119–21
VE (virtual-environment) technologies, 89
videotapes, 51
virtual-environment (VE) technologies, 89
volleyball: analyzing practice, 94; building foundation, 55; Coach Rodriguez on, 1, 18–19; designing practice, 88; feedback, 172, 174, 175; games-based activities, 209; repetitions, 140, 144, *145*, 146, 155, 156–57, 158, 160; science of transfer, 41; skill instruction, 116

wait times in questioning, 128
weightlifting, 140, 156
Weinberg, Robert, 50
"whole" *vs.* parts practice, 154–58, 162
Winkelman, Nick, 119–21
Wooden, John, 2, 14, 15, 46
working memory, 37, *37*

Zaharias, Babe Didrikson, 151

About the Authors

Gibson Darden is professor of motor behavior at Coastal Carolina University. Dr. Darden has taught courses in motor learning, motor development, sport psychology, youth sport, and coaching education at four different universities. He has served on several national task forces to establish best practice standards and assessment in teacher, sport, and coaching education. A former collegiate athlete, he has coached at the middle school, high school, and collegiate levels. Darden has authored over 30 publications and conducted more than 35 presentations related to practice and motor skill learning.

Sandra Wilson is an associate professor of kinesiology at Coastal Carolina University. Dr. Wilson has taught courses in coaching education, sport psychology, youth sport, physical education, and motor learning. She has 25+ years of experience training, supervising, and mentoring preprofessional coaches and teachers at three different universities. A former collegiate All-American field hockey athlete, Dr. Wilson is an accreditation portfolio reviewer for the National Council for Accreditation for Coaching Education, has authored over 15 publications, and has conducted over 60 presentations related to teaching and learning sport skills.

Ingram Content Group UK Ltd.
Milton Keynes UK
UKHW011258180423
420365UK00013B/58